SHULCHAN HALEVI

Halachic Responsa
From the Desk of

HAGAON HARAV
Yisroel HaLevi Belsky, ***shlita***

שמחת התורה
SIMCHAS HATORAH

Edited & Arranged by
Moshe Armel & Reuven Mathieson

Annotated by
Daniel Price

Executive Editor
Rabbi Reuven Noach Cohen

MACHON SIMCHAS HATORAH
36/1 S'dei Chemed Street
Kiryat Sefer
Eretz Yisroel
Tel. 972 8 979 8047

Cover design: R. Moses
Typesetting: KPS

In loving memory of our beloved parents:

William Kriger

ר׳ **זאב** בן ר׳ יעקב **מאיר**, ז״ל

Hannah Kriger

מרת **חנה הינדה** בת ר׳ **יצחק אייזיק**, ע״ה

Arriving in America at a young age, our father was מוסר נפש to be *Shomer Shabbos*. He was a man of noble character and great integrity, committed to Torah values and learning. He taught us respect for Torah and *Talmidei Chachamim*. Despite great hardship, he ensured that we receive a yeshiva education. No sacrifice was too great for his family.

Our dear mother, his devoted עזר כנגדו was a paragon of loyalty and love for her husband and family. She was a vibrant woman, who instilled *simchah*, joy for life, within all of her children, and taught us the true meaning of *chesed*. Mother imbued us with love for *Yiddishkeit*, *Shabbos* and *zemiros*, as well as the importance of family ties.

Their example inspires us all.

With everlasting love and admiration

Mordechai and Miriam Kriger and Family

Marion Talansky and Family
Tzipi and Dr. Howard Cedar and Family
Dr. and Mrs. Jacob Kriger and Family

In loving memory of our beloved mother

Anne Fuchs

מרת חיה חנצע בת ר׳ נפתלי הרצל, ע״ה

A true *Aishes Chayil*. She combined beauty, wisdom, strength of character, and a great passion for living.

A survivor of the Holocaust, her faith never wavered. She and her loving husband, R. Chaim Meyer Fuchs, *shlit"a*, were happily married in August 1945. Mother cared for her family with great love and dedication as she guided us on the proper path. Love, warmth, and intelligence emanated from her special *neshamah*. She brightened the lives of all those around her. We were privileged to have had such a great human being as a mother.

קמו בניה ויאשרוה בעלה ויהללה

"Her children arise and praise her, her husband lauds her." (Mishlei 31:28)

With love and respect

Chaim Meyer (Henry) Fuchs
Miriam and Marty Kriger and Family
Irving and Rena Fuchs and Family
Susan and Dr. Larry Bernstein and Family

Grandchildren: Rabbi Naftali and Ziva Kriger, Debra Kriger, Monica and Rabbi Dr. Robert Goldstein, Lisa, Atara and Yakira Fuchs, Rabbi Jacob, Danny and Annie Bernstein

Great Grandchildren: Shimon Yehuda, Zev, Chananiah, Ezriel Gedaliah, Yisroel, and Tehila Chana Kriger,
Akiva, Zev, Yosef, Esti, Shifra, Yehuda, and Shira Goldstein
Aryeh Leib, Avrohom, and Dina Scheininger
Yoni, Ari, and Devorah Bernstein
Dara Bernstein

Dedicated in memory of our dear cousin

הרב יונה אסטראו זצ"ל

An eminent *talmid chacham* educated in the great European yeshivos. My father and I were fortunate to learn with him and be the beneficiaries of his great knowledge.

Rav Yonah was my first mentor and had a great influence in developing my approach to learning Torah. He encouraged me to originate novel Torah thoughts, always being mindful of the Torah context.

I have great *hakaras hatov* for the profound impact that he had on my life.

ת.נ.צ.ב.ה.

In everlasting gratitude and respect

Mordechai Kriger and Family

Contents

AUTHOR'S PREFACE

WHILE I WAS PERUSING the "Question and Answer" exchanges gleaned from several years-worth of shiurim, I realized that there was a considerable amount of material that could be collated into a sefer, and be presented to the Torah world and the general Jewish public.

All of the topics under discussion are of major concern to those for whom the Torah is quite literally, "their lives and the length of their days." New issues constantly arise which require in-depth analysis, and which directly affect daily activity. These issues need resolving, and clear halachic guidance given to clarify what otherwise would be sources of doubt and confusion. Indeed, the Rambam once wrote, "There is no greater joy than that of resolving doubts." It brings happiness because it allows a person to pursue his life without a heavy cloud of confusion troubling him from morning to evening. This collection provides answers and guidance which will hopefully allay much of that confusion.

I wish to express my thanks to R' Moshe Armel and R' Reuven Mathieson, who arranged and edited the material contained in this volume, and rewrote it in a way that would be clear, precise and not least, enjoyable reading. This was carried out under the guidance of my esteemed son-in-law, Rabbi Reuven Cohen, who oversaw the development of this sefer from beginning to fruitful end.

I would like to state clearly, that I have read every word carefully, and made changes and additions where necessary, so as to preserve the clarity and accuracy of the halachic material presented. The final "nusach" accurately expresses my opinions on the subjects discussed therein.

The original 'question and answer' sessions were conducted in English, hence the use of that language for this sefer. I hope, *b'ezras Hashem*, to soon be able to present a number of volumes in Hebrew, including in-depth *sha'alos* and *teshuvos*.

I am overjoyed to share with my Jewish brethren, what I perceive to be a clear guide to halachic issues of our day. My heartfelt and fervent prayers are extended to Hashem Yisborach, for His guidance and *siyata d'Shmaya,* and I pray that no mistake has unwittingly crept into this work. Should any reader notice what he considers to be an error, I beg him to please inform myself directly, or Machon Simchas HaTorah, and I will *b'ezras Hashem* consider his words carefully, and re-examine my writing where applicable.

A warm personal note of thanks to my close and dear friend who has been with me from early childhood until this very day, HaRav Mordechai Aharon Kriger. It is a credit to his unbelievable generosity and appreciation for Torah that these volumes have been able to see the light of day. May Hashem Yisborach bless him and his with His bountiful *brachos*, which are so richly deserved.

I close with an earnest expression of thanks to those who assisted and encouraged me in the arduous task of editing of this sefer until its completion. Foremost among them are Rabbi Naftali Leshkowitz, Rabbi Yosef Chaim Perlman, Reb Tzvi Adams, and Reb Dov Goldbrenner. Their assistance was carried out with the faithfulness and friendship that characterize true devotion, and it is this that inspired me to go steadily forward. May they be rewarded from Heaven in every manner possible. Among the other notable individuals whose help is appreciated in a major way are Rabbi Avi Neuhouse, Rabbi Michoel Styller, and Rabbi Yitzchok Cohen.

Yisroel Belsky
12th of Menachem-Av 5768

Publishers Preface

IT IS A PRIVILEGE and an honor to present the first volume of the *Shulchan HaLevi* series of responsa to the Torah world. *Shulchan HaLevi* is the first of its kind, and its release is a milestone for the English-speaking Jewish community.

The great majority of halachah sefarim in the English language concentrate on a single topic, such as Shabbos, kashrus, brachos and so forth. The authors of these works study the topic for many years, and then present a comprehensive discussion of all its facets in written form. In contrast, the *Shulchan HaLevi* series is a genuine English-language collection of halachic responsa. This is significant in several ways.

Firstly, the author of *Shulchan HaLevi*, HaGaon HaRav Yisroel HaLevi Belsky, *shlita*, is known throughout the Torah world as one who has a ready teshuvah for, literally, any question proposed to him.

Secondly, within each volume are questions that span the length and breadth of Torah topics, and address many of the questions raised in modern-day society. The series will cover questions from all four sections of the *Shulchan Aruch*, hence the name *Shulchan HaLevi*.

To date, all responsa sefarim that share *Shulchan HaLevi's* format have been written exclusively in Hebrew. Yet, there are currently tens of thousands of English-speaking, Torah observant Jews, who would certainly be more comfortable reading responsa in the vernacular, so that they might clearly comprehend the finer points of the halachic issues they face. This raises the question as to why there has been a paucity of similar sefarim written in English.

One reason for the dearth of English responsa, is that until recently, *Gedolei Torah* who were capable of writing responsa from the vantage point of *kol haTorah kulah*, that is, whose command of every Torah discipline made them capable of rendering halachic decisions on every contemporary issue, had grown up in Europe, and their native tongue was Yiddish, not English.

HaRav Belsky, however, was raised on American soil, and has answered tens of thousands of *sheilos* in English over the past forty-five years, many of them recorded both by individuals and major organizations, such as the Orthodox Union which supplied several discs of the Rav's shiurim, and Irgun Shiurei Torah from whom we have received numerous tapes of the Rav's halachic discourses, and to whom we extend our heartfelt thanks. This places HaRav Belsky, *shlita*, in a unique position to author a set of responsa in English.

After three years of painstakingly transcribing, organizing, researching and annotating this wealth of information, the dedicated and professional team of editors at Machon Simchas HaTorah has the great privilege to present to the Torah world, the first volume of HaRav Belsky's responsa series, *Shulchan HaLevi*!

Shulchan HaLevi makes available Rabbi Belsky's erudition and wisdom to the wider Jewish community. The entire English-speaking Torah world will now be able to find the answers to hundreds of pertinent questions that have been presented to the Rav over the years, covering a broad and comprehensive range of topics.

I once merited visiting the *Posek Hador*, HaGaon HaRav Elyashiv, שליט"א, together with HaRav Belsky, at which time I gained a deeper understanding of the magnitude of Rav Belsky's true stature. Rav Elyashiv, already well into his nineties, tried to stand up by himself to honor the Rav, and with a beautiful smile called out twice, "Rav Belsky! Rav Belsky!" I watched, as these two giants of Torah engaged in a discussion surrounding a Gemara in *Avodah Zarah*, and its application to modern-day halachah. (See "Sheitel Controversy", p. 154.)

What was clear to me, was that the *Posek Hador* considered HaRav Belsky eminently capable of determining *halachah lemaaseh*, practical Torah guidance, even in the most difficult cases.

Shulchan HaLevi in Lashon HaKodesh

During this period, the Machon has also been busy producing the Hebrew version of Shulchan HaLevi, the first volume of which is set for release in the very near future. I would like to take this opportunity to clarify some important differences between these two editions.

The main purpose of the English edition of *Shulchan HaLevi* is to present HaRav Belsky's responsa in a clear and understandable format, so that each person, whether an accomplished scholar, a layman, or a home-maker, may speedily find answers to many pressing issues. The responsa are generally brief, and have often been embellished to give a general description of the halachic issues involved. Every attempt was made to maintain the personable style of the author, which reflects his profound concern for every Jew. It is as if one had presented his question to the Rav personally.

In contrast, the Hebrew edition is closer in style to traditional responsa sefarim. Many of the responsa were set down in writing by HaRav Belsky himself, and are replete with *pilpul* and proofs from the wealth of his knowledge of Torah and *metzius*. Other responsa are shorter, having been delivered orally, or when time for a more comprehensive treatment was lacking. The Hebrew edition is intended for the more serious student, looking not only for the Rav's answers, but to study the topic in depth.

How to use this sefer

The reader can gain much from the present volume in one of two ways. HaRav Belsky's style is friendly and clear, making casual reading enjoyable and informative. One can gain jewels of insight into any topic just by opening the sefer and starting to read.

The reader might also use this sefer exactly as if he were consulting the Rav in person, by looking up a specific question or topic. To this end, we have spent considerable time on preparing a detailed index to enable readers to easily find each *sheilah* as quickly and easily as possible.

It is our hope and prayer that both the Hebrew and English editions of *Shulchan HaLevi* will faithfully serve the halachic needs of Klal Yisroel until the coming of the Moshiach, may it be speedily and in our days.

Appreciation

It is my special honor to thank one whom I consider to be a good friend, Mr. Mordechai Kriger, for not only sponsoring the Kriger Edition of *Shulchan HaLevi*, but also for his inspiration and encouragement throughout the hard work over the past three years. In all my many meetings with Reb Mordechai, I have found him to be a man of Torah; one who spends time diligently and productively in the Beis Midrash. Indeed, Mr. Kriger has enjoyed a long and close relationship with the author, going back to the days they were classmates in Torah VoDaath elementary school. Even when Mr. Kriger took his considerable talents into the business world, this did not detract at all from his love of Torah learning, and he has been learning and writing *sefarim* all throughout his career. Just recently, HaRav Belsky conferred upon Mr. Kriger the coveted *semichah* of *Yoreh Yoreh*, after years of diligent study.

To him I say, "Great is your portion, in this world, and the Next!" *Chazal* say, "Privilege is given to the meritorious." This is certainly appropriate in Mr. Kriger's case, for he has already proven his commitment to Torah study, both in terms of his personal diligence and in his generous support of Torah institutions. It is only fitting that someone of his caliber would merit being the driving force behind the *Shulchan HaLevi* series.

Additionally, I would like to take this opportunity to extend my gratitude to Mr. Kriger's very special *chavrusa*, and my own dear friend, HaRav Moshe Bergman. Reb Moshe has been a fount of the deepest friendship to both myself and Mr. Kriger, and has given the most encouraging inspiration throughout this project.

Heartfelt thanks are extended also to Mr. Kriger's son, Rabbi Naftali Kriger. Reb Naftali has contributed some very pertinent and useful suggestions, some of which were incorporated into the *sefer*, and enhanced it considerably, notably, the inclusion of English terms in the Hebrew volume, for the sake of clarity.

I am both indebted to, and extremely impressed with, the dedication and professionalism of Moshe Armel and Reuven Mathieson, the Machon's editors. Both worked tirelessly to hone and clarify the wording of HaRav Belsky's responsa. Indeed, the entire staff of Machon Simchas HaTorah made a rich contribution to this flagship publication, each doing his or her job with skill and attentiveness. A special thank you goes also to Rabbis Dovid Goldstein and Avi Neuhouse, Reb Tzvi Adams, Reb Shloimie Ettinger, and Reb Zev Weinberger in Yeshiva Torah VoDaath who liaised with the Machon and took their time to sit and review each draft of the sefer with HaRav Belsky, faithfully noting the Rav's comments, and additions.

With our hands outstretched to Hashem Yisborach, I thank Him for the opportunity to increase the knowledge of Torah among Klal Yisroel, and humbly request that He continue helping us in all our future endeavors.

בברכת התורה
Rabbi Reuven Cohen
Menachem-Av 5768

Shulchan Halevi

REGARDING TRANSLITERATIONS:

Our policy throughout the book has been to italicize the first instance of oft-repeated transliterations of Hebrew words and phrases in each question, and thereafter set them in standard font (roman). Transliterations seldom used or less familiar to English readers are always set in italics.

ORACH CHAIM

NEGEL VASSER NEXT TO THE BED[1]

Is there any leniency for those who do not wash their hands (*negel vasser*) next to the bed, or for those who do not wash as soon as they wake up, if washing next to the bed might wake up someone else in the room who rises later?

ANSWER

The consensus of the Mishnah Berurah[2] and Shaarei Teshuvah,[3] following the Zohar, is to wash by the bed immediately upon awakening. There is mention of a serious punishment for leaving the unclean spirit on one's hands. Therefore, it is very important to wash one's hands next to the bed and to do so immediately upon arising, in order to avoid leaving the *tumah* on one's hands for the time it takes to walk four *amos*. This applies to both men and women.

On the other hand, in some situations it may be better to forego this important halachah and rely instead on the view of the Tanna, Rebbi Shimon ben Elazar, who holds that an entire house (*bayis*) is

1. או"ח סי' א'
2. סי' א' סק"ב
3. שם אות ב'

halachically considered as four *amos*.[4] There are several yeshivos, for example, where having negel vasser by the bed resulted in water fights at night. The Roshei Yeshivos examined the situation and instituted a rule that negel vasser be done at the sink.

Sometimes, the presence of negel vasser in crowded sleeping quarters may result in the spillage of water that carries a *ruach ra'ah*, which would remain until the water dries up.[5] The Mishnah Berurah says that if the water should touch food, the food item should be washed three times before being eaten. Additionally, the activity of washing negel vasser might rob light sleepers of their much-needed rest. Here too, it may be better to wash at the sink.

Nevertheless, the Mishnah Berurah makes it very clear that in general one should not rely on leniencies regarding negel vasser. Therefore, in the absence of a specific *heter*, the proper course of action is to wash by the bed in the morning.

OVERSIZED TALLIS FOR SIMCHAS TORAH

There is a custom on Simchas Torah to lift a tallis above the heads of all the children during the *aliyah* of *kol hane'arim*. Someone is marketing a new extra-large tallis, ten feet by thirteen feet, for this purpose. Does this qualify as a *tallis shel shutafim* (a jointly-owned tallis), which requires tzitzis, or, since it is not made to be used as a garment but as a canopy, does it require tzitzis at all?

ANSWER

The minhag is to be under a *chuppah*, and we use a tallis to simulate the chuppah. It does not actually have to be a wearable garment; it could even be a blanket. With regard to a blanket, the Mishnah

4. ברכות כה:
5. עי' אשל אברהם

Berurah[6] recommends, but does not require, that one round the corners of a woolen blanket even though it is only intended to be used at night and is not worn but rather placed atop a person. This is because there is an opinion in the Rishonim (Tosafos[7] and the Rambam[8]) that requires tzitzis on blankets by day.[9] Even according to this opinion, there is no reason to place tzitzis on the corners of the extra large tallis under discussion, as it is not even being placed upon anyone, just held above the heads of the children and the *baal kriah*. Therefore, there is no requirement for this tallis to have tzitzis, as they serve no purpose except to create an atmosphere suitable for Simchas Torah. What is more, putting tzitzis on such a large tallis may create a misunderstanding of what the mitzvah of tzitzis requires. The traditional practice of holding several regular talleisim to serve as a 'chuppah' is probably more appropriate.

BUYING TEFILLIN AND MEZUZOS[10]

Due to the discovery of fraudulent *tefillin* and *mezuzos* that had been machine-printed instead of hand-written, how can one ensure that the parchments (*parshiyos*) being purchased are kosher?

ANSWER

The discovery of the fraudulent mezuzos referred to here, occurred several years ago, in the year 5758 (1998). It is a good thing that the incident is still remembered and recounted, despite the fact that the *sofer* (scribe) in question was caught and put out of business.

6. או"ח סי' י"ח סק"ח
7. עי' ברכות יד: תוס' ד"ה ויאמר. והמעיין יראה דס"ל דלמ"ד ציצית חובת גברא הוא חייב ביום בכל הבגדים ופטור בלילה בכל הבגדים, ודווקא למ"ד חובת טלית הוא חייב בכסות יום ופטור בכסות לילה (ובלי זה אין פירוש לדברי התוס').
8. עי' פרק ג' מהל' ציצית הל' ז'
9. מ"ב שם
10. או"ח סי' ל"ב, ל"ט

A person should only buy his tefillin and mezuzah parshiyos from a dealer he trusts. The dealer should be able to tell you exactly who wrote the parshiyos and that the sofer can be trusted. The parshiyos should then be checked for errors.

Problems with mezuzos: Many Orthodox Jews who make a trip to and from Eretz Yisroel, look for ways to subsidize the expense by purchasing mezuzos in Eretz Yisroel and reselling them in America for a profit. There is no problem with doing this, but if one is not careful, a dealer in Israel may supply mezuzos written by inexperienced scribes (*sofrim*), or mezuzos whose origins are not definitively known. It is advisable for those wishing to offset their travel expenses in this way to verify the origins of the mezuzos and tefillin parshiyos they purchase, and to procure a letter of endorsement from the supervising Rabbi (*Rav Ha'machshir*) attesting to the kashrus of the tefillin and mezuzos that they plan to resell in the States. This will help ensure that the mezuzah and tefillin market in the United States remains free of problematic parshiyos.

Most people think that a sofer must be God-fearing (a *Yareh Shamayim*) to ensure that he has the proper focus and concentration when he writes Hashem's holy Name. This is not the most important consideration. A sofer can declare the proper intentions and go to the mikvah once at the beginning of the day and write twenty mezuzos relying on that single declaration. The most important reason that one must be particular to buy a mezuzah written by a God-fearing scribe, is that we rely on his honesty that the mezuzos and tefillin are kosher.[11] All tefillin and mezuzos have to be written *kesidran*, in their proper order. This means that if even one letter is omitted, everything that has been written subsequently must be erased in order for the forgotten letter to be inserted,[12] and this is not always possible. One is not allowed to erase Hashem's Name,[13] and if it has already been writ-

11. עי׳ או״ח סי׳ ל״ב סע׳ כ׳
12. או״ח שם סע׳ כ״ג לענין תפילין, יו״ד סי׳ רפ״ח סע׳ ג׳ לענין מזוזה
13. עי׳ מ״ב שם ס״ק ק״ח

ten after the necessary insertion point, the sofer will have to discard hours of beautiful handiwork and put the invalid mezuzah in *genizah* (concealed storage). It is also a common occurrence that two letters will inadvertently touch, and depending on the circumstances, it may or may not be permissible to separate them.[14] If the sofer is not God-fearing, he could easily correct the errors without anyone knowing and pass off an invalid (*posul*) mezuzah as a kosher one.

Thus, the dealer must know the sofrim from whom he buys, and possess some proof that they are honest and God-fearing.

It should be mentioned that the incident referred to above was an extreme case of fraud, and thankfully such occurrences are rare. That particularly talented sofer wrote six beautiful mezuzos. They were works of art; a true fulfillment of the dictum, "*zeh Keli v'anveihu* – This is my God and I shall beautify myself before Him." Unfortunately, this sofer's talent was lost to the world. He took those mezuzos and photocopied them onto ruled parchment using a process that left a raised layer of ink. The market was flooded with hundreds of posul mezuzos that appeared to be of the highest quality (*mehadrin*) in every way. The only way he was caught was through computerized checking. The programs that are used to check parshiyos register duplicates when the same mezuzah is scanned twice. When dealers began to report frequent and unexpected duplicates, their suspicions were raised, and the sofer producing the posul mezuzos was eventually tracked down.

Tefillin: There is an additional concern with regard to tefillin. It is common for tefillin to be shipped from Eretz Yisroel ready to wear. The parshiyos are inserted into the *batim* (the square leather boxes that house the parshiyos), the batim are closed and sealed, and the finishing touches and painting are all done in Israel. The finished set is sent to the buyer abroad.

Unfortunately, this system lends itself to a certain amount of abuse. Due to modern-day advances in the field of tefillin manufacture, once

14. ע"ש סע' י"ח

the parshiyos are inserted into the batim, and the batim are sealed and filled, people generally do not open them up to inspect the parshiyos for many years. The dealer in Israel knows this, and every dealer and sofer has sets of parshiyos that are sloppily written and are thus difficult to sell. Local buyers take the parshiyos to their Rav for inspection before purchasing them, and they are advised accordingly. Therefore, the foreign purchaser who does not plan on inspecting the parshiyos beforehand will likely end up being the owner of these second-rate parshiyos, even if he is paying the full market rate. By the time the parshiyos are inspected years later, no one will even remember where they came from or who the sofer was.

The best way to ensure receiving quality parshiyos from Israel is to arrange for the parshiyos and batim to be shipped separately, and have the parshiyos inserted and the batim sealed locally, after inspection. There are many experienced tefillin craftsmen in the United States who can skillfully seal and paint tefillin.

The invention of segirah – sealing tefillin: As an aside, the custom of beautifying tefillin by sealing the unsightly split between the upper section of the *titura* (the wide base of the tefillin) and its lower cover is a recent innovation. It is a skilled craft and must be done in a precise way in order to not invalidate the tefillin. The tefillin must be first sewn up, then the *soger*, or sealer, uses various glues and paint to eliminate the split.

Years ago, many people would glue the *titura* before stitching the tefillin closed. However, the Mishnah Berurah writes that it might not be permissible to apply glue before first making the *tefiros*, the stitches that hold the tefillin closed.[15] Leaving the gap unglued thus became a badge of honor for those *b'nei Torah* who were careful to avoid having their tefillin glued shut, in deference to this opinion. The *segirah* as it is carried out today does not violate this view because it is done after the tefillin have been sewn up, although it does deny the wearer the opportunity to carry the aforementioned badge of honor.

15. ביאור הלכה סוף סי' ל"ב ד"ה יתפור

The Chazon Ish[16] goes further than the Mishnah Berurah, reasoning that tefillin have to be held together by the sinews with which they are stitched. Thus, whether glue is applied before or after stitching, it renders the sinews useless and the tefillin are invalid. According to this view, even today's *segirah* is invalid. The custom, however, follows the Mishnah Berurah.

SILKSCREENING[17]

Is it permissible to produce Torah scrolls, *tefillin*, and *mezuzos* using the process of silkscreening?

ANSWER

Theoretically, *stam* (an acronym for **S**ifrei Torah, **t**efillin, and **m**ezuzos) made by silkscreening could be kosher. Many people have argued that it could standardize the industry and virtually eliminate errors. Nevertheless, the leading Rabbis of our generation (*Gedolei Hador*) were unhappy about adopting this technique for several reasons. To understand this we must discuss how silkscreening is done.

A silkscreen is essentially a very accurate stencil or pattern that is used to ensure an even and consistent application of ink or paint. The silkscreen is laid on top of the surface upon which the image is to be applied. Then, paint or ink is spread on the silkscreen, which is designed to allow the ink to penetrate to the surface only in the desired areas. The process is used extensively in the garment industry to apply lettering and designs to clothing. Once designed, the silkscreen can be used numerous times.

Kesidran: The problems with adopting silkscreening for producing *stam* are as follows. First, tefillin and mezuzah parshiyos must be

16. חזו"א או"ח סי' י"א ס"ק י'
17. או"ח סי' ל"ב

written one letter at a time in their proper order.[18] With silkscreening, the ink would have to be carefully controlled to ensure that each letter was produced in the proper order, something that would be extremely difficult to accomplish. For this reason, silkscreening should not be used for tefillin and mezuzos.

Forgeries: Regarding Sifrei Torah, Nevi'im, and Megillos, all of which do not have to be written in exact order, the reason for avoiding silk-screen techniques has less to do with the kashrus of the sefarim, and more to do with preventing forgeries. As we mentioned, forged mezuzos have been made by quality photocopying. The only way to rule out the possibility of such swindling is to ensure that each mezuzah and every Sefer Torah is hand-written. If we were to allow silk-screening techniques, the market would quickly be filled with duplicate Sifrei Torah and megillos all based on the same silkscreen, and there would be no way to ascertain if the producer used the kosher, but more expensive silkscreen method, or if he simply photocopied them.

Sirtut: Another deficiency of silkscreening has to do with the requirement of *sirtut*, scoring the parchment with lines to guide the writing of the letters and ensure that the rows of text are straight and even. Rabbi Akiva Eiger[19] demonstrates from the Gemara[20] that if a scribe (*sofer*) first writes a mezuzah and only afterwards scores the parchment, even if the scored lines are properly placed, the mezuzah is invalid, for the tradition Moshe Rabbeinu received on Har Sinai (*halachah l'Moshe m'Sinai*) requires that the sirtut actually assist in keeping the writing straight. Since the sofer wrote the mezuzah before the sirtut was applied, they did not perform their function and the mezuzah is invalid. Rabbi Akiva Eiger writes further, that the logic here applies even to a case where the scored lines were applied first, but that the sofer paid no heed to them when he wrote the letters. Because the

18. או"ח סי' ל"ב סע' כ"ג
19. שו"ת סי' נ'
20. מנחות לב:

sirtut were not instrumental in producing the evenness of the writing, the mezuzah is invalid.

Most Poskim (including Tosafos),[21] maintain the requirement of sirtut applies only to mezuzos but many Poskim and Rishonim insist that Sifrei Torah must also be written with sirtut.[22] The Gemara says that a Megillah must be written with sirtut, "*ka'amitah shel Torah* – like the truth of Torah." Tosafos says that this is referring to the parshah of Shema that is written on a mezuzah.[23] The custom is to apply sirtut to all sifrei kodesh. Consequently, a silkscreened Sefer Torah or Megillah might very well be invalid, because the evenness of the lettering is not a result of following the scoring, but rather of the placement of the silkscreen. This is true, even though the original writing was straight because of the sirtut with which it was written.

Some read into the ruling of the Magen Avraham[24] that permits reading from printed sifrei Nevi'im, that sirtut is not required for printed books of Torah, Nevi'im, and Kesuvim, because the printing machine will ensure that the lines are straight and neat to the same degree that sirtut does. According to this logic, silkscreened Sifrei Torah, Nevi'im, and Kesuvim would also be acceptable. It is incorrect, however, to draw this conclusion from the Magen Avraham's leniency (*heter*). He permitted printed Nevi'im only as a last resort, and in consideration of the dire poverty of the European Jewish communities of his time. His *heter* in this regard cannot, therefore, be taken to imply that sirtut is not required when writing *sifrei kodesh*, even with a device that ensures straight and neatly written lines.

Innovations: A time-tested guideline for this type of question is, "*Chadash assur min HaTorah* – What is new is forbidden by the Torah." A person should be wary of introducing new methods and techniques or altering the traditional ways of performing or preparing for any

21. גיטין ו: ד"ה א"ר
22. יו"ד סי' רע"א סע' ה'
23. עי' מגילה טז:
24. הקדמה לסי' רפ"ד

mitzvah. Any new idea must first gain the approval of the Gedolei Hador, who are entrusted with the protection of the Torah and our traditions. Even with the best intentions, it is not the place of any single individual to introduce revolutionary changes into the traditional methods of performing mitzvos.

TEFILLIN STITCHING[25]

Must *tefillin* be sewn together in such a way, that the lines of the stitching follow the perfectly square shape (*ribua*) of the *tefillin* boxes (*batim*) themselves? On many older pairs of handmade *tefillin*, the stitching is not exactly centered, either forming a square of its own which is not parallel to the lines of the box, or, even if the rows of stitches are parallel, they do not share the same center-point as the box.

ANSWER

It is definitely a *hiddur*, a beautification of the mitzvah of tefillin, if the *ribua* of the stitching matches that of the *bayis*. The centers of the two squares of stitching should coincide precisely. Nevertheless, the kashrus of the tefillin is in no way compromised if they do not exactly match.

DRYING HANDS FOR NETILAS YADAYIM[26]

Need one be sure that his hands are completely dry before washing for bread?

ANSWER

Strictly speaking, a person does not have to dry his hands before

25. או"ח סי' ל"ב סע' ל"ט
26. שו"ע או"ח סי' קס"ב וקס"ה

performing *netilas yadayim*. Nevertheless, the *minhag* mentioned by the Magen Avraham is to dry one's hands anyway.

Tumas yadayim: The Sages decreed a special *tumah* on a person's hands in order to protect the purity of *terumah*. The Biblical impurities of *tumas meis*, imparted by the corpses of humans; *tumas neveilah*, that of dead beasts; *tumas sheratzim*, conveyed by certain types of small, dead creatures; or any other *tumah* found in the Torah, do not interfere with netilas yadayim.

Water for netilas yadayim: Only water that was contaminated by the Rabbinically-ordained *tumas yadayim* interferes with netilas yadayim. This can occur when water is poured on the hands to remove this tumah, but fails to do so. For instance, if a person washed his hands with less than the necessary quantity (*pachos mi'keshiur*), or poured water on only half a hand, the dampness from his hands on the washing cup and whatever else he touches becomes contaminated with tumas yadayim.

Water or any other liquid that touches the hands for any reason other than *netilas yadayim* does not become *tamei*.

Leniency when in doubt: Tumas yadayim is, as we have said, a Rabbinic ordinance. Therefore, if a person knows that the water on the cup and around the sink is not tamei – or even if he is in doubt as to its status – he may be lenient. Even if his hands are wet, he is not required to dry them first. If, however, there is a reasonable concern that the water is tamei, there is room to conduct oneself with extra caution by drying off the cup before washing.

Washing for cleanliness: Even the Magen Avraham does not require drying one's hands if the water was used to prepare the hands for *netilas yadayim*. There are two common examples of this:

If a person washes his hands in order to remove a foreign substance (*chatzitzah*) so that he may wash his hands for bread, it is considered part of netilas yadayim, and he does not have to dry his hands. Foreign substances also include liquids such as oil, grape or fruit juice, blood, and milk. That it is unnecessary to dry one's hands after cleaning them in preparation for netilas yadayim is evident from the Shulchan Aruch,[27] which mentions that a person should ideally wash each hand three times. The first washing is intended to remove foreign matter, and twice more for netilas yadayim. He makes no mention of drying the hands between the first and second washings.

Washing for bread after using the restroom: When a person performs netilas yadayim after using the facilities, immediately prior to washing for bread, he is presented with a halachic dilemma.[28] He is obligated to say '*asher yatzar*' which he can only do after performing netilas yadayim. Once he performs netilas yadayim, however, he becomes obligated to also say the brachah '*al netilas yadayim*,' as he has now purified his hands prior to breaking bread. If he says '*asher yatzar*' first, then he effects an interruption between the *netilah* and its brachah. On the other hand, if he says '*al netilas yadayim*' first, then he would have to wait until after *hamotzi* to say '*asher yatzar*,' so as not to create an interruption between washing the hands and breaking bread, which is also unacceptable.

Although there are several different customs, the opinion of the Magen Avraham, cited by the Mishnah Berurah and many other later Poskim, is that one should first wash his hands in a way that does not fulfill the requirements of netilas yadayim for bread, that is, with the tap, as one would wash his hands for cleanliness, thereby avoiding the obligation to recite '*al netilas yadayim*'. This method is sufficient for washing one's hands when coming out of the bathroom, even for people who ordinarily wash with a *keli* (a halachically defined vessel). Then one should say '*asher yatzar*,' wash for bread with a *keli*, and recite '*al netilas yadayim*'. In this way, the halachic difficulties are avoided. In this situation, he is not required to dry his hands after the first washing, prior to washing for bread.

27. סי' קס"ב סע' ב'
28. עי' סי' קס"ה סע' א' ומ"ב שם סק"ב

SHIFSHUF[29]

Why is it that *shifshuf* seems to be neglected these days by many religious Jews?

ANSWER

The halachah of '*shifshuf*' applies today as always. After washing one hand twice and the other hand twice, one is supposed to then rub his hands together. This is brought as the halachah in the Shulchan Aruch.[30]

Two reasons are mentioned as to why *netilus yadayim* was instituted. Some Rishonim[31] explain that the *takanah* of netilas yadayim was meant to ensure cleanliness and sanctity on the part of Klal Yisroel.

Most Rishonim say that netilas yadayim was a *gezeira meshum srach tumah*, a decree to ensure that Kohanim would wash their hands before partaking of terumah. The decree was extended to all of Klal Yisroel that no one should partake of bread without first washing his hands. This decree remains in effect even today, so that Klal Yisroel will be accustomed to eating in purity when the Beis HaMikdash will be rebuilt, *bimheirah b'yameinu*.

Even according to this reason, Rashi (*Shabbos* 14a), explains that the Kohanim were initially required to wash their hands before eating terumah for the sake of cleanliness, without which there would be a degradation of the holiness of terumah. (Other reasons for the *takanah* are suggested by the Poskim[32]) Thus, the act of shifshuf ensures that netilas yadayim fulfills its primary purpose, that of leaving the hands clean of any foreign substance.

It is possible, therefore, that people neglect shifshuf nowadays because it is unnecessary to ensure the hands are clean. People nowadays

29. או"ח סי' קס"ב
30. סי' קס"ב סע' ב'
31. ראב"ד הובא בב"י
32. עי' מג"א ופמ"ג ועוד

have become accustomed to washing their hands with soap before sitting down to eat, and no longer need to rub them together after netilas yadayim to make sure they are clean. One should not draw any mistaken conclusion from the above discussion that shifshuf is unnecessary. On the contrary, one should always abide by what Chazal instituted without applying innovations.

BRACHAH IN FRONT OF ERVAH[33]

Is one permitted to make *brachos*, *daven* or learn in a place where women walk around without stockings or with their hair improperly covered? Is it sufficient to close one's eyes or face the other way?

ANSWER

As a general rule, a Jewish man cannot learn Torah, pray, or recite blessings in view of the parts of a woman's body that are considered *ervah*. This can be loosely defined as any part of the body that is usually covered by God-fearing Jewish women in that locality.

In certain communities, it is considered acceptable for women and girls who are generally careful to stay properly covered to walk about the house without stockings or socks. The men who live in these communities and are accustomed to this behavior, are permitted to say Krias Shema and study Torah inside the home in full view of these women. If a woman's leg is uncovered above the knee, it is always considered a makom ervah, regardless of the local standard, and it is forbidden to make a blessing in her presence. If only the lower part of the leg below the knee is exposed, it is not a makom ervah. This is the generally accepted opinion of the Mishnah Berurah.[34]

Others hold that the portion of the leg Chazal refer to as the *shok*, is between the knee and the ankle, and that section is therefore ervah.

33. או"ח סי' ע"ה
34. שם סק"ב

They wonder if it is possible that the Mishnah Berurah overlooked a number of Mishnayos[35] which clearly identify the lower leg as *shok* with respect to the part of the korban given to the Kohen. The Chafetz Chaim undoubtedly knew these Mishnayos, just as he knew every other aspect of Torah. "*Kol raz lo anis lei* – no secret was hidden from him." Rather, the Chafetz Chaim felt that the usage of the word changed over time. There are many instances of this, which can be attributed in large part to the catastrophic destruction of our Beis HaMikdash.[36] When the Written Torah and the Sages of the Mishnah spoke of *shok* they meant the lower part of the leg. Subsequently, the word's meaning came to mean the upper leg, which is how the Mishnah Berurah used it.

Closing the eyes: In many cases, it is not sufficient to simply close one's eyes in the presence of an immodestly clad woman.[37] Rather, a person should go into another room, though turning completely around to face the opposite direction is also acceptable. If he is in another room and the improper sight is in view through the door, then closing one's eyes is sufficient.[38] Closing one's eyes or turning the head the other way would also help in the presence of a married woman's exposed hair.[39]

RECITING 'MEZONOS' ON NON-GRAIN FOODS

If someone mistakenly recites '*mezonos*' on a cake that has no flour, must he then make the correct blessing? If not, is he exempt from making blessings on foods requiring '*mezonos*' that are eaten subsequently?

35. עי' חולין פ"י מ"ד
36. עי' שבת לו., סוכה לד.
37. עי' מ"ב שם סק"א וס"ק כ"ט
38. עי' מ"ב ס"ק כ"ט וצ"ע
39. מ"ב שם סק"ה

ANSWER

A general blessing: He does not have to recite another blessing on that cake. The Chaye Adam[40] equates the blessings of '*mezonos*' and '*shehakol*.' '*Shehakol*' is an all-inclusive blessing, as is apparent from the phrasing of the blessing itself: "For *everything* came into existence through His word." It may, therefore, be used to exempt any food where some question exists as to the proper blessing, as a last resort, or even if it was mistakenly recited upon food that requires a more specific brachah.

'*Mezonos*', too, is a general blessing of sorts. The formula for this blessing, "Who has created types of nourishing substances," generally describes all nourishing foods, and therefore exempts any food upon which it was recited, with the exceptions of water and salt. The Mishnah Berurah[41] cites this halachah in the name of several Poskim. Thus, if '*mezonos*' was recited unintentionally, the proper brachah need not be repeated.

Does not extend to other foods: Normally, any brachah recited exempts all similar foods that will be eaten at that sitting. In the case presented here, this holds true only for any real mezonos he will subsequently eat, and only if he had in mind to eat this when he recited the mistaken '*mezonos*'. His mistaken '*mezonos*' will not have exempted items that require a different blessing, other than the original piece of food in question, and he must make sure to recite the proper blessing on any additional items he might wish to eat, such as fruit or chocolate.

PRIMACY OF THE FIVE GRAINS[42]

There are many foods that contain flour from one of the five

40. כלל נ"ח סע' ג'
41. ביאור הלכה סי' קס"ז סע' י' ד"ה במקום
42. או"ח סי' קס"ח, וסי' ר"ח

species of grain (wheat, barley, rye, oats and spelt). Under what circumstances does the addition of these grains elevate the blessing of that food to '*borei minei mezonos*?' Examples include: gefilte fish, schnitzel, breaded fish, soup containing barley or noodles, cookie crumbs, ice-cream sandwiches and ice-cream eaten with cones.

ANSWER

The Gemara[43] states, "The blessing '*borei minei mezonos*' is made on any food containing (*kol sheyeish bo*) ingredients from the five species of grain." The term, "*kol sheyeish bo*" applies to food where the mezonos content is mixed or blended into the food (*ta'aroves*). As we shall see, there are combinations of foods that are not considered mixed, and in these cases, the mezonos does not automatically overpower the blessing of the food eaten with it. Yet, even when the mezonos is mixed into a food, it only converts the food to mezonos when the grain is intended to satiate, to noticeably enhance the flavor, or to impart a grain-like texture.

When used as a binder: Frequently, grain flour is added only to serve as a binding agent (*d'buki be'alma*). Gluten, a protein found in the five grains, effectively 'glues' the other ingredients together. In this case, the blessing is not 'mezonos', even if the food contains a large amount of flour. This is because the grain product is nullified (*batul*) to the primary ingredient of the foodstuff.[44] An example of this is gefilte fish, where the flour or matzah meal is used solely to bind the fish together, and not as a flavor enhancer. In such a case, the blessing would be '*shehakol*.' Licorice is another example where the flour is used primarily as a binder and the blessing remains '*shehakol*.'[45]

As food coloring: Often, grain flour is added only to give food a

43. ברכות לו:
44. או"ח סי' ר"ח סע' ב' ומ"ב סק"ח
45. שמעתי מהר' יעקב קמינצקי זצ"ל

certain color. In this case, too, the mezonos is nullified to the food itself. The blessing is not elevated to '*mezonos*.'

Coated shnitzel and fish: Shnitzel or fish which is fried in a coating of flour and/or breadcrumbs is a little more complicated. The coating makes the fish or shnitzel crispy and therefore tastier, which would suggest that the brachah should be 'mezonos'. But this is not always the case, as we shall now explain.

There is another, more basic rule, which governs this case and similar cases, and which takes precedence over the rule of "*kol sheyeish bo*" mentioned earlier, and that is the rule of "*ikar v'tafel*." Where one food is clearly subordinate to another, serving only to enhance the flavor of the main food, it almost never receives a brachah of its own. (The single exception is where the subordinate food is eaten first to prepare the mouth to receive the main food, in which case a '*shehakol*' is recited on the *tafel*.[46])

With regard to fried schnitzel or fish, if the coating is very thin, even though it adds to the taste, it serves only to enhance the flavor of the meat, and remains subordinate (*tafel*) to the chicken or fish, which is the primary food. In this case, the blessing is '*shehakol*,' for the fish or meat, and the coating is exempt. If the coating is thick, and it serves to satiate one's appetite or considerably adds to the flavor of the dish, then the coating is not tafel, and the proper blessing is 'mezonos'. In a borderline case when one cannot be sure how much satiation the coating provides or whether the taste of the mezonos is desirable in its own right, it is better to first make a blessing on a separate piece of mezonos and then make '*shehakol*' on the chicken or fish itself.

As an aside, one should beware of making a '*shehakol*' on water to exempt the meat, as water only requires a blessing if it is drunk to quench one's thirst.[47] Here, the reason for drinking the water is to exempt the fish or chicken from the blessing, and the water may therefore not require a blessing at all. It is a good idea to keep certain

46. סימן רי"ב ס"א

47. או"ח סי' ר"ד סע' ז'

foods in store, such as soda, mayonnaise, apples, carrots, and biscuits, which are readily available and upon which the appropriate blessings can be recited when questions arise, and in this way many halachic dilemmas can be avoided.

Cereals: A great deal of research goes into determining the correct brachah on breakfast cereals such as cornflakes. It is not always easy to determine the function of a grain ingredient. Often, grains are added to enhance the cereal's flavor. At other times, they are added simply as a binder. To help determine the grain's function it is necessary to consult with the technicians who developed the formulas. In cases of uncertainty, it is better to conduct oneself according to the guidelines in the previous paragraph and satisfy the obligation to recite a brachah over the grain content with a blessing on something else.

Noodle soup: Many thin soups contain an added mezonos ingredient, such as farfel (egg barley) or noodles. According to the Magen Avraham, if the quantity of mezonos in the soup is relatively small, the soup is considered a drink and is unaffected by the farfel or the noodles. One should then make two separate blessings: one on the farfel and one on the soup.

According to the version of the Magen Avraham that we find printed in the standard Shulchan Aruch,[48] the '*shehakol*' should be made first, since there is a possibility that a '*shehakol*' made afterwards will be a '*brachah levatalah*' (blessing made in vain) because the soup could very well be considered to be *tafel* to the mezonos, which is the *ikar*, the principle ingredient.

Reb Moshe Feinstein, *zt"l*, ruled that '*mezonos*' should be said before the '*shehakol*,' as '*mezonos*' is the more important brachah.[49] His opinion is supported by the first-edition printing of the Magen Avraham which states that '*mezonos*' should be said first.

Ideally, one should make the blessings on separate foods requiring

48. סי' ר"ח סק"ז
49. אגרות משה, אורח חיים, ח"א סי' ס"ט

'*mezonos*' and '*shehakol*,' thus including all the items in the soup. In many cases a soup will contain vegetables. This converts the brachah on the soup from '*shehakol*' to '*ha'adamah*', if the flavor of the soup is strongly affected by the vegetables.

Cooked barley: Most commercially available barley available today is known as 'pearled barley'. Whole barley grains are spun in rough-walled containers that remove the husks and polish the barley, giving it a pearl-like appearance. Some opinions maintain that this process is equivalent to grinding, which gives the barley the status of 'flour'. Cooked grain flour has the status of mezonos, and pearled barley would be no different.

Others maintain that pearled barley cannot be considered flour, and when cooked should be treated as a whole-grain dish, whose brachah is '*ha'adamah*'.

The halachic dispute as to the correct blessing for cooked pearled barley is unresolved. Since both opinions can be shown to be correct, the Mishnah Berurah states that either blessing is acceptable. (One who wishes to eat uncooked pearled barley should recite '*shehakol*.'[50])

Barley soup: The correct blessing on barley soup is determined by the two considerations discussed above. According to the Magen Avraham, a thin barley soup with some barley added would require two blessings. Thick barley soup would require a single blessing on the barley. The blessing on the barley is dependent on the status of 'pearled barley' outlined in the previous paragraph, and the choice is up to the individual whether to recite '*mezonos*' or '*ha'adamah*.'

Cholent and vegetable-barley soup: If barley constitutes one of the ingredients in cholent or thick vegetable-barley soup, the aforementioned rules do not apply.

If the cholent contains a negligible amount of barley, and it does not affect the taste or consistency of the cholent, then no separate

50. רמ"א סי' ר"ח סעי' ד' ועי' מג"א שם סק"ד

blessing is made on the barley at all. Instead, one makes a brachah on the primary or majority ingredient; either '*ha'adamah*' for vegetables, or '*shehakol*' for meat, and this brachah exempts the rest of the cholent.

If the cholent contains a sizeable amount of barley, however, one is faced with the following dilemma: If pearled barley requires a '*mezonos*' blessing, then it is primary (the *ikar*), and the entire cholent becomes a single item requiring the blessing of '*mezonos*.' However, according to the opinion that the brachah on cooked barley is '*ha'adamah*,' then the barley combines with the beans and potatoes to make the mainstay (*rov*) of the cholent '*ha'adamah*.' Thus, the *safek* as to the status of the barley creates an additional *safek* as to what the primary ingredient of the cholent truly is, and one may not simply choose the blessing of his choice. To avoid the dilemma, one should make a blessing on a separate item of mezonos, and recite '*ha'adamah*' on a bean or potato prior to eating the cholent. The other sure way to avoid this problem is to eat the cholent as part of a meal that is eaten with bread, as is done on Shabbos.

The same dilemma applies to a thick vegetable-barley soup. With regard to soup of thinner consistency, see the Mishnah Berurah.[51]

Ice-cream sandwiches: Ice-cream is often eaten together with various types of mezonos, and is another example of a combination of primary and secondary foods. When asked about ice-cream sandwiches, Reb Moshe Feinstein, *zt"l*,[52] reasoned that the ice-cream could not be considered secondary to the mezonos of the biscuits. At the same time, the biscuits on the top and bottom add to the taste and satisfaction of the product, and are valued in their own right by the people who eat them. He therefore held that one must separate some of the wafer from the ice-cream and recite the appropriate brachah on each item.

Ice-cream cones: In the case of ice-cream cones, Reb Moshe differentiated between two distinct types of cone. One is a sugar cone which is

51. סי' ר"ח ס"ק כ"ג

52. אגרות משה, או"ח, ח"ד סי' מ"ג

enjoyable in its own right. Here, both '*mezonos*' and '*shehakol*' should be made, as with the ice-cream sandwich.

The second type is a plain, tasteless wafer cone whose purpose is chiefly to hold the ice-cream. In this case, only a '*shehakol*' is made on the ice-cream. He compared these wafer cones to very thin crackers (*rakikin dakin me'od*) used to eat a dip or compote (*merkachas*). The wafer's function is essentially to hold the food and keep the hands clean. The Shulchan Aruch[53] states that in this case, the blessing on the *merkachas* also covers the wafer. Examples of this include the very thin crackers seen at buffets and smorgasbords. Even though the cracker itself may add to the enjoyment of the food, its main purpose is to hold the herring or the dip and therefore the cracker itself warrants no independent brachah. It is permissible to eat the remainder of the cracker alone after the *merkachas* has been eaten, without making a '*mezonos*.' This holds true unless a person derives special pleasure from eating such a cone or cracker.

Cookies and cream: As we have mentioned, in any mixture containing mezonos, it must be determined what function the mezonos is serving. If it is there to add grain flavor or satiation, then we invoke the principle of "*kol sheyeish bo*" and the blessing is '*mezonos*.' However, if the mezonos is *tafel* to the primary food, as above, then the principle of "*kol sheyeish bo*" does not apply.

The status of cookies crumbled into ice-cream is unclear. If the crumbs simply enhance the flavor of the ice-cream, they are *tafel*, and the ice-cream remains the single primary ingredient that defines the mixture. The blessing would therefore be '*shehakol*'. If the cookie taste is desirable in its own right, then the cookie crumbs are also a primary ingredient, and the blessing on the ice-cream would therefore be '*mezonos*'. Since the status of the cookie crumbs is unclear, a separate '*mezonos*' should first be made on a different item, followed by a '*shehakol*' on the ice-cream. It is similar to the case of farfel soup mentioned above.

53. או"ח סי' קס"ח סע' ח'

Learn the halachos: The brief treatment given here cannot do justice to the principles that govern the blessings to be said on food in all cases. Every Jewish person should make it a personal goal to learn and be knowledgeable in all of *hilchos brachos*, starting with a careful study of *perek Keitzad Mevarchin* (the sixth chapter of Tractate Brachos) and then following the principles through to the Mishnah Berurah and recent Poskim. Where this is not possible, a person should verify the appropriate brachah in each and every case by asking a competent Rav.

MEZONOS ROLLS[54]

Which brachah should be said on mezonos rolls that are sold as ready-made sandwiches, or served on airplanes as part of a meal?

ANSWER

Practically speaking, all mezonos rolls require the brachah, '*Hamotzi lechem min ha'aretz*', even on less than a *kezayis*. There are three types of mezonos, based on the dispute amongst Rishonim in Maseches Brachos (36b–37a).[55] We refer to these types as "pies, cakes, and crackers." "Mezonos rolls" are a misnomer, for they do not fit into any of these categories.

The Shulchan Aruch[56] does write that if honey or some other flavoring is added to bread, and the taste is apparent, then the brachah is '*mezonos*.' This, however, only applies to Sefardim in certain situations. (The author is not aware of any 'mezonos bread' currently produced which fulfills the requirement for Sefardim.) For Ashkenazim, none of the supposed 'mezonos rolls' even approach the texture, consistency, or flavor of cake, as the Rema clearly states.[57] A careful study of the

54. או"ח סי' קס"ח
55. הובא בשו"ע או"ח סי' קס"ח סע' ז
56. שם
57. עי' רמ"א שם

Poskim makes it extremely difficult, at best, to find any basis for the thinking that rationalizes mezonos rolls. A lengthy discussion of the subject may be found in the Hebrew edition of Shulchan HaLevi.[58]

As in all areas of halachah that have applications on a daily basis, every person should take the time to learn the *sugyos* and the Shulchan Aruch, and familiarize himself with the appropriate precepts.

Pizza: Unlike regular pie, whose filling is enclosed inside the dough, a pizza's 'filling' is spread on top of the dough. Therefore, it has been suggested that pizza should not be viewed as a pie, and its blessing should be '*hamotzi*.' This argument is incorrect. It is irrelevant whether the filling is inside, underneath, or on top.

The nature of the filling, not its location, is halachically significant. The Shulchan Aruch[59] states that fillings such as meat or cheese, which are commonly eaten with bread as a meal, bestow upon the bread-like component, a greater *kevius* than ordinary un-filled, bread-like pastries. This is because the combination of such a filling and the bread-like dough together is a meal in itself, a true *seudas keva*, and the proper brachah is therefore '*hamotzi*.' According to this, pizza should be '*hamotzi*' even if less than a *shiur* was eaten. In contrast, the Taz[60] maintains that any kind of filling should change the brachah of the bread to '*mezonos*.'

The Mishnah Berurah[61] says we should only follow the opinion of the Taz with small hors d'oeuvres type pastries and doughs such as 'franks-in-blankets' that are designed as snack-food and not as meal-food. Thus, any ordinary size pie with a bread-like component that is primarily eaten as a meal, requires '*hamotzi*' if the filling is cheese or meat.

Pies with a cake-dough crust have the brachah of '*mezonos*' regardless of the filling, though one might be required to recite '*hamotzi*' if

58. עי' שו"ת שולחן הלוי ח"א
59. שם סע' י"ז
60. סק"כ
61. ביאור הלכה שם ד"ה פשטיד"א

intending to eat a sufficient quantity. (See page 35, for the definition of cake-dough.)

Is pizza, therefore, considered meal-food or snack-food? This is a difficult question to answer definitively, but the custom in most places is to make a '*mezonos*' on pizza. One must nevertheless keep in mind that if enough pizza will be eaten to establish a *kevius*, one should wash and *bentch*.

It should also be kept in mind that some brands of frozen pizza are made differently, and require *hamotzi* under all circumstances. The dough is baked alone without any toppings, and is considered bread according to all opinions. The sauce and toppings are applied only after the baking, and this does not affect the brachah.

ESTABLISHING A MEAL ON BAKED MEZONOS[62]

How much baked mezonos must an adult eat to require the blessings of 'hamotzi' and Birkas HaMazon?

ANSWER

Exactly how much mezonos one must eat in order to bentch depends upon the circumstances. In any given case, it must be enough to have the status of *kevias seudah*, of establishing a set meal in order to require Birkas HaMazon. These halachos are discussed by the Mishnah Berurah[63] and many other Poskim at great length. Essentially, there are three ways to 'establish a meal' on mezonos.

Case 1. If a person is eating only mezonos, he must eat the volume equivalent to all the food he would normally eat in a regular, satisfying meal. For example, if a person's whole meal consists of pie or cake, he becomes obligated to recite Birkas HaMazon only if the pie he eats is

62. או"ח סי' קס"ח
63. סי' קס"ח ס"ק כ"ד

equal to the total volume of the bread, main course, and side dishes that he normally consumes in a regular meal. Reb Moshe, *zt"l*, held that three slices of pizza is the equivalent of a full meal.

Case 2. When mezonos is eaten together with other foods, it is regarded as a bread substitute, and the *shiur* that establishes *kevias seudah* is significantly less. One need only eat a volume of mezonos equal to the volume of the *bread* normally consumed with a regular meal. For example, one ordinary slice of pizza is generally equivalent to two slices of rye bread. If one would normally eat two slices of bread with cheese, fries, and a salad, then a slice of pizza eaten with the same foods would require washing for '*hamotzi*' and the recitation of Birkas HaMazon.[64]

Case 3. This category is a combination of the conditions set out in cases 1 and 2. If one eats mezonos alone (case 1), but becomes satiated by eating a quantity of mezonos equivalent only to the volume of bread eaten with a full meal (case 2), *bentching* is still required. This category is unique because the obligation to bentch depends on the subjective criterion of individual satiation, and not simply according to a standard volume normally eaten by others. For example, if one ate cake, and nothing else, and ate enough to feel fully satiated, as if he had eaten a full, regular meal, he must recite '*hamotzi*' and Birkas HaMazon, even if the total volume of cake is less than the full volume of a regular meal, but equal to at least the amount of bread eaten with a regular meal.

It is important to note that nowadays, people usually eat a far smaller

64. מקור קביעת סעודה ע"פ ב' השיעורים האלו תמצא בגמ' ערובין כט: "אמר רב יהודה אמר שמואל כל שהוא ליפתן – כדי לאכול בו; כל שאינו ליפתן – כדי לאכול הימנו." ופרש"י ז"ל: "כדי לאכול בו – כל שהוא לפתן שיעורו כדי לאכול בו ללפת בו את הפת מזון ב' סעודות: כדי לאכול הימנו – שיהו כל שתי הסעודות ממנו: ע"ע כתובות סד. המשרה את אשתו על ידי שליש לא יפחות לה משני קבין חטין וכו' ונותן לה חצי קב קיטנית וחצי לוג שמן וקב גרוגרות או מנה דבילה וכו'. משמע מהכא ששיעור של ד' ביצים הוא כדי לאכול בו, היינו הכמות של לחם הנאכל עם סעודה של כמה מיני מאכלים ביחד.

quantity of bread with their meal than was the norm in past times. It used to be customary to eat five or six slices of bread at one sitting. One reason for this change is the increased availability and affordability of other foodstuffs such as fish, meat, and cheese. The result is that a standard meal today consists of a large main dish with a small amount of bread, since the main dish itself provides a significant amount of satiation. Consequently, the amount of cake required for kevias seudah in the second case above, should be determined by the amount of bread that is normally eaten under contemporary conditions, which is about two slices. This is discussed more fully in Iggros Moshe.[65]

How much is the 'shiur'? **The Mishnah** (*Uktsin* 2:8) states, "פת ספוגנית משתערת בכמות שהיא, אם יש בה חלל ממעך את חללה – Sponge-cake is measured as-is; if it contains a pocket of air-space, its air-space should not be counted into the Shiur." To determine if a spongy piece of bread is of sufficient volume to become *tamei*, the bread should not be compressed; it is measured as-is. This is true even though it can be squeezed and reduced into a small fraction of its present volume.

The Shulchan Aruch[66] states that this method of measuring applies also to determining the shiur of kezayis for a mitzvah such as eating matzah on Pesach. Thus a kezayis of matzah even if it is light and puffy will suffice, even though when chewed and swallowed it will be equal to a fraction of the original amount.

The Mishnah Berurah[67] states that uncompressed volume applies also for measuring a kezayis for Birkas HaMazon. Therefore, even a puffy kezayis of bread requires Birkas HaMazon.

Measuring 'shiur' for kevias seudah: None of the well-known Poskim discuss whether uncompressed volume can be used with *pas haba'ah b'kisnin* to determine the quantity for kevias seudah. It

65. או"ח ח"ג סי' ל"ב
66. או"ח סי' תפ"ו
67. שם סק"ז

stands to reason, however, that it should not be enough to simply measure the uncompressed volume of mezonos to determine if the requirements of kevias seudah have been met. This is because kevias seudah is a result of the satiation-power of the mezonos, which is not accurately reflected by its volume alone. A piece of very light and puffy cake may be very large, but contain only a small amount of actual food. Its correct shiur can only be determined by measuring the amount of actual food it contains; it cannot be measured strictly in terms of halachic volume. In this respect, measuring the quantity of *pas haba'ah b'kisnin* for the purposes of Birkas HaMazon differs from the method of measuring the quantity of food regarding the other mitzvos discussed above.

The Shabbos kiddush: It should be taken into account, that once a person begins eating he may change his mind as to the quantity he intends to consume. Often, he intends to eat a small piece of cake, but, as is well known, the very act of eating stimulates the appetite and he may go on to eat a quantity that requires him to *bentch*. A typical Shabbos kiddush is a good example of this. Not wanting to fill himself up before his regular seudah, a person may join the kiddush with the intention of eating only a small amount, but once he begins eating the various types of kugel, and has a few slices of cake and so on, he will have definitely exceeded the shiur that requires bentching. If someone knows that he will likely end up eating mezonos to satiation, or the volume equivalent to a meal, the proper thing to do is to wash, recite '*hamotzi*,' and bentch at the kiddush, and afterwards go home and eat his regular Shabbos seudah.

If he realizes in the middle of a kiddush that he has consumed the amount of food described above, he must bentch even though he had neither washed nor made '*hamotzi*' to begin with. If he had not yet consumed the amount of food described above, but is planning on continuing to eat an additional quantity of mezonos that would require him to bentch, (i.e. outside of what he ate until now), he must also wash and make '*hamotzi*.' There is no need to make '*al hamichyah*.'

Learn the halachos well: "*Eizehu chacham, haro'eh es hanolad*, he who is wise will consider the consequences."[68] Since eating is a daily necessity, questions in *kevias seudah* will frequently arise. It cannot be overstressed that a person must take the time to become knowledgeable in this area of halachah and make himself familiar with its complexities and applications. By doing so, he will remove the doubt from many common situations.

A CHILD'S MEAL OF BAKED MEZONOS

Is the shiur of mezonos that would require a child to wash and bentch dependent on his size and age, or is it the same as an adult?

ANSWER

Every father is obligated in *chinuch habanim*, to teach his children the proper way to fulfill the mitzvos. To fulfill this obligation, he must be sure his child performs the mitzvah in the same way as an adult. Therefore, if the mitzvah requires a shiur, the mitzvah of *chinuch* is not fulfilled unless the minor (*katan*[69]) performs the mitzvah with the required shiur.

For example, the mitzvah of matzah on the first night of Pesach can only be fulfilled by eating a kezayis of matzah. Even though a kezayis may be a large amount for a child, chinuch requires that he eat the same amount for his mitzvah.

Likewise, just as an esrog must be owned by an adult on the first day of Sukkos, most Poskim maintain that a child is not properly trained in the mitzvah unless he too owns the esrog that he waves. This is true even though it may result in a hardship. Once the *katan* owns it, it remains his forever. A minor can acquire ownership, but

68. תמיד לב.
69. בן שלא הגיע ליום הולדת הי"ג שלו, או בת שלא הגיעה ליום הולדת הי"ב שלה נחשבים לקטנים.

cannot transfer ownership to others (*katan koneh v'eino makneh*). This means that the esrog may not then be used by any other adult to fulfill the mitzvah on the first day of Sukkos.

This principle applies also to the obligation to recite Birkas HaMazon after eating bread; a child must eat a kezayis of bread in order to bentch Birkas HaMazon. This applies even if the *katan* is fully satisfied after eating less than a kezayis, because the obligation to bentch is dependent on two requirements: *achilah* and *sevi'a* (eating and satiation). To satisfy the condition of *achilah*, a kezayis is required, even if one is fully satisfied from a smaller quantity of bread.[70]

With regard to washing and reciting '*hamotzi*' and Birkas HaMazon on mezonos, the main consideration is whether or not the person eating has fulfilled the requirements of *kevias seudah*, establishing a set meal. There is no fixed volume of food that creates kevias seudah. Rather, this is done by eating a "*shiur she'acheirim kovin alav*," the amount of food that others would consider a satisfying meal. For instance, in order to make a meal out of heavy cake, a person might need to eat a volume of four eggs' worth (*beitzim*). However, a similar quantity of a lighter cake would not be sufficient to create kevias seudah, because the shiur of kevias seudah depends on the satiation the food provides rather than its volume.

With regard to the shiur for *brachah acharonah*, the volume is always the determining factor. With regard to the shiur of kevias seudah it is the 'satiation quotient' or '*kevius*-value' that counts. Indeed, whenever volume is used in sefarim and charts to measure kevias seudah it only represents the amount of satiation-per-volume that the food ordinarily provides, and must be adapted according to the actual density of the food being eaten.

Returning to our question, chinuch requires that the shiur for a child be determined in the same manner as for an adult, and for kevias seudah, this is according to the '*shiur she'acheirim kovin alav*.' This means that in order to recite '*hamotzi*' and bentch on mezonos, the child would have to eat a quantity that would normally satisfy other

70. עי' אג"מ, או"ח, ח"א סי' ע"ו

people of his age and build. The volume of a satiating meal varies not only with the type of food eaten, but also according to the satiation threshold of the type of person eating the meal, such that the '*shiur she'acheirim kovin alav*' will yield a smaller volume for a child of ten than it will for a fully-grown adult. [71]

If, for example, a father and son sit down to eat pizza, it might be that the father would have to eat two slices in order to recite Birkas HaMazon, yet for the child, only one slice of the same pizza would require him to bentch.

It should again be stressed that whenever halachah specifies an absolute shiur of a specific volume there is never any variation, regardless of the age or size of the person, nor does the shiur vary with the texture and density of the material measured. A kezayis of airy matzah has the same shiur volume as heavy, thick matzah. A *k'beitzah* of bread requires '*al netilas yadayim*' whether or not the loaf is light and spongy or heavy and dense. It should be kept in mind that the custom is to wash even before eating a piece of bread less than a kezayis, barring certain exceptional considerations, such as where the bread is in any case secondary to some other food or drink.[72]

CONDITIONS THAT CHANGE THE STATUS OF BREAD TO MEZONOS[73]

What blessing should be made on matzah when it is ground up or soaked in milk and sugar – '*hamotzi*' or '*mezonos*'?

ANSWER

There are specific conditions whereby bread is relegated to the status of mezonos. First, the pieces of bread must be less than a *kezayis*. Pieces of bread larger than a kezayis never lose their status of bread

71. ביאור הלכה סי' קס"ח סע' ו' ד"ה אע"פ
72. עי' מ"ב קנ"ח ס"ק י'
73. או"ח סי' קס"ח

even when cooked, even if they lose their bread-like appearance. Pieces of bread smaller than a kezayis can be reduced to mezonos if one of two conditions is met. If they are cooked in a liquid over the fire, or even simply put into a hot *keli rishon* that is off the fire, then they automatically become mezonos. It is not necessary to check and see if they still have a bread-like texture. If they are placed in a liquid that cannot cook, then the pieces of bread must lose their bread-like texture before becoming mezonos.

Hot matzah cereal: Therefore, if matzah meal or small broken up pieces of matzah are cooked in milk to make a hot breakfast cereal, there is no question that the brachah is now '*mezonos*.' The same would apply to adding matzah meal or crushed matzah to very hot soup.

Cold matzah cereal: If matzah is soaked in cold milk to make a breakfast cereal, then one has to check to see that the matzah has lost its bread-like appearance before '*mezonos*' may be recited. Matzah meal or very small crumbs will become mezonos in cold liquid after only a minute or two, as by then it will have become soft. Larger pieces (though still less than a kezayis) will take longer. The Shulchan Aruch[74] mentions that bread has lost its appearance when the water in which it is soaking turns white.[75]

Re-baking bread: It is important to remember that re-baking bread that was reduced to mezonos can reinstate the blessing of '*hamotzi lechem min ha'aretz*.' A common example is a recipe for challah kugel, where the soaked challah is baked once again. If the challah is shredded into pieces that are each less than a kezayis, and the recipe contains a significant amount of sugar or spices and has a sweet taste, then the blessing would remain '*mezonos*', like any sweet cake. However, many recipes produce kugel that is similar in sweetness to standard

74. שם סעיף י"א
75. עי' ברכות דף לז. תוס' ד"ה תוריתא דנהמא, בשם רבינו דוד ממיץ

challah. It is like making challah from a dough of old challah instead of flour, and such a kugel requires '*hamotzi*.'[76]

As in so many areas of halachah, it is worthwhile for every person to take the time to learn the guidelines well. Situations arise literally every day regarding the laws of mezonos and bread. Every *ben Torah* should therefore be well-versed in the appropriate halachos and be able to recall them with ease.

DESSERT BLESSINGS[77]

Which blessings, if any, must be recited over desserts served at the end of a meal over which '*hamotzi*' has been recited?

ANSWER

Dessert at a standard meal: After a standard meal, where the table is cleared and the dessert is served, the basic halachah is that a blessing should be made on whatever dessert is served, whether it be apple pie, cake, fruit, or jello.[78] Generally, one hears that if the dessert consists of pastries or cake, one does not recite '*mezonos*.' This is because there is usually a question (*safek*) as to whether these baked grain products are considered '*pas haba'ah b'kisnin*' which requires '*mezonos*,' or if they are forms of bread, which would be covered by the '*hamotzi*' recited at the beginning of the meal.[79] One opinion maintains that pastries consisting of bread-like dough with sweet fillings, are *pas haba'ah b'kisnin*, and require a blessing of '*mezonos*.' Others maintain that the dough or batter itself must contain oil, sugar or juice to warrant a blessing of '*mezonos*.' A baked item of this description is commonly referred to as cake. A third opinion defines *pas haba'ah b'kisnin* as hard and brittle crackers. Each opinion maintains that its definition is the exclusive

76. עי' מ"ב שם ס"ק נ"ט
77. או"ח סי' קס"ח, קע"ז
78. או"ח סי' קע"ז סע' א'
79. או"ח סי' קס"ח סע' ז', וע"ע ביאור הלכה שם סע"ח

one for *pas haba'ah b'kisnin*,[80] that any other bread-like mezonos is simply another form of bread, and that one does not make an extra '*hamotzi*' on a different type of bread served at the end of a meal.

A pie which satisfies all three definitions of *pas haba'ah b'kisnin*, that is, the crust is hard and crispy, its dough was mixed with sugar or oil, and it has a filling, requires '*mezonos*' according to all opinions.[81] A blessing should be made on such a pie, provided that it is not being eaten for satiation. If one is still hungry, the pie would be considered a primary part of the meal, no different from meat or fish, and does not warrant its own blessing.

At a wedding: At a formal affair, where the tables and chairs are cleared away after the main course, the situation is different. Rightfully speaking, this is called "after the meal (*le'achar hamazon*)," and people do not intend to eat any more bread after this point, even if they have not yet recited Birkas HaMazon. The Gemara[82] states, "Rav Pappa said: the halachah is, after the meal [all food served] requires a blessing both before and after." In such a case, a person should make a '*shehakol*' on a piece of chocolate, and if he ate a sufficient amount, '*borei nefashos*' after finishing – all before Birkas HaMazon.

There is a dispute regarding the definition of the term '*le'achar hamazon*.' Some say it means that the tables are physically removed.[83] Others hold it means that the diners have completely stopped eating bread (*mashchu yedeihem min ha'pas*[84]). Thus, the Poskim[85] write that in their time, it was uncommon to find a case of '*le'achar hamazon*' before Birkas HaMazon.

Although these criteria are not met at the conclusion of a regular formal meal, at a wedding nowadays, the tables are often removed

80. כ"כ רעק"א בח' (קס"ח במג"א סכ"ב). ועי' בה"ל מה שהביא ממאמר מרדכי.
81. סע' ח' ביה"ל ד"ה טעונים
82. ברכות מא:
83. אליה רבה סי' קע"ז בשם הרשב"א הכלבו ורבינו יונה
84. תוס' שם ד"ה לאחר, רא"ש שם פ"ו סי' כ"ו וע' שו"ע סי' קע"ז סע' ב'
85. תוס' שם ד"ה לאחר

along with the bread. This is similar to the situation discussed in the Gemara, and therefore, Rav Pappa's halachah applies.[86]

The Viennese table: At such a wedding, the arrival of the Viennese table brings with it a number of halachic complications. The array of desserts on the standard Viennese table includes cakes and pastries. Many of these items are considered bread according to one or the other of the opinions mentioned above, and their presence raises a question as to whether or not bread is still being served. This in turn, calls into question whether or not the meal is considered to have finished, and the guests are thus confronted with a dilemma.

If the meal is officially over, one is required to say blessings before and after everything eaten, but if the meal is not yet over, one is only required to say initial blessings on the non-mezonos items and crusty pies that meet the criteria of *pas haba'ah b'kisnin* according to all opinions. Some opinions hold that the only way to resolve this dilemma is for the host to arrange that all the mezonos being served is *pas haba'ah b'kisnin* according to all opinions, or that the Viennese table should contain no cakes at all. In either of these two cases, the situation is similar to that described in the Gemara, and blessings would be required both before and after.

It is reasonable to suggest, however, that even if there are cakes and pastries on a Viennese table, Rav Pappa's halachah applies. This is because the type of eating that is done around a Viennese table always occurs after the guests have "withdrawn from bread." "*Mashchu yedeihem min ha'pas*" means the end of formal, meal-like eating indicated by the presence of bread. The presence of cake or pastries on the Viennese table is no indication of formality in any way. On the contrary, they are a convincing display of informality and a sure sign that the meal is over. Therefore, blessings should be said before and after every type of food.

In former years there was much discussion as to whether or not the brachah on desserts should be omitted altogether, in consideration

86. עי' ביאור הלכה שם ד"ה שאין

of an opinion stated in Tosafos,[87] that food which is eaten with the meal is considered part of the meal itself. Despite the clearly stated *psak* of the Mishnah Berurah[88] to the contrary, a number of authoritative people would make a brachah on something else so as to avoid making a brachah on the dessert. The poskim from whom the author learned, held that a brachah should be said. This included Reb Moshe, *zt"l.* They maintained this position even at a time when dessert was a required dish at every standard meal.

Today, the issue is irrelevant because dessert is no longer de rigueur at most regular meals and has long ceased to be a must for normal dining. Hence, there is no question that brachos should always be recited on desserts as per the *Poskim*.

BLESSINGS ON GRAINS AND CEREAL[89]

What are the correct blessings to recite on puffed wheat, puffed rice, and cornflakes?

ANSWER

Individual whole grains, even when cooked, are always '*ha'adamah*,' as are all brands of puffed wheat sold in the United States made from whole grains of wheat. Therefore, these cereals require the blessing of '*borei p'ri ha'adamah*.'

Of the many companies that produce puffed wheat cereal, some put the wheat through a process that removes a portion of the endosperm, the outer layer of the edible part of the grain. A suggestion was circulated that this is enough for the cereal to warrant a '*mezonos*' blessing, as only whole grains require '*ha'adamah*,' and cooked partial grains are sometimes elevated to '*mezonos*.' However, such a distinction between whole grains and those missing a small amount

87. עי' דברי תוס' ברכות מב. בתחילת העמוד
88. סי' קע"ז שעה"צ אות ז'
89. או"ח סי' ר"ח

of the endosperm is not made by any of the Rishonim or Poskim. Reb Moshe, *zt"l*,[90] held that puffed wheat always requires a blessing of '*borei p'ri ha'adamah*.'

Puffed rice: The appearance of all brands of crisped rice cereal is somewhat deceptive. The individual "crispies" appear to be whole puffed kernels of rice, but are actually made from a rice-flour paste. The proper blessing is '*mezonos*.'

Cornflakes: Cornflakes also present a halachic question regarding the proper blessing. Certain brands, such as Kellogg's, make cornflakes from kernels of corn that have been flattened and toasted. Corn cereals made in this way require the blessing of '*ha'adamah*.' Other brands are manufactured using dough formed from corn paste, which is then fashioned into a cornflake shape. These require the brachah of '*shehakol*.' If the listed ingredient is milled corn, then it was certainly made with rolled kernels and the blessing is '*ha'adamah*.' If the ingredients mention corn flour or some variation, the blessing is '*shehakol*.'

Cracked grains and split grains: Even cracked or split grains may sometimes require the blessing of '*ha'adamah*' and not '*mezonos*.' Split or cracked grains of wheat, barley, rye, oats, and spelt that are cooked in a way that the grains do not adhere to one another, require only the blessing of '*ha'adamah*'; the requirement for the higher blessing of '*mezonos*' only begins if they are cooked in a way that causes them to stick together.[91]

In the case where grains stick together through the cooking process, then the halachah is more complicated. With regard to rice, the fact that the grains are somewhat distended and stick together is enough to warrant '*borei minei mezonos*.'[92] With other grains, however, this

90. אגרות משה, או"ח, ח"ד סי' מ"ד–מ"ה
91. עי' סי' ר"ח סע' ב' ומ"ב סק"ו, וכן בסע' ד' ומ"ב סקט"ו
92. שו"ע שם סע' ז'

might not be sufficient. Rabbeinu Yonah[93] mentions that other grains must also be crushed to warrant the blessing '*mezonos*.' Thus, many grain products require '*ha'adamah*' and not '*mezonos*.'

Wheat germ: The Poskim have concluded that wheat germ requires '*ha'adamah*'.[94]

Muesli: Although the addition of milk to muesli somewhat softens the oats therein, the blessing of '*ha'adamah*' is required. If by soaking it in cold milk the oats stick together and lose their form and shape, the muesli then requires '*mezonos*.'

Granola bars: Granola bars containing whole or split grains of oat require a '*ha'adamah*.' Though the grains are stuck together, this is accomplished by the sugar or honey, and not by the grain itself. Even if flour were to be added to the mixture, the blessing would still be '*ha'adamah*' because the flour is secondary to the grains. This would be true even if there would be a significant amount of flour added to thicken or solidify the mixture, because it would still be secondary to the granola. According to the information available to the author, all granola bars on the market today are '*ha'adamah*.'

The after-blessing: The Shulchan Aruch[95] notes a dilemma regarding the *brachah achronah* on whole grains. Tosafos[96] mentions in the name of Rabbeinu Tam that the blessing for whole wheat kernels should resemble the formula of *birkas me'ein shalosh*. This is because wheat is one of the types of food for which the Land of Israel is praised. On the other hand, whole grains are not 'mezonos', or 'of the tree', or 'of the vine'. Thus, the standard formula of *birkas me'ein shalosh* does not accurately describe whole grains and cannot be recited upon them.

93. ברכות לז. ד"ה והפת
94. אגרות משה שם סי' מ"ו
95. שם סע' ד'
96. ברכות שם ד"ה הכוסס

Rabbeinu Tam initially included a special formula in *birkas me'ein shalosh* for whole grains: "*Al ha'adamah ve'al p'ri ha'adamah*," but he later removed it, remaining doubtful of the propriety of reciting such a formula, as it had not been composed by Chazal.

The Shulchan Aruch therefore states that the appropriate '*brachah achronah*' on whole grains is '*borei nefashos*,' but that a God-fearing person will only eat such foods as part of a meal served with bread, or will eat less than the amount requiring an after-blessing.

That being the case, the best thing is to be sure never to eat an entire *kezayis* of these foods within the time it takes to eat a certain portion of bread (*bichdei achilas pras*). Eat less than that amount, take a break for a few minutes; partake of another dish. Then have more of the questionable grains. Indeed, a person can learn to derive great pleasure from eating in a way that is consciously guided by a clear understanding of the questions and opinions of our halachic authorities; a greater pleasure perhaps, than that derived from the taste of the food itself.

Nevertheless, since a person is not obligated to avoid these foods, nor limit himself in any way, he can choose to follow the accepted halachic ruling and simply say '*borei nefashos*.'

POTATO FLAKES

What blessing should be recited on mashed potatoes made by adding water to dehydrated potato flakes?

ANSWER

When Reb Moshe Feinstein, *zt"l*, was first approached with this question, he maintained that the blessing was '*shehakol*.' However, many years later he reversed his opinion, saying that it had become the normal way (*derech*) to make mashed potatoes using flakes. This follows the logic of the Trumas HaDeshen,[97] who holds that the primary blessing of a food is maintained when prepared in any of the normal

97. סי' כ"ט הובא ברמ"א סי' ר"ב סע' ז'

ways. Even caterers often use flakes or powder rather than fresh potatoes, for the extra smooth texture they provide. Additionally, the flakes contain no additives at all. The blessing is therefore '*ha'adamah*.'

TORTILLA CHIPS AND CORN CHIPS

What is the correct blessing on tortilla chips and corn chips?

ANSWER

Most tortilla chips are made entirely from inedible corn, known as "cow corn," which is processed and rendered suitable for human consumption. Furthermore, most sweet, edible corn in the United States is not grown to be used for tortillas. Food prepared in a non-standard or unusual way loses its primary blessing if it is ground up and made to lose the appearance of the fruit or vegetable from which is was made. Therefore, the blessing on tortillas is '*shehakol*.' In countries such as Mexico, where tortillas are a common and major source of sustenance, this may be considered a standard way of preparing corn. Indeed, corn might be grown in such countries primarily for the purpose of making tortillas. If this is true, then the blessing on tortillas in Mexico would be '*borei p'ri ha'adamah*.' However, in the United States and elsewhere, the blessing remains '*shehakol*.'

EATING FOLLOWING AN AFTER-BLESSING

If a person sits down to eat a piece of chicken with a cup of hot tea, may he recite '*borei nefashos*' once he has finished the chicken, lest he forget to recite the blessing later, and then continue to drink his tea?

ANSWER

There are many instances where one might desire to follow a snack with some type of food which takes a long time to eat. Such foods or drink are not consumed quickly enough to warrant a *brachah acharonah*, yet an obligation exists from a previously eaten food to recite a *brachah acharonah* in any case. It may be that a person who nonetheless continues to eat might forget to recite the *brachah acharonah* in the end, or sufficient time might pass (*shiur ikul*) by the time he completes his tea that he may lose the opportunity to recite the *brachah acharonah* entirely.

Theoretically, someone in this situation might think to recite '*borei nefashos*' on all he has eaten until that point, and then recite a new '*shehakol*' on whatever he wishes to continue to eat. This is unacceptable, for had he waited to recite '*borei nefashos*' until he had finished all his food, it would never have been necessary to recite the second '*shehakol*'. He has intentionally created a situation where he will be required to recite a blessing that he was not initially required to recite, and this is an unnecessary blessing (*brachah she'einah tzerichah*).

Another possibility is that which is described in the above question: Let him recite '*borei nefashos*' on what he has eaten thus far, having in mind that the *brachah acharonah* should only exempt the particular food he has finished (the chicken), allowing him to continue sipping his tea on the basis of his original '*shehakol*'.

To evaluate the feasibility of this approach we must determine what a *brachah acharonah* accomplishes. Does it simply exempt the food upon which it is recited, or does it terminate the *brachah rishonah*?

There is a Gemara that discusses a similar case to ours. If one should drink wine prior to a bread meal, such as *kiddush* on *leil Shabbos*, he recites '*borei p'ri hagafen*.' After the *seudah*, he recites Birkas HaMazon over a cup of wine. The Gemara deliberates over whether or not this man's original '*borei p'ri hagafen*' can exempt the wine he is about to drink.

On the one hand, Birkas HaMazon was only recited upon that which was eaten at the meal, and does not exempt the wine he drank for kiddush. This would suggest that his original *brachah* over the wine remains unaffected by the recital of Birkas HaMazon, and that he should not be required to recite another '*borei p'ri hagafen*' on the wine after the meal.

On the other hand, perhaps Birkas HaMazon divides between

the initial blessing over the wine and the wine he is now drinking, terminating the effectiveness of that original blessing. The Gemara[98] concludes that one must recite a new '*borei p'ri hagafen*' on the wine over which he recited Birkas HaMazon. This suggests that any *brachah acharonah* terminates a *brachah rishonah*.

In our case too, '*borei nefashos*' should serve to permanently divide between the '*shehakol*' and the rest of the food he wishes to finish, terminating the effectiveness of his original *brachah rishonah*. This holds true even if one were to make a verbal declaration that he was only reciting a *brachah acharonah* on a portion of his food, just as Birkas HaMazon terminates the *brachah rishonah* on the wine, even though it does not exempt the wine.[99]

If a person has already recited a *brachah acharonah* over the chicken before finishing his tea, he must recite another *brachah rishonah*. Though the additional *brachah* had initially been unnecessary, and though he himself was the cause of the obligation to recite this additional blessing, under no circumstances may he eat food that is not covered by a blessing.[100]

BLESSING ON FRAGRANCES[101]

Must one recite a blessing on the fragrance of bushes and flowers in a botanical garden?

ANSWER

A general rule regarding *birchos hare'ach*, blessings over fragrances,

98. פסחים קג:
99. כן נראה לעניות דעתי.
100. עי' פרי מגדים באשל אברהם סי' ר"ז סק"א וז"ל: "אם אכל ושתה הרבה מינים ובירך ברכה אחרונה בנ"ר אדעתא למפטר רק מין אחד פטר הכל ואסור לברך שוב על שאר המינים". היינו שאסור לברך עוד הפעם ברכה אחרונה שכבר נפטרו כל המינים שאכל מהם לפני כן. נמצא שהוא נחשב כסיים אכילתו הראשונה, וממילא אסור לו להמשיך ולאכול מן המאכלים האלו בלא ברכה ראשונה חדשה. וברוך שכוונתי.
101. או"ח סי' רט"ז–רי"ז

is that an item set aside for some purpose other than its fragrance is called *lo avida l'reicha*, not designated for its scent, and does not require a brachah. This applies only where the intention of setting aside the fragrant item is specifically for some other use than its scent. If the item is displayed for a dual purpose, for instance, to be sold to the public and also to provide a pleasant smell so as to entice customers, it is considered *avida l'reicha*, designated for its scent.

It is also possible that a fragrant object's status can change. A case in point would be where flowers or spices are placed next to a dead body as a show of honor, or to negate its foul smell. These flowers are considered *lo avida l'reicha*. Nonetheless, if one takes one of these flowers or spices in his hand in order to smell it, it becomes *avida l'reicha* and it requires a brachah.[102]

Sweet-smelling flowers growing in the wild or displayed in a botanical garden are considered *avida l'reicha* and a brachah must be made when one inhales the smell for his enjoyment. In such a situation it is advisable to approach the fragrant shrub to demonstrate his specific intent to enjoy its smell, while having in mind the other scents that he will enjoy along the way. This practice takes into consideration the existence of a slight possibility that these flowers are actually considered *lo avida l'reicha*.

It is important to point out that in a botanical garden, the correct blessing in the vast majority of cases is not '*borei minei besamim*.' Though we recite this blessing at havdalah even on items that strictly speaking require different blessings, this is only in deference to the standard Ashkenazi *nusach* of havdalah, which stipulates that '*borei minei besamim*' always be recited.[103] In a garden where there are various species, a number of brachos should be made where applicable. One should recite '*hanosein re'ach tov hapeiros* – Who has placed a goodly scent within fruits', on any edible fruit or herb. If the fragrance comes from an inedible plant, if it grows from a woody stem which remains in the ground the whole year, the blessing is '*borei atzei be-*

102. מ"ב סי' רי"ז סק"א
103. עי' מ"ב סי' רצ"ז סק"א

samim – Who has created fragrant woods'. If the scent derives from a grass or similar plant that withers away in the winter, then the blessing is '*borei isvei besamim* – Who has created fragrant grasses '. '*Borei minei besamim*' is made on a scent derived from animals, such as musk, or a mix of spices ground into a powder that cannot be separated, or during havdalah, as mentioned above.

These halachos are treated in the Shulchan Aruch,[104] and carry a special importance. Chazal[105] tell us: "'*Let all souls praise God, Halleluyah.*' What thing does the soul benefit from [in this world, that it should praise Hashem]? I would say, this refers to fragrance." Fragrance is something the soul itself enjoys. It is certainly worthwhile to know the precise blessing to recite on a pleasure that even the soul enjoys. As we have often indicated, the halachos presented here are only a basic outline. A proper understanding of these halachos can only be reached by studying and reviewing them thoroughly.

ERUV IN BUNGALOW COLONY AND CITY[106]

Is it preferable to be stringent (*machmir*) and avoid carrying within the eruv of a city, bungalow colony, or camp?

ANSWER

If the *eruv* in question is known to be kosher, and under reliable supervision, then there is no problem making use of it. There are some who wish to follow the opinion of the Rambam,[107] who holds that the distance of the enclosure covered by actual *mechitzos* (halachic 'barriers') should be greater than that covered by *tzuros ha'pesach* (halachic 'doorways'). This principle is called "*omed merubah al haparutz*," that is, the real barriers must be greater than the open

104. או"ח סי' רט"ז סע' ב'
105. ברכות מג:
106. או"ח סי' שמ"ה
107. מובא בשו"ע או"ח סי' שס"ב סע' י'

areas in which doorways are used to complete the enclosure. Most eruvin do not adhere to this restriction, and those who wish to be *machmir* should consult with the Rav in charge of the particular eruv they wish to use.

Bungalow colonies: In a bungalow colony, as long as the eruv was installed correctly (*al pi din*), there is almost never a question as to its kashrus. This is because these small collections of summer cabins are usually not considered to be a proper public domain (*reshus ha'rabbim*), even considering the country road that might bisect it. Even in the view of the Mishkenos Yaakov,[108] such an area is not a public domain, and the eruv is kosher. Some bungalow colonies may nevertheless have public domains running through the area enclosed by the eruv, so it is always advisable to consult with the Rav in that colony for specific information regarding each eruv.

City eruv: Determining the halachah regarding a city eruv is far more complex. It is clearly established in halachah, that a series of *tzuros ha'pesach*, or open doorways, in a public domain (*reshus ha'rabbim*) cannot be used for an eruv. What remains as a matter of dispute is precisely what the Torah considers to be a public domain.

The early Rishonim disagree on whether a domain must contain six-hundred thousand people to be considered 'public'. Rashi[109] and Tosafos[110] hold that it must, while most other Rishonim disagree, and maintain that even if there are not six-hundred thousand people in a particular area, it may still be a full-fledged public domain.

About one hundred and seventy-five years ago, two major responsa were written regarding eruvin. The Mishkenos Yaakov[111] wrote against the practice of building eruvin in large cities, even if their population did not reach six-hundred thousand, while the Beis Ephraim[112]

108. עי' להלן
109. עירובין ו. ד"ה ר"ה, ו: ד"ה ירושלים, נט. ד"ה עיר
110. שבת ו: ד"ה כאן
111. שו"ת חלק או"ח סימנים קכ–קכב
112. שו"ת חלק או"ח סימנים כו–כז

justified the construction of such eruvin, as long as the population did not exceed six-hundred thousand people, based on Rashi and Tosafos. The custom in Europe in most communities was to rely on the Beis Ephraim, Rashi, and Tosafos, that a Torah-sanctioned reshus ha'rabbim must be populated by six-hundred thousand people. Since most European towns did not meet that criterion, eruvin were permitted during that period.

With the passing of time cities became larger until it became common for Jews to live in cities with populations in the hundreds of thousands and even millions. This means that even Rashi and Tosafos would consider these cities full-fledged 'public domains,' and the main *heter* of the Beis Ephraim no longer applies.

In the interest of maintaining the viability of eruvin in large cities, some modern-day Rabbanim began to search for various rationales to avoid classifying large cities as bona-fide public domains.

Sidewalks: One suggestion that has been made is that sidewalks are not public domains, but simply "edges of the public domain" (*tzidei reshus ha'rabbim*). If this were indeed the case, it would be permissible to set up an eruv on the sidewalk. Presumably, the rationale is that cars and other vehicles do not generally drive on the sidewalk; they usually drive on the paved road, which contains no obstacles and upon which it is easier to travel. On the other hand, the Gemara[113] defines *tzidei reshus ha'rabbim* as a market place where peddlers sell their wares and pedestrians cannot pass through with ease. With this in mind, it becomes very difficult to classify our sidewalks, which were made for the express purpose of permitting the free flow of pedestrian traffic (*hiluch ha'rabbim*), as *tzidei reshus ha'rabbim*, where pedestrian traffic is limited.

Individual streets: Another mistaken idea is that individual streets which cannot accommodate six-hundred thousand people at a time are not considered reshus ha'rabbim, even if they are part of a city

113. עי' שבת ח.

whose population exceeds that number. This innovative distinction fails when subjected to halachic scrutiny. The undisputed halachah is that an alley-way open on both ends (*mavui mefulash*) to a public domain is also classified as a public domain. Side streets are no better than alley-ways, and open-ended side-streets must also be classified as a part of the public domain. Thus, the argument for constructing an eruv on side-streets becomes completely baseless. More fundamentally, the fact that open-ended alley-ways are considered part of the public domain negates the notion that for any particular street to be deemed a public domain, it would need to have six-hundred thousand residents. It is unthinkable that an alley way could accommodate such a number, yet it certainly forms part of the public domain.

Number of passersby: Others set on finding a loophole for eruvin in large cities looked to the wording of the Shulchan Aruch,[114] who writes that a reshus ha'rabbim is one that is traversed by six-hundred thousand people each day. This, they suggested, means that even if an area or thoroughfare was potentially capable of handling the traffic of six-hundred thousand people, if the number of actual passersby each day was fewer, it could not be classified as a public domain. This would allow the construction of halachic 'doorways' in and along such thoroughfares. The Mishnah Berurah[115] takes issue with this interpretation, saying, "I have looked through all the Rishonim who discuss this view, and this precondition is not mentioned by them. [The Rishonim] only say that a city must be populated by six hundred thousand." Given this, all of a large city's roads and thoroughfares are to be considered a reshus harabbim, even if no existing street carries six-hundred thousand people daily.

As an aside, the idea that there are streets through which 600,000 people traverse daily gives credence to a fantasy. No such street ever existed and imagining this to be a requirement for a reshus ha'rabbim is essentially an attempt to institute a halachic reform for

114. סי' שמ"ה סע' ז'
115. שם ס"ק כ"ד

the sake of modern convenience. The danger of such an approach is self-evident.

The law of the land: In one city, a certain Rav justified the building of an eruv based on the halachah of *dinna d'malchusa dinna*, that the law of the land is halachically binding. It is the law of the land that all people, pedestrians and vehicles alike, are required to come to a full stop at a red light. Therefore, this Rabbi opined that the barrier of the traffic signal should be considered a halachic 'wall' separating one city block from the next, breaking up the city into hundreds of separate blocks. On the basis of this idea, one which was never previously mentioned in halachic literature, he permitted the construction of an eruv in an area where the Torah prohibition to carry remained.

The severity of hotza'as Shabbos: It is one thing if a person relies on an established leniency among the Rishonim, such as Rashi and Tosafos. No one will be taken to task by the Ribbono Shel Olam after one hundred and twenty years for carrying in an eruv that was built in consideration of the *minhag ha'kehillos*, the custom of the European communities, and founded on the opinions of Rashi and Tosafos.

Even so, when it comes to relying on the city-wide, European eruvin, the Mishnah Berurah often repeats the telling phrase, "*uba'al nefesh yachmir* – and a sensitive soul should be stringent." In our times, it is no longer a question of stringency. With city populations easily exceeding six-hundred thousand, it is a genuine matter of a Torah prohibition. Creative rationales have no place anywhere in halachah, especially when we are dealing with a serious *issur* like *hotza'as Shabbos*.

The prohibition of *hotza'ah*, of carrying on Shabbos, is one of the most serious prohibitions in the Torah. Family purity, which is dear to everyone (and no one would ever think to be lenient in this), carries a punishment of *kareis*, spiritual severance from HaKadosh Baruch Hu. Hotza'ah is far more serious, and carries the death penalty of *skilah* – stoning, in addition to *kareis*.

The issur of carrying is unique amongst all the thirty-nine *melachos* of Shabbos. The discussion of hotza'ah in the Talmud is ten times longer than the next most extensive topic. Over two hundred pages of Gemara are dedicated to the intricacies of forbidden hotza'ah. No other *issur d'Oraisa* is protected by so many Rabbinical ordinances and stringencies. We refrain from performing two Torah mitzvos, and one ordinance of the Prophets – shofar, lulav, and megillah – in deference to the issur of hotza'ah on Shabbos. According to most Rishonim, the entire edifice of *muktzah*, the restriction of handling unnecessary items on Shabbos, is to guard against accidental hotza'ah. Shlomo HaMelech wisely developed the requirements of eruvin even in non-public areas, and Hashem approved it, as a safeguard against violating the Torah prohibition of hotza'ah.

If anyone would ask why the first Beis HaMikdash was destroyed, the natural response would be to quote the Gemara in *Yoma* (9b): "Because of three things…idolatry, immorality, and murder." But Yirmiyahu HaNavi gave another reason altogether:

> *Thus says Hashem, "Guard your lives and do not carry any object…do not take out from your homes any object on the Sabbath day…. If you do not heed Me to sanctify the Sabbath day and not to carry objects, and you come to the gates of Jerusalem on the Sabbath day, I shall kindle fire in her gates, and I shall consume the palaces of Jerusalem, and it will not be extinguished"* (Yirmiyahu 17:21–22,27).

Instead of seeking leniencies and finding rationales to permit what is *assur*, we should take *Chazal* as our guide and guard ourselves from the issur of hotza'ah, relying only on the solid views of the Rishonim. We should shun modern-day excuses for carrying on Shabbos Kodesh.

The Gemara (*Eruvin* 101a) states, that when Yerushalayim was completely surrounded by walls, it was rendered a *karmelis*. The question then arises, why indeed did they not make *eruvei chatzeiros* or *shitufei mevo'os* to permit carrying on Shabbos? Many *mefarshim* answer that it was an accepted *minhag* not to build *eruvin* in large cities even where it was permissible.

It should be noted when making eruvin in cities where the population is less then 600,000 one must be on guard for an increase in population which would render the existing eruvin invalid. Furthermore, almost all of the creative reasons invented to permit eruvin in large cities today would result in rules that would make it impossible for the existence of a *reshus ha'rabbim*, even those surrounded by walls, such as Yerushalayim, and the Babylonian city of Mechuza. It is self-evident that reasoning which leads to absurd conclusions is flawed by definition. It is surely the most ridiculous absurdity to imagine that there were never any public domains when so many of them are actually identified by Chazal and in light of the many decrees that were made by Chazal to prevent carrying on Shabbos. This alone is proof enough to invalidate this entire modernistic approach to halachah.

It is painful to observe how the groups who wish to construct these eruvin insist that the Chassidic custom has always been to seek any justification to allow eruvin any place, when in fact all historical evidence points to the contrary. As we mentioned above, it was the Beis Ephraim, a staunch *misnaged*, who permitted eruvin in Europe.

In Warsaw, Poland, the Rav who permitted an eruv, even when the population of the city grew to exceed 600,000, was Rav Shlomo Dovid Kahane, a Lithuanian Jew who never identified with Chassidism. The Chassidic population of Warsaw never used the eruv, and considered carrying in Warsaw on Shabbos to be prohibited.

Those who today wish to permit eruvin, who in every other respect are faithful to time-honored traditional custom have in this case availed themselves of an approach to halachah that has no precedent and has never before appeared in any reputable Torah work.

FISH ON PESACH

Should one be concerned about the rumor that large frozen fish vendors sprinkle starch, which might be chametz or kitniyos, on the fish to keep them from freezing together?

ANSWER

In Europe many years ago, live carp were often transported by packing them in wet straw, and placing an alcohol-soaked swab of cotton in their mouths. Since the fish did not always survive the journey, the concern that they absorbed the *chametzdike* alcohol moved the Rabbanim in some regions to prohibit the use of fish on Pesach. Refrigerated freight has made this concern a thing of the past, but some people might still avoid using fish on Pesach on account of this once common custom.

The author looked carefully into the situation and asked people knowledgeable in the industry, and they are not aware of any starch whatsoever used in the processing of frozen fish. The circumstances surrounding the recent rumor suggest that it was an attempt to justify the old custom to prohibit fish as being somehow applicable today. There is nothing to be concerned about at this point in time. Continuous investigation is always necessary in all areas of food production, because of the ever-changing nature of manufacturing processes.

WATERING LAWNS[116]

Is it permissible to water houseplants, flowerbeds and lawns on *Chol HaMoed*?

ANSWER

Maseches Moed Katan (2a) begins with a discussion of this very subject: "It is permissible to water a *beis hashlachin*…on Chol HaMoed." A *beis hashlachin* is a field that depends on irrigation for survival. It will wither and die without a constant supply of water. The Gemara[117] limits this leniency, however: "But not with rainwater or trough-water… which require an excessive amount of effort (*tirchah*)." Thus we derive two of the great principles that can be applied to many questions of

116. או"ח סי' תקל"ז
117. מועד קטן ד.

work on Chol HaMoed: 1) Work is permitted to prevent potential loss, and 2) the work cannot involve excessive strain or inconvenience.

When it comes to houseplants, gardens, and lawns, there is no question that they will suffer from lack of water, and there is usually little effort in watering them. It is therefore permitted. For the sake of clarity, the permissibility stands only for Chol HaMoed. Watering of any kind is forbidden on Shabbos and Yom Tov.

FILLING IN TAX FORMS[118]

The last day for submitting tax returns sometimes falls immediately after Pesach. If a person did not manage to fill out and send in his return before Yom Tov, may he do it on Chol HaMoed, lest he miss the deadline and incur a loss?

ANSWER

Filling out tax returns on Chol HaMoed should be strongly discouraged.

There are leniencies when it comes to informal writing on Chol HaMoed, and the custom is to rely upon them. Nevertheless, the Mishnah Berurah[119] writes that many Poskim (including the Rema) forbade even informal writing on Chol HaMoed, except in clear cases of financial loss. The Mishnah Berurah therefore advises that, wherever possible, a person should try to refrain from writing for any reason on Chol HaMoed. One noteworthy exception to this rule is writing down *chiddushei Torah*, which is always considered a *davar ha'aveid*.

In the case of tax returns, the writing might even be considered formal. People are extremely careful to fill out tax forms in clear, block letters. Formal writing is certainly forbidden on Chol HaMoed, barring a clear and significant financial loss. The penalty for late filing is

118. או"ח סי' תקמ"ה

119. סי' תקמ"ה סע' ה' ס"ק ל"ה וביאור הלכה ד"ה אפילו

a percentage of the tax owed (as of this writing: 5 percent, for a delay of up to 30 days), and does not always result in a significant loss.

Alternatives to writing: With taxes, there are three options that should be seriously considered before concluding that there is no choice other than writing on Chol HaMoed. First, there is plenty of time before Pesach to prepare the forms, and a person has only to organize himself in a way that he can take care of his taxes beforehand. A person should also consider just how much time he needs to prepare the forms. It could very well be that if a person is willing to stay up extra late, he will be able to finish preparing the forms after Yom Tov, before midnight of April 15th, and personally bring them to the Post Office to be stamped and mailed on time. Anyone who has ever visited the Post Office on the eve of April 15th will see that many people do just that. A person should certainly consider this possibility in order to protect the sanctity of the Moed.

The next best possibility is to request an extension from the Internal Revenue Service. There is a small fee for the extension, but again, it is not a great financial loss and the honor of the Moed is worth the expense. Failing that, he can prepare the returns on a computer, leaving the printing for after the holidays.

If the deadline for filing tax returns falls on Chol HaMoed itself, then there are more grounds to permit filling out the forms due to the potential financial loss. Here too, applying for an extension would still be the best approach.

One may also prepare the returns on a computer, but they should not be printed on Chol HaMoed unless it would result in serious financial loss (*davar ha'aveid*). Typing on a computer is not 'writing' in the true sense of the word, as the letters are not considered permanent until they are printed. There are even programs available especially for the purpose of preparing tax forms which eliminate much of the need for typing. Nevertheless, even a computer should only be used when there is a genuine need.

As mentioned above, writing on Chol HaMoed is only forbidden if the writing is both a creative act (*melachah*), and done in the manner of *ma'aseh umman*, a skilled craft. Typing words into a computer is most certainly a *ma'aseh umman*, but cannot be considered a creative act, because the letters are not printed. The *melachah* of writing is only accomplished when the words are actually printed out. This being the case, a skilled craft alone, if it is not a *melachah*, is not forbidden.[120] Therefore, typing the words and keeping them in the computer's memory without printing them would be allowed on Chol HaMoed, but should only be done in a case of necessity. It is forbidden to type and then print information from a computer. This is *ma'aseh umman* and a *melachah*, even though it is a two-step process.

PLAYING GAMES[121]

May one play scrabble or other games that involve keeping score or jotting down words or numbers on Chol HaMoed?

ANSWER

Keeping score: One may write words and numbers in an unusual, informal manner.[122] Yet with a little ingenuity, even keeping score can be done without any writing at all. The best arrangement for keeping score is to provide each player with a small calculator. In this way no writing at all is taking place, as the numbers on the display are not permanent.

Be safe: A person should train himself to live well within the letter of the law. The Rema[123] states that a person who is ill (but not dangerously so) is allowed to eat the burnt remains of vermin (*sheretz hasaruf*) as a cure, if there is no kosher remedy available. If there is

120. דומיא דשופר, עי' ראש השנה כט: "תנא דבי שמואל כל מלאכת עבודה לא תעשו יצתה תקיעת שופר ורדיית הפת שהיא חכמה ואינה מלאכה".

121. או"ח סי' תקמ"ה

122. עי' או"ח סי' תקמ"ה סע' ה' ומ"ב שם ס"ק ל"ה

123. יו"ד סי' קפ"ה סע' ג'

an alternative cure available that is kosher, he should take that one, even if he will have to wait a while longer or pay more to acquire the kosher medicine. This is true even though the *sheretz* has been rendered permissible because of its destruction through burning. The sentiment of the Rema should be also applied to the question of writing on Chol HaMoed. It may be permissible to write in an unusual manner (*shinui*), but wherever an alternative exists, one should avail himself of it. Writing, after all, is one of the things expressly forbidden by Chazal on Chol HaMoed.[124]

WRITING AND CRAFTS FOR CHILDREN

May children play games on Chol HaMoed that involve writing, drawing, or other arts-and-crafts activities?

ANSWER

It may be that a child's writing, drawing, and craft-making can be considered a *ma'aseh hedyot* (unskilled) and strictly speaking there is no need for a parent to instruct his children to refrain from these activities on Chol HaMoed, except for children whose drawing is done skillfully. On the other hand, there are so many activities available today that do not involve writing or crafts, that it is not really necessary to specifically choose games that require writing, and drawing.

Writing should be reserved for those things that require it. If a person had to hire a repairman on Chol HaMoed, he would be allowed to write him a check so as to pay him on time. There is no way of avoiding the need to write in that case. But parents should choose games and activities for their children that preserve the sanctity of Chol HaMoed.

One should follow a path in life which avoids making use of *heterim*, unless there is a pressing necessity, and the *heter* is based on solid, unquestionable ground. When something comes along which

124. מועד קטן יח:

seems to be in conflict with the tried and tested way of doing things, it should sound the alarm button.

DOING BUSINESS[125]

Must a store or business that is permitted to operate on Chol HaMoed indicate in some way that it is Chol HaMoed?

ANSWER

Stores and professionals that provide essential goods and services necessary for the Festival are allowed to open on Chol HaMoed. However, business should be done in a modest fashion (*b'tzinah*). If the store has two doors, one of them should be left shut. If the store has only one door, then some other indication can be made.[126] Nowadays, the metal gate that protects the storefront is left partially extended, or the displays normally set up outside the store are kept inside.

The Jewish community has grown more sensitive to the sanctity of the Moed over the past several years. Still, open breaches of halachah do arise. Frequently, Rabbanim receive calls from distraught employees whose observant employers are demanding that they show up to work, even when there exists no leniency for that type of business to operate on the Moed.

Occasionally, someone will contract for the construction of a large building in the middle of a Jewish community. Construction is prohibited on Chol HaMoed even outside the community, where no one will see it and even if the job is contracted out to a gentile (*kablanus*), which removes the problem of the gentile working on behalf of the Jew (*shlichus*).[127] This is a stricture that is more exacting on the Moed than even on Shabbos. On Shabbos a person does not have to require

125. או"ח סי' תקל"ט, תקמ"ג
126. או"ח סי' תקל"ט סע' י"א
127. או"ח סי' תקמ"ג סע' ב'

a non-Jewish contractor to desist if their work is being carried on outside the city limits (*techum Shabbos*).[128]

Chazal (Avos 3:11) say, "One who disgraces the Festivals (*Moados*)... even should he possess Torah and good deeds, has no portion in the World to Come." The Bartenura tells us that the Mishnah is discussing Chol HaMoed. By far the greatest disgrace to Chol HaMoed is to neglect the study of its laws. Thus, it behooves every Jew to take the time to familiarize himself with these halachos.

RENOVATING AN APARTMENT[129]

An engaged couple who are getting married soon after Yom Tov, finally manage to find an appropriate apartment a few days before the Festival. The apartment needs some repairs and a paint job. If the repairs are not done over Chol HaMoed, then they will likely have to pay to stay in a hotel for a week or two. Must the couple pay for the hotel to avoid doing the repairs during Chol HaMoed?

ANSWER

According to the strict letter of the law, it may be permissible for them to have the repairs done on Chol HaMoed. A young couple may not have much money, which will make the expense of an extended hotel stay a significant loss (*davar ha'aveid*) for them. Thus, even though property repairs are expressly forbidden, as is any work involving land and the buildings situated upon it (*meleches karka*),[130] in a case of financial hardship even this is permissible.

On the other hand, the seriousness of the prohibition compared to the relatively minor real-dollar expense of the hotel stay might still make it worthwhile for the couple to honor the Moed and do the

128. או"ח סי' רמ"ד סע' א'
129. או"ח סי' תק"מ
130. עי' או"ח סי' תק"מ סע' א'

repairs afterwards. It may even be possible for the couple to find other, albeit less convenient accommodations.

A similar question once arose regarding renovations to the top floor of a brownstone that a certain Ben Torah bought over forty years ago. He arranged for a contractor to do the renovations in Ellul with the understanding that the work would be finished before Rosh Hashanah. Unfortunately, the work dragged on. In the meantime, this *yungerman* found two yeshivah students who agreed to rent out the newly renovated upper floor of the house after Sukkos, for sixty dollars a month – a sizeable sum of money in those days. Of course, they would only move in once the work had been finished and the heating installed. On Chol HaMoed Sukkos, the contractor called the man and told him that all his workers were available and that he could finish the work in just three days. "Besides," the contractor mentioned, "it's a *davar ha'aveid*. If I can't do the work now, I won't be able to finish it until mid-December, which means you will lose three months of rent."

The *yungerman* called Reb Yaakov Kamenetzky, *zt"l*, and asked him what to do. Could he have the work done on Chol HaMoed, considering the loss of one hundred and eighty dollars of rent?

Reb Yaakov said, "*Chas vechalila*, it's *meleches karka*, and for this amount of money it is not considered a *davar ha'aveid* and it is *assur* on Chol HaMoed, and even if one wanted to make a case for *davar ha'aveid*, for you it would be a *chillul Hashem*. You're a yeshivah man, and others will say, '*hitiru ha'prushim es hadavar*,' like they said regarding Pinchas." The *yungerman* refrained from doing the work, and the contractor finished the work at the end of December.

In the end, the honor this fellow gave to Chol HaMoed saved him far more money than he lost from the rental. The heating in the house was provided by a water-heating boiler system. In such a system, the hot water flows through the pipes and radiators and heats the house. Up to two levels above the boiler, the system needs no pump; the heated water naturally rises and the cooler water naturally returns to the boiler to be reheated. In this case, however, the upper storey of the house was three levels above the boiler. At the beginning of the winter, when the weather is mild, the natural circulation is sufficient to heat the top floor, but it is not enough to properly heat it during the bitterly cold mid-winter months. The system requires a mechanical pump to make sure the hot water speedily reaches even the top floor.

As it was, the contractor did not install a pump. By standing by the honor of Chol HaMoed, the work was only finished in the deep of winter, and it was quite obvious that the contractor had done an improper job by not installing a pump. The contractor had to spend almost two-thousand dollars to remove parts of the system and install the pump. Had the yungerman agreed to have the work done in the milder weather of Chol HaMoed Sukkos, he would not have realized that the system was improperly installed. The contractor would have finished the job and probably never have come back, and this expense would have fallen squarely upon his shoulders.

The Ribbono Shel Olam will surely assist those who protect the honor and sanctity of the Festivals, who do not rush to save themselves from every minor loss they might incur, at the expense of the holiness of the Moed.

KASHERING A KITCHEN[131]

May one kasher a kitchen and eating utensils on Chol HaMoed in order that they should be ready for use after Yom Tov?

ANSWER

If the family living there is becoming religious (*ba'alei teshuvah*), then the painstaking work of kashering the kitchen is a tremendous mitzvah. It will undoubtedly be accompanied by a feeling of simchah and will bring them encouragement. What better way to celebrate the Moed than with the *simchah shel mitzvah* that kashering their kitchen will engender?

131. או"ח סי' תקל"ה

On the other hand, for a frum family, kashering the kitchen of a new house is part of the ordinary work done to facilitate kosher meals. It is painstaking, involved, and a *tirchah*, and might thus be forbidden. There may be mitigating circumstances, of course. If they have nowhere to eat in the meantime, or if the kashering is also necessary for Yom Tov, these might be reasons to permit it. It must then be determined if the kashering is considered a skilled craft (*ma'aseh umman*) or an unskilled craft (*ma'aseh hedyot*). Each question should be addressed according to its unique combination of circumstances, by applying the principles of Chol HaMoed. As far as actually moving into the new apartment, it is generally forbidden to move during Chol HaMoed.[132]

INSECT EXTERMINATION[133]

May one perform insect extermination on Chol HaMoed?

ANSWER

Professional extermination: Professional extermination is a skilled craft (*ma'aseh umman*). The chemicals used are potent and even dangerous. To become certified, exterminators must take a course and receive a license to practice. It is therefore forbidden on Chol HaMoed.

Amateur extermination: Buying a can of insect spray from the local hardware store and spraying down areas of the house is something anybody can do. It is also not very effective in the long run. This is considered an unskilled craft (*ma'aseh hedyot*), and is permissible on Chol HaMoed.[134] In any event, if a person has a serious bug infestation,

132. או"ח סי' תקל"ה סע' א'
133. או"ח סי' תקמ"א
134. או"ח סי' תקמ"א סע' ה'

it was probably known about even before Yom Tov. It should have been taken care of then.[135]

MINOR REPAIRS[136]

May one change a washer to stop a dripping faucet on Chol HaMoed?

ANSWER

Changing a washer is not usually a skilled craft (*ma'aseh umman*). Standard faucets do not require more than a straightforward repair to stop a leak. But there are new styles of faucets today that are much more complicated. These might require professional skill to repair.[137] Of course, if the faucet is dripping unbearably then one may have it fixed on Chol HaMoed even if a ma'aseh umman is required. A ma'aseh umman is allowed in a case of great discomfort (*tza'ar gadol*). If the faucet was dripping before Yom Tov, then it should have been taken care of beforehand.[138]

LAUNDERING[139]

Is a person permitted to wash his shirts on Chol HaMoed if he does not have enough? If it is permitted, must he wash one at a time, or may he wash as many as he needs for Yom Tov at one time?

ANSWER

Washing a shirt or other garment that does not require dry cleaning

135. מ"ב סי' תק"מ סק"ט
136. או"ח סי' תקמ"א
137. או"ח סי' תקמ"א סע' ה'
138. סי' תק"מ סק"ט
139. או"ח סי' תקל"ד

was restricted by Chazal on Chol HaMoed. This is true even though standard laundering is an unskilled craft (*ma'aseh hedyot*) and it is generally permissible to perform an unskilled craft in order to care for Yom Tov necessities. The exceptions to this rule are laundering clothes and taking a haircut, which Chazal specifically forbade. Even these activities can be allowed in a case of unexpected need (*o'nes*), as Chazal did not make their decrees binding in such a case.[140] When the need to wash clothing arises on Chol HaMoed, a Rav should always be consulted in order to safely navigate the halachic complexities of laundering.

Adult garments: The Rema[141] states that one should only wash, "what he needs at the moment, that is, one outfit at a time." Still, the permissibility of washing any shirts on Chol HaMoed for adults remains questionable. Shirts can usually be worn for more than one day, and even if a person is too sensitive to wear a shirt twice, it is preferable to buy a few more shirts than to seek leniencies regarding the *kedushah* of Chol HaMoed. With the hundred dollars he will spend on the extra shirts, he will be investing in the honor of Yom Tov. He will also be freeing himself to learn Torah and spend time with the family in a Yom Tov-dik way.[142]

Children's clothes: Laundering the clothes of very young children is generally permissible on Chol HaMoed. The Rema[143] writes: "It is permissible to wash the clothes of very small children who soil their clothing, even four and five at a time, as a ready supply is always needed." When it comes to older children who tend to soil their clothes, a person can wash, but not dry-clean, only as many articles of clothing as are absolutely necessary to make it through Yom Tov.

140. סי' תקמ"א סע' ה'
141. שם סע' א'
142. ירושלמי מועד קטן פ"ב ה"ג ועי' רא"ש פ"א אות א'
143. או"ח סי' תקל"ד

If a need to launder clothing should arise, one should ask a *sheilah* to determine what is permissible and what is not.

Ironing: It should be noted that there is no restriction at all regarding ironing a shirt or other articles of clothing on Chol HaMoed, unless there is some very complicated process involved, such as in the case of certain frills rarely seen today.[144]

DRY-CLEANING

If someone has only one Shabbos suit which becomes soiled, may he bring it to the dry cleaners on Chol HaMoed?

ANSWER

In the case of an accident, where something unexpectedly spilled on a person's only Yom Tov suit, the situation is complicated, because dry cleaning a suit on Chol HaMoed is restricted by several decrees (*gezeiros*) of Chazal. For one, dry-cleaning is a skilled craft (*ma'aseh umman*), and Chazal instituted that a ma'aseh umman cannot be done, even for the necessity of the Moed.[145] It is likewise forbidden to drop off or pick up clothing from a professional cleaner.[146] Additionally, Chazal decreed that one cannot wash clothing on the Moed.[147] Even where it might be considered a significant loss not to have the suit, a ben Torah should seek every alternative so as not to bring his suit in for cleaning, lest others see him and think that it is permissible (*hitiru perushim es hadavar*). Thus, it is not a simple thing to permit the dry cleaning of a suit.

In the case of an adult, he might be able to wear last year's Shabbos suit. For a child, last year's suit will be too small, but it might be

144. סי' תקמ"א ס"ג ברמ"א ובמ"ב סק"ט
145. או"ח סי' תקמ"א סע' ה'
146. מ"ב סי' תקל"ד ס"ק ט"ו
147. סי' תקל"ד סע' א'

possible to spot-clean the suit with a wet towel until it is wearable. Alternatively, one can borrow an old suit from a relative or friend.

As a rule, a person can often avoid putting himself into a difficult halachic situation with a little forethought. If the family is going on a Chol HaMoed picnic, he might choose to wear an old suit or piece of clothing which he does not mind getting soiled, and keep his good one clean.[148] In general, one should wear clothing fit for Shabbos on Chol HaMoed, but when one will be doing some activity which may result in soiled clothing, it neither brings honor to the Moed nor is it wise to put on one's Shabbos best.

BUYING ARBA MINIM[149]

Is it permitted to purchase a *lulav* and *esrog* from an unfamiliar vendor, relying only on the vendor's word that his produce is halachically acceptable, or should we be concerned that they may have been grafted (*murkav*) or stolen?

ANSWER

Lulavim: Practically all *lulavim* are picked from date palms, and there is very little concern that they may have been grafted. Occasionally, non-kosher lulavim from non-fruit bearing trees make their way onto the market. When this is the case, warnings are posted, and they do actually look different from the kosher varieties. The most important thing is to look at the *shedrah*, the spine of the lulav to make sure it is completely straight; then one should look at the *tiomes*, the double center leaf. It is a special *hiddur* for the tiomes to be completely closed.[150]

148. עי' מ"ב סי' תק"ל ס"ק א' שכתב דחייב לכבד חוה"מ במאכל ובמשתה וכסות נקיה שלא ינהג בהן מנהג חול. ומהרי"ל לבש הקט"א של שבת, עכ"ל. וע"ע בשה"צ אות ד' שמצדד דלא בעינן להחמיר בזה כ"כ כמו ביו"ט עצמו, רק שלא ינהג בו מנהג חול. ולכן בעת הצורך מותר ללבוש מלבושים שאינם ממש של יו"ט ובלבד שהם מכובדים ואינם נראים כבגדי חול.

149. או"ח סי' תרמ"ה, סי' תרמ"ח, סי' תרמ"ט

150. או"ח סי' תרמ"ה סע' ג' וברמ"א

Esrogim: The problem of grafting *esrog* trees is well documented, and many of the esrogim offered for sale are indeed from grafted trees. Some Poskim permit grafted esrogim, but the majority, including the Mishnah Berurah,[151] do not. To avoid problems, it is important to buy only from those vendors who receive their esrogim from supervised orchards that are known (*muchzak*) to only have non-grafted trees.

Theft: With regard to theft, the author is not aware of any serious concern that vendors are peddling stolen wares. It would be proper to ask someone who knows the esrog market well.

PURCHASING FROM A MINOR

Is there a problem if the lulav vendor is under the age of bar-mitzvah?

ANSWER

Someone who is under the age of bar-mitzvah (a *katan*) has the ability to acquire (*koneh*) property, but he cannot release ownership (*makneh*) of his possessions to someone else.[152] The Torah stipulates that on the first day of Sukkos, the *arba minim*, the four species, must be completely owned by the one who shakes them. "ולקחתם לכם ביום הראשון – And you shall *take for yourselves* on the first day" (Vayikra 23:40). Therefore, one should not purchase a lulav or esrog from a minor under the age of thirteen. If he does, he will not be able to fulfill the mitzvah of lulav on the first day. If there is an indication that the minor is simply manning the booth, and the transaction (*kinyan*) is being performed by an adult, then it would be permissible. The author believes this is true in most cases.

151. שם ס"ק ס"ה
152. סוכה מו:

A DISCARDED LULAV

Are surplus lulavim that vendors did not manage to sell considered muktzah, or may one use them on Yom Tov?

ANSWER

The larger, more established *lulav* vendors are aware of the fact that people often discover they need a new lulav, even on the first days of Yom Tov. Therefore, even if one should find lulavim outside, it is unreasonable to think that these vendors intended to discard the lulavim and render them *muktzah*, unless there is some indication that the lulav was actually discarded.

In addition, one might argue that it is proper to consider lulavim on erev Sukkos similar to items (*keilim*) which never become refuse even when discarded because they retain their usefulness. Surplus lulavim are quite useful, as they can be used to fulfill the mitzvah, or to make *kaishelach*, the woven *hadas* and *aravah* holders people attach to their lulavim. Thus, it would be similar to someone who throws away a perfectly good mat (*machatzeles*). The act of throwing it away cannot remove its status as a usable object, and its does not become *muktzah*.

This would permit the discarded lulavim of even the less established vendors, who literally throw away the remaining lulavim just before the onset of the holiday without any thought of saving them. According to this reasoning, it would be permissible to handle such lulavim, even if they might be found in the garbage can itself.

VERY THICK SCHACH (SCHACH M'UBEH)[153]

May a person use the European type of *schach*, where thin layers of large leaves are placed on a slanted frame in order to keep out the rain?

ANSWER

Tosafos[154] tells us that even though the walls of a sukkah can be made in a permanent manner, the thatching (*schach*) of a sukkah must always be temporary. Rain-proof schach is considered to be permanent, house-like roofing, and does not qualify for a sukkah. Tosafos[155] mentions the possibility of covering the schach with a sheet to protect the people inside from the heat of the sun or placing a sheet under the schach to keep leaves from falling on the people in the sukkah, and this might be permissible. Yet if the schach itself is made to withstand the rain, then it is invalid (*posul*). This is the opinion quoted as halachah by the Be'er Heitiv.[156] The Mishnah Berurah[157] mentions that if one has no other sukkah to use but one with a very thick layer of schach which does not let in the rain, he can rely on the opinion of those who permit it.

It seems clear to the author, however, that the lenient opinion only applies where the schach material is not waterproof and it is only its thickness that prevents water from seeping through. In our case, the schach itself is arranged and constructed to be waterproof and should be considered an actual roof according to every opinion. Such a sukkah is almost certainly *posul min haTorah*.

Much has been written to justify the use of rain-proof schach in rainy climates, and to show how these are not truly rain-proof and therefore not considered to be roof-like structures. Nevertheless, these arguments themselves are not watertight. Therefore, it is far better to

153. או"ח סי' תרל"א
154. סוכה ב., ד"ה כי
155. שם י., ד"ה פירס
156. סי' תרל"א סק"ג
157. שם סק"ו

make use of the standard schach that lets in the rain, and cope with the weather conditions as they develop.

DRILLING HOLES IN RAIN-PROOF SCHACH

Does it help to drill a few holes in the rain-proof schach that are big enough to let in some rain?

ANSWER

If there are enough holes, yes. If there are not enough holes, then no. It would be very difficult to determine exactly how many holes are necessary to make the schach kosher for a sukkah. If a person wants to do it that way, then he should drill as many holes as he feels will certainly let in the rain without a doubt, and then drill a few more for good measure. The Pri Megadim[158] says, it is possible that a stretch of waterproof schach four *tefachim* wide can invalidate the sukkah. Therefore, one should be sure to drill holes in every area of the schach.

It is important to keep in mind that the mitzvah of sitting in a sukkah is to remind us of the sukkos in which HaKadosh Baruch Hu placed *Klal Yisroel* while they wandered in the desert. "*That your descendants may know that I placed the Children of Israel in sukkos when they went out of Egypt*" (Vayikra 23:43). The surest way to fulfill this mitzvah is to use what has always been used as schach so that his sukkah will resemble the sukkah of his ancestors.

158. פמ"ג אשל אברהם סימן תרל"א אות ב'

MAKING SCHACH WITH TWINE[159]

May twine be used for schach?

ANSWER

Rashi's position: The opinion of Rashi is that only twine which is fit to be *mekabel tumah* is invalid for schach.[160] Accordingly, a thread of twine would only be posul if it could become *tamei* from *tzara'as*.[161] The Torah stipulates that these threads must be made specifically from wool or linen. Other types of thread do not become tamei from tzara'as, unless they are part of a piece of material. Standard twine is not made from wool or linen, and it does not become tamei by Torah law. However, Chazal decreed that any type of thread accepts tumah, as long as it is made by a process called spinning, which Chazal refer to as *teviyah*. Twine made from spun thread, therefore, can become tamei by Rabbinical decree (*miderabbanan*), and cannot be used for schach. "Thread" here refers to fine and very narrow yarns, the like of which are used for garments and in sewing.

A rope, on the other hand, never becomes tamei, as its fibers are not spun before being twined. There are many types of string and rope on the market, and a person needs to determine regarding each one, whether its fibers are spun or if they are twined without being spun first.

The Shulchan Aruch's psak: The Shulchan Aruch[162] follows the opinion of the Rambam,[163] and paskens that any type of rope or twine is posul for a sukkah, since it is changed so radically from its natural state. Therefore, no twine or rope should ever be used for schach

159. או"ח סי' תרכ"ט
160. עי' סוכה יב: רש"י ד"ה סיככה
161. עי' שבת כז:
162. או"ח סי' תרכ"ט סע' ה'
163. פ"ה מהלכות סוכה הל' ד'

unless it is made from certain reed-like fibers that are not changed greatly from their natural state.[164]

TYING DOWN SCHACH MATS[165]

Is there a problem in tying down schach mats to the sukkah with string in order to prevent them from flying away in strong winds?

ANSWER

Using string to tie down a schach mat does not usually present a problem. Reb Moshe, *zt"l*, ruled that the use of string only invalidates the schach when the entire mat is held together with a spun type of string. In that case, the schach mat is completely dependent on the string for its integrity since the string 'holds up' (*ma'amid*) the mat. Since such string is unacceptable, as explained above, the entire schach will then become posul because of *ma'amid*.[166]

However, if the string is only used to secure kosher schach which already lays nicely on the sukkah, it presents no problem, for the schach retains its integrity even if it is not tied down. Fastening the schach is done simply as a convenience, to eliminate damage to the sukkah and the need to replace the schach after a strong gust of wind (*ruach she'einah metzuyah*).

If one knows that the schach will not remain in place under normal wind conditions (*ruach metzuyah*), then the schach is not kosher (*Sukkah* 23a).[167] To make the schach kosher, it must be weighed down or fastened to the sukkah. In this case, tying the schach down with regular string so that it will not fly away would present a problem, as

164. סי' תרכ"ט סע' ה'
165. או"ח סי' תרכ"ט
166. עי' או"ח סי' תרכ"ט סע' ז'
167. עי' או"ח סי' תרכ"ח סע' ב'

the only reason the schach does not fly away is due to the string, which is not kosher for schach. This is a form of ma'amid.

SCREWING DOWN SCHACH MATS

May one use screws to fasten the schach, or would this give it the status of a permanent roof?[168]

ANSWER

Beams and lattices: Screws do not make kosher schach into a roof. Chazal only prohibited making schach out of material that is suitable for roofing. The Shulchan Aruch[169] mentions beams (*koros* or *ra'afim*) that are four *tefachim* wide, but the Mishnah Berurah[170] adds that even the thinner beams (lattices) are forbidden today because they are commonly used in roofing. If these are laid down in such a manner as to prevent any rain from entering the sukkah, their use is prohibited whether there are screws or not. This issue is discussed at length on page 69.

In contrast, if one attached bamboo or reed mats with screws, rain could still enter the sukkah. Such schach would also never be confused with standard roofing and is kosher.

Ma'amid: There may still be a problem with using screws, however. If the only reason a person wants to screw down the schach is because he is afraid that even a normal wind might blow it off, there is a problem of ma'amid. If the schach would fly away were it not for the screws, it is not kosher.

168. או"ח סי' תרכ"ט, תר"ל
169. או"ח סי' תרכ"ט סע' י"ח
170. שם ס"ק מ"ט

A MISTAKEN LEISHEV BASUKKAH

If someone recited '*leishev basukkah*' with Kiddush, and then after reciting 'hamotzi' he mistakenly began reciting 'leishev' a second time, remembering his error after he had already pronounced Hashem's Name, what should he do?

ANSWER

Generally, when someone mistakenly begins to recite an unnecessary blessing (*brachah she'einah tzerichah*), he can avoid having uttered a Name in vain (*Shem Shamayim levatalah*) in several ways, depending upon how much of the blessing he has recited. If he realized his error after reciting, '*Baruch Atah Hashem*,' then he should finish with '*lamdeini chukechah*,' thus completing possuk 12 in Chapter 112 of Tehillim. If he has already said "*Elokei*," and did not yet pronounce the last syllable ('*nu*'), then he should continue "*Elokei Yisroel Avinu me'olam v'ad olam*", thus completing possuk 10, Chapter 29, in I Divrei HaYamim. If he is holding past that, then he should say, "*Baruch Shem kevod Malchuso le'olam va'ed*."[171]

The case in question is more complicated, for the inadvertent brachah might be an interruption (*hefsek*) between '*hamotzi*' and partaking of the challah (*achilah*). If reciting the three words, "*Baruch Atah Hashem*," is an interruption, then the brachah said before would be lost and all the options above would apply.

However, in this case the interruption might not be halachically considered a *hefsek*. First of all, if he recited these words quickly, the interruption is less than *toch kedei dibbur* and too short to be of any consequence. Furthermore, not every interruption between the blessing and the bread is classified as a *hefsek*. The Gemara[172] tells us that if one spoke regarding something necessary for the meal, it is not considered an interruption. If a person forgot to bring salt to the table, and said, "Bring the salt," after reciting '*hamotzi*,' it is not

171. או"ח סי' ר"ו סע' ו' וע"ע חיי אדם כלל ה' סע' א'

172. ברכות מ.

considered an interruption, though one should not do so *lechatchilah*. In the above case too, this person began reciting '*leishev*' thinking that it was necessary before eating the challah. Thus, his '*hamotzi*' might still be valid.

One cannot knowingly invalidate a blessing by creating a hefsek. In our case, this means that one may not choose to protect the Shem Hashem of his mistaken '*leishev*' by completing a possuk, as mentioned above. Were he to do this, it would automatically invalidate his '*hamotzi*' and render it a *brachah levatalah*. It is true that the words '*lamdeini chukecha*' are within the range of *toch kedei dibbur*, and not enough to create a hefsek, but reciting the complete possuk, "*Baruch Atah Hashem lamdeini chukecha*," is certainly enough to create a *hefsek*.[173]

This is not comparable to the interruption one is required to create in Shemoneh Esrei, such as where one forgot '*ya'aleh v'yavo*' and began saying '*Baruch Atah Hashem*' at the end of '*retzei*.'[174] In such a case, the words '*lamdeini chukecha*' prevent the completion of the brachah of '*retzei*' and the possuk that was said, is at worst considered as though he spoke in midst of his tefillah (*sach b'emtza hatefillah*). Words spoken in the middle of davening are not enough to invalidate the tefillah.[175]

In our case, though, the completion of the possuk would result in a full-fledged *hefsek* between the brachah and the *achilah*. This would turn the brachah of '*hamotzi*' into a *brachah levatalah*. According to some opinions, he would thereby transgress the prohibition of taking Hashem's Name in vain (*lo sissa es Shem Hashem...l'shav*).[176]

One might seek to claim that saying "*lamdeini chukecha*" should not be considered a hefsek, for it is required to prevent '*lo sissa*,' and by definition, any necessary interruption should never be considered a hefsek, just as we see by an interruption to request salt. Following

173. כן נראה לי, לעניות דעתי.
174. ביאור הלכה סי׳ קי״ד סע׳ ו׳ סוד״ה בלא, מ״ב סי׳ תכ״ב סק״ה
175. עי׳ או״ח סי׳ ק״ד סע׳ ו׳, ומ״ב ס״ק כ״ה
176. ברכות לג.

this reasoning, one should be allowed to go on an errand of *pikuach nefesh* immediately after reciting '*hamotzi*,' tarry for a number of hours, and return to partake of bread without reciting a second brachah (so long as one took the pains not to be *mesiach da'as*). This cannot be, of course, as such a major interruption is a *hefsek* by any definition. This demonstrates that necessity alone is insufficient grounds for discounting an interruption. Any principle that may easily be stretched to the point of absurdity (*ein l'davar sof*) cannot hold true even where it seems to be reasonable.

Thus, in order to disregard an interruption between '*hamotzi*' and *achilah*, it would have to specifically serve the needs of the *seudah* in some way. This is the true understanding as to why requesting salt is not considered a *hefsek*. Even this legitimate interruption cannot be extended indefinitely, however. The rational mind will set reasonable limits.

The only remaining option is to recite '*Baruch Shem kevod*,' after he eats a piece of the challah. When a person utters Hashem's Name unnecessarily, it demonstrates a lack of sensitivity to the holiness of His Name. To show that it was unintentional, and to restore the lost honor to His Name, we recite, "*Baruch Shem kevod malchuso le'olam va'ed*." While it is obviously better to recite this immediately upon becoming aware that one has mistakenly uttered Hashem's Name, if circumstances arise such as those in the case under discussion, then the honor may be restored to Hashem's Name at the earliest opportunity. In our case, as soon as the one reciting the mistaken '*leishev*' becomes aware of his error, he should immediately eat the challah to fulfill his '*hamotzi*,' and then after swallowing, restore the honor to Hashem's name by reciting '*Baruch Shem kevod*.'

YOREH DE'AH

COMMON QUESTIONS REGARDING POULTRY

When one finds broken bones or bruises on a chicken, under what circumstances must one ask a *sheilah*?[1]

ANSWER

Years ago, bringing a chicken to the Rav on Thursday or Erev Shabbos was commonplace. Nowadays, with the amount of supervision in the poultry slaughterhouses, chickens of questionable status are generally removed before packaging.

Nevertheless, there are still a few sheilos that can come up, namely, in the *tzomes ha'gidim*, a dense network of muscle tendons at the narrow end of the drumstick; and with a *buka d'itma*, a dislocated thighbone, where the thighbone is connected with the spine. The thighbone runs through the triangular piece of dark meat which forms the upper part of the leg, and ends in a ball and socket joint that attaches it to the pelvic bone which connects to the spine. Once in a while, one might discover a leg that was broken from before *shechitah*.

It is a valuable experience to bring the first few broken bones and bruises you discover to a Rav, and ask him to take the time to explain

1. יו"ד סי' נ"ג

where to look for a real sheilah. This way you will get a proper picture of what to look for.

PERIODIC VERSUS CONTINUOUS SUPERVISION[2]

It is common to enter stores, restaurants or bakeries that are under official Rabbinical supervision, and find that the only staff in attendance are either not Jewish, or are non-observant Jews. Should an observant Jew avoid such establishments due to potential problems relating to the halachos of: (I) *Bishul akum* (food prepared by a non-Jew); (II) *Pas akum* (Bread baked by a non-Jew); and (III) *Basar she'nisalem min ha'ayin* (unsupervised meat), since constant supervision is not in place?

ANSWER

According to the strict letter of the law (*me'ikar hadin*), it is not necessary for food-service establishments to have constant supervision (*mashgiach temidi*) in order to obtain kosher certification. Periodic supervision (*yotzei venichnas*) is sufficient. The effectiveness of *yotzei venichnas* supervision is established clearly in the Gemara.[3] A mashgiach who periodically visits in a random fashion, is enough to ensure compliance to kosher requirements. Few proprietors would risk losing their lucrative kashrus certification by using non-kosher ingredients, knowing that the mashgiach could walk in at any time.

Having said this, many years of practical experience have shown that the situation is, in reality, far more complicated and problematic. For many years now, responsible Rabbis have required that there be permanent supervision in establishments that sell and serve meat products. The halachic minimum is satisfied, strictly speaking, by the

2. יו"ד סי' קי"ח, קי"ט
3. חולין ג.

principle of '*yotzei venichnas*,' but those who wish to be more careful, should take into account the following concerns.

Ingredient substitution: It is common in restaurants that certain ingredients run out. Restaurants generally prepare a certain amount of each menu item every day. If a group arrives unexpectedly and orders a large quantity of a particular entrée, the proprietor may be tempted to send out for unsupervised ingredients so as not to turn away customers. There was a known case where a kosher restaurant ran out of duck sauce and brought in a supply from a nearby non-kosher Chinese restaurant. The restaurant had a permanent mashgiach on staff who prevented the duck sauce from being used. Had this restaurant employed only a periodic mashgiach, the customers would have been served something that might have been non-kosher. Unfortunately, incidents like these are not uncommon.

Guarding kosher meat: Another consideration is the requirement to provide a scrupulous watch over kosher meat intended for Jewish consumption.[4] Kosher meat is significantly more expensive than non-kosher meat, and there is always the worry that unscrupulous proprietors will substitute the cheaper *treif* meat for the kosher meat. Meat that has not been properly guarded is called '*basar she'nisalem min ha'ayin*,' literally, 'meat that has been out of view'. The propriety of securing a *mashgiach temidi* is evident.

Bishul akum[5]**:** Avoiding the restrictions of food cooked by a non-Jew (*bishul akum*) is another urgent concern. According to Ashkenazic custom, as long as the mashgiach ignites the flame and/or the oven before cooking begins, all the food is considered cooked by a Jew (*bishul Yisroel*).[6] This requirement can theoretically be satisfied by a mashgiach who visits periodically, giving the impression that the

4. עי' יו"ד סי' קי"ח
5. יו"ד סי' קי"ג
6. יו"ד סי' קי"ג סע' ז' ברמ"א

requirements necessary to remove the restrictions of bishul akum can be easily applied. In practice, *bishul Yisroel* proves to be quite difficult to implement. The mashgiach must be especially alert to many possible problems, and *bishul akum* remains an issue of major concern in kashrus today. There are opinions that allow food to be cooked by gentiles as long as the pilot light had originally been lit by a Jew, though one should rely on this only in exceptional circumstances.

For Sefardim, the requirements for *bishul Yisroel* are more stringent. The Mechaber of the Shulchan Aruch maintains that the actual cooking must be done by a Jew. Thus, the preparatory act of igniting the flame is insufficient to render the food permissible.

Practically all meat dishes are fit to be served at a formal dinner (*oleh al shulchan melachim*),[7] and therefore require bishul Yisroel. Special care must also be taken to prevent mixing meat and fish, which is a *sakanah* (harmful). This would almost certainly be neglected without proper hashgachah.

Although there is halachic basis to take a more lenient approach to the above issues, experience has clearly shown, that to ensure that basic standards of kashrus are consistently maintained, permanent supervision of restaurants serving meat is required.

Dairy restaurants: Until only a few years ago, most Rabbis were satisfied with periodic (*yotzei venichnas*) supervision at dairy restaurants. The assumption was that there is comparatively little risk of bishul akum, since most of the food is not *oleh al shulchan melachim*, and the potential for genuine kashrus concerns is minimal from the outset. The fact is, however, that many egg, fish, potato, vegetable, and grain dishes are subject to the restrictions of bishul akum. Additionally, *bishul akum* aside, experience has clearly shown that serious kashrus concerns do develop, and there is a real need for permanent supervision, even in dairy restaurants.

An example of the type of problem that may arise was related by a Rav Ha'machshir a number of years ago. Upon returning home from

7. ע"ש סע' א'

a simchah in the early hours of the morning, he happened to pass by a dairy restaurant that was under his personal supervision. Noticing that the lights were on and that there appeared to be activity inside, he entered unannounced, and found several members of the kitchen staff grating large blocks of non-kosher cheese for the next day's pizza. To complete the illusion, a few packs of kosher cheese were open, ready to be displayed the next morning in order to give the impression that this was the cheese that had been used. This is just one of many similar examples that have led responsible Rabbis to conclude that constant supervision is as necessary in dairy restaurants as it is in meat restaurants.

Without *hashgachah temidis, bedikas tola'im* (careful preparation of vegetables to remove insects) would also likely be neglected. Even in a case of religious ownership, the chances of the owner himself providing adequate supervision whilst running the business and serving customers, are very slim.

PICKLE BARRELS[8]

Many food stores that are owned by non-observant Jews are known to sell sour pickles from open barrels, which originally came from kosher companies. In addition, they often sell olives and hot peppers from open cans that came with a hechsher from Eretz Yisroel. Is it permissible to purchase such products?

ANSWER

A God-fearing Jew should avoid buying unpackaged food unless the store has proper kashrus supervision and there is no suspicion that kosher items are being switched or mixed with non-kosher ones. It is unreasonable to rely on the original hechsher on a barrel of pickles that has possibly been filled and refilled over the years.

8. יו"ד סי' קי"ח

There is a story of a store that carried the sign "*tachas hashgachas harabbanim hagaonim shlita*, under the supervision of the illustrious Rabbis" over the door, bearing testimony to the fact that kosher certification had been granted to the great-grandfather of the present owner. The 'supervising' Rabbis had long since ceased to perform their functions in this world, and Jews careful to eat only kosher knew the sign was meaningless. The same may be said of the open pickle barrel in a non-kosher store. The certification on an open can or barrel does not guarantee the kashrus of the contents therein.

RANDOM INSPECTIONS[9]

To have reliable kashrus supervision in a plant that produces smoked fish, is it sufficient for the kashrus inspector to visit the site twice a week, considering that all the parties involved know that he will never inspect more frequently, and never on Shabbos and Yom Tov?

ANSWER

The Gemara[10] observes that a *mamuneh haba lekitzin greiusah hi*, a mashgiach who comes at set times is not effective, as the workers will not be afraid of getting caught. The Gemara concludes that it is imperative to have a *mamuneh she'eino ba lekitzin*, a mashgiach that does *not* come at set times. If the mashgiach only comes twice a week, and the staff at the plant know that he will not visit a third time, it is as if there is no hashgachah at all. A mashgiach must time his visits in a random, unpredictable manner, and additionally, must occasionally visit on Shabbos and Yom Tov. This is the practice carried out by responsible kashrus agencies. The mashgiach stays in a nearby hotel and walks into the plant on Shabbos. Once or twice a year is sufficient,

9. יו"ד סי' קי"ח
10. ע"ז סא:

as long as it is known that such a visit may take place unexpectedly, and at any time.

The effectiveness of periodic supervision (*yotzei venichnas*) is an issue that kashrus agencies deal with on a constant basis. It applies to all areas of food production, smokehouses being only one of thousands of real-life examples of the need for truly random supervision. A judgment has to be made on the basis of each individual case as to how inspections can best assure compliance.

The mashgiach's responsibilities: Hashgachah work involves much more than a serious inspection of the premises. A mashgiach must understand the workings of the industry in minute detail. He should be aware of every possible avenue of substitution, go through sales and inventory records, check the computer databases, and be there to inspect deliveries of supplies. He has to regularly inspect freezers and storage areas, and have access to order slips and all other office paperwork. Indeed, he should not need to ask permission to inspect any area of the facility he oversees, and any resistance on the part of the staff is a clear sign that things are not as they should be. Anything suspicious must be researched and brought to the attention of the supervising Rabbis.

PROMOTING ACCOUNTABILITY

How can we be sure that the scallions that are added to products such as tuna fish and egg salad have been properly checked?

ANSWER

The best thing to do is to call the supervising mashgiach and ask him personally if he has made such a check. The greatest assurance that a mashgiach will do his job and maintain the standards he sets out to apply, is accountability. Indeed, when there is more than one mashgiach involved in a particular area of supervision, each must justify his actions to the other, and in the process, the level of kashrus is preserved. Consumer inquiries also add to the sense of accountability, which will encourage the mashgiach to be uncompromising in his standards.

DELIVERIES[11]

Is it permissible for a kosher bakery or fishmonger to use a non-religious Jew or non-Jew to make its deliveries?

ANSWER

Sealed packaging: All kosher items must be sent with a trustworthy person who is beyond suspicion that he may tamper with or switch the goods on route. If this criterion cannot be satisfied, then the food must be closed with a seal. A valuable or expensive item requires two seals.[12]

Fish: Fish is one of the items that the Gemara[13] mentions as requiring two seals to attest to its kashrus. (The others are meat, wine, and *techeiles*, the blue thread used to make tzitzis.) One reason for this is the great expense involved in supervising the production of kosher fish. This is necessary because it is impossible to distinguish between pieces of kosher and non-kosher fish once they have been skinned and supervision is required from the beginning of the preparation. Because of this, the price differential between kosher and non-kosher fish is great, and an incentive to switch the fish exists. Therefore, two seals are required.[14]

Baked goods: Baked goods do not generally require the same level

11. יו"ד סי' קי"ח
12. יו"ד סי' קי"ח סע' א'
13. ע"ז לט.
14. יו"ד סי' קי"ח סע' א'

of protection against substitution as fish,[15] though there are a number of factors to consider. Certain kosher bakeries make products that are easily identifiable as their own, which lessens the need for a seal, as any substitution would be obvious.

Baked products that are less common, that come from a lesser-known bakery, or whose shape is common to many bakeries, require supervised delivery. They must have a seal to protect them from being exchanged, unless it is clearly recognizable that they have come from a kosher source. Generally, we are less concerned that non-kosher baked goods have been switched for kosher goods, since the price differential is negligible. Therefore one seal is sufficient.

Indirect monitoring: There are some circumstances where it is impossible to place a seal on the goods. Instead, the kashrus agency monitors the delivery system indirectly. They routinely time the deliveries, and the results enable them to determine, in any given case, whether or not there was sufficient time for the drivers to switch the goods. However, using such a system on a regular basis, especially in a large business, would be highly impractical, expensive and time-consuming, not to mention, open to abuse. At this scale of operation, food products need to be sealed.

Scored tape: The simplest, most inexpensive way to seal packages of kosher food is by using scored tape that, once attached, cannot be removed without coming apart. This will ensure that the food is neither touched nor switched. In a case where food has already been sent without these precautions, an experienced Rabbi needs to be consulted.

15. ע"ש

BAKED GOODS IN OPEN BAGS

Is it halachically acceptable to leave early-morning deliveries of baked goods in open bags in front of the stores?

ANSWER

Bakeries deliver bread in open bags to allow the steam from the fresh loaves to escape, which prevents it from becoming damp or soggy. There may be room to rely on the principle of periodic supervision (*yotzei venichnas*), as the (Orthodox Jewish) owner may turn up to open his store at any moment, and will occasionally inspect the deliveries. Ideally, however, there should be a seal to eliminate even the slightest chance of substitution, even if it means that there is a chance that the bread will be slightly less tasty.

FOOD COLORINGS[16]

Do all products containing food colorings require proper kosher certification?

ANSWER

Any product containing food colorings, even in small amounts, is potentially problematic. The Pri Megadim[17] maintains that if food contains a non-kosher ingredient that was less that one-sixtieth of the total volume, and would ordinarily be nullified (*batul*) by virtue of taste, it would still not be considered batul if it imparts color to the food (*chazusah d'tarfus*), and the mixture would be forbidden for consumption.

By purchasing only those products with proper kosher certification, one may be assured that all ingredients, including the colorings, are scrutinized to ensure their permissibility. When inspecting a product for certification, a kashrus agency will be on the lookout for specific

16. יו"ד סי' ק'
17. יו"ד סי' ק' משבצות זהב סק"א

food colorings that are known to be non-kosher and are therefore entirely unacceptable.

Carmine red: A bright red food coloring known as carmine is made from crushed beetles, and is, of course, non-kosher. Carmine can be distinguished from other red dyes because its color does not dissolve or run, and is a very bright red color. Maraschino cherries are usually colored by a cheaper variety of dye that can be identified by the telltale ring of red dye in the surrounding food. In contrast, fruit-cocktail cherries dyed with carmine will never leave any mark on adjacent food. Despite this difference, no one should judge for himself whether or not the red coloring is kosher. Hashgachah is required.

Enocianina: There is also a brownish-purple food coloring, known as enocianina, which is mainly produced in Italy. It is a forbidden derivative of the grape skins used in manufacturing non-kosher wine.

Other food dyes: The above dyes are used to produce red, purple, and brown colored food products. Any product containing these colors is therefore suspect. Other food dyes and colorings are usually kosher, and do not generally pose kashrus issues.

Some people are under the impression that natural coloring is kosher and that the only problem is with artificial coloring. This argument can be easily refuted by pointing out that beetles, cows and grapes are all completely natural.

BEER

Does beer manufactured in the United States require a hechsher? If not, does this also hold true for imported beers?

ANSWER

The concerns we have nowadays regarding the kashrus of beer are the same ones addressed by the Poskim for hundreds of years. Although it is uncommon these days, certain substances can be put into beer such as flavor enhancers, clarifiers or coloring agents. One of these additives is known as isinglass, a type of gelatin made from the swim bladders of sturgeon, which is a non-kosher fish. Some Rabbis nevertheless permit this substance since the change brought about from the drying process permanently destroys the bladder tissue to the point that it cannot simply be reconstituted or restored by the reintroduction of water, such as is done, for example, with dried instant coffee. Thus, it can no longer be considered a derivative of non-kosher fish, and is acceptable according to these opinions.

Dark beer without a hechsher should generally be avoided, since the dark color can be produced by many different types of additives. Some of them are colorings taken from wine and other substances that absolutely require supervision. It is preferable to look for a hechsher even on light beer.

The differences between American beer and European beers are very slight, though in one respect it is possible to rely on American beer without a hechsher if the label includes the words 'contains no additives'. The laws governing the production of alcoholic beverages are very comprehensive and strictly enforced by the regular presence of government officers. This is due to the government's interest in collecting the taxes it imposes upon alcoholic beverages. Therefore, we can be certain there are no additives in products thus labeled.

COFFEE

Certain famous brands of coffee have manufacturing plants throughout the world. The coffee produced by the American plants carries a hechsher, but is more expensive. Coffee produced abroad, in Brazil and Mexico for example, is imported and sold at a lower price, but does not carry a hechsher. Can one assume that imported packages of coffee are kosher nonetheless?

ANSWER

'Fresh-ground' coffee: Standard ground coffee, which is neither flavored nor decaffeinated, presents no problems whatsoever. It can be assumed to be kosher for year-round and Passover use.

Problems in the past: Years ago, it was the practice to add roasted barley to coffee as a flavor enhancer, and the coffee had to be checked before grinding to ensure that there was no danger of chametz. The equipment also had to be checked or kashered because of the possibility that barley had been used in previous runs. Rabbi Moshe Leiber, *zt"l*, one of the pioneers in preparing kosher food in America, used to personally check whole sacks of coffee, bean by bean, to be used for *kosher l'Pesach* coffee.

Nowadays, barley grains are never roasted with the coffee beans, and all flavorings and additives are introduced only after the beans are roasted. Consequently, plain coffee is roasted on machinery that is free of chametz and free of *tarfus* (non-kosher substances).

Instant coffee: Regular instant coffee now requires kosher supervision for Passover use. An additive by the name of maltodextrin is now an occasional ingredient in instant coffee, and it may be made from wheat starch.

Flavored coffees: It goes without saying that all flavored coffees need kosher supervision to ensure that the flavors do not contain *tarfus*.

Decaffeinated coffee: Decaffeinated coffees need reliable Pesach supervision to rule out chametz. The common procedure of removing caffeine from coffee involves soaking the beans in ethyl acetate. This chemical is a combination of alcohol (that may be made from grain), and vinegar (that may even be produced from non-kosher wine).

While it is true that concentrated ethyl acetate is inedible (*nifsal me'achilah*), nevertheless, in a diluted form it is used as an effective vanilla flavoring. In the process of extracting the caffeine, a trace amount of ethyl acetate flavor is absorbed by the beans, and this flavor is most definitely edible, if not desirable. Therefore decaffeinated coffee, whether instant or ground, should never be used for Pesach without special Pesach supervision.

KASHERING A MICROWAVE OVEN

Can a treif microwave oven be kashered? If so, could it then be used alternately for milk and meat, kashering between each use?

ANSWER

There are two concerns with kashering a microwave oven.

Kashering a treif microwave oven: Firstly, we must examine how a microwave becomes treif. There are two ways in which non-kosher flavor (a *beliyas issur*), or any other flavor, might get absorbed into surfaces of a microwave oven. When food spills onto the floor or the turntable of the microwave, it is similar to the absorption that occurs in a *keli rishon*, a pot of boiling liquid on the fire. At the very least, it would be treated as *irui keli rishon*, the absorption that takes place when pouring from a boiling pot onto another surface. The second, less severe type of absorption (*beliya*), is from the steam that fills the oven and penetrates the walls. The following steps should therefore be taken to *kasher* a treif microwave:

To remove the *beliyas issur* from the turntable, it should be immersed into a pot of boiling water as is done with regular *ha'agalah*. If the turntable is plastic, a *sheilah* should be asked to one's personal Rav, as there are Poskim who object to the kashering of plastic items. The prevailing view among the Poskim, though, including the final view of Reb Moshe, *zt"l*, was to permit the kashering of plastic.

Boiling water should be poured onto the floor of the microwave oven after it has been thoroughly cleaned, and twenty-four hours have passed since the microwave was used.

A large bowl of water should be placed in the microwave oven and heated on the highest setting for at least twenty minutes. The chamber will fill with very hot steam and the walls will become piping hot. This is akin to doing ha'agalah on the walls of the microwave. The door of the microwave should not be opened during the steaming process, as the accumulation of heat will be lost.

Kashering with steam: Generally, heat created by steam cannot be used for kashering. Only boiling water may be used. Here, however, Reb Moshe, *zt"l*, applied the principle of *kebol'o kach polto*, "as it was absorbed, so it may be released." In a microwave, the flavor of the food penetrates the walls solely through the buildup of steam. Furthermore, microwaves are used more for heating up food than for actually cooking them, such that the amount of beliya is relatively small. Furthermore, we generally need not be concerned about boiling hot food that occasionally splatters onto the walls of the microwave. It is sufficient that ha'agalah removes the flavor absorbed during the course of standard usage (*rov tashmisho*). Thus the use of steam is sufficient to kasher the walls of a microwave. In cases where a microwave is also used for cooking, or where spills and splatters are frequent, a competent Rav should be consulted.

One oven for milk and meat: Kashering a microwave oven between alternate milk and meat uses is not recommended, since it is generally forbidden to use the same vessel for both meat and milk. The Magen

Avraham[18] writes specifically that one should have two distinct sets of utensils; otherwise there is great potential for confusion and therefore, mistakes. If it is necessary to switch any utensil's use from milk to meat, or vice-versa, the custom (*minhag*) brought by the Magen Avraham is to kasher it for Pesach, at which point it is *parve*. It can then be designated either for milk or for meat.

Reb Yaakov Kamenetzky, *zt"l*, related that the Rabbanim of Europe would offer an alternative method for someone who had a special need to switch a utensil from milk to meat. They would advise waiting until the utensil is *eino ben yomo*, that is, it had not been used for milk within twenty-four hours, then to pour a few drops of hot meat gravy onto it, which rendered the utensil *assur* for use by Rabbinical decree (*miderabbanan*) according to most Poskim. (This cannot be done within twenty-four hours of being used for milk, because that would be tantamount to cooking the milk flavor in the utensil with the hot meat gravy, which is forbidden by the Torah.) Once the utensil is forbidden to use, one is allowed to kasher it.[19]

Kashering conventional ovens between milk and meat: When it comes to conventional ovens, the *minhag* in Klal Yisroel was always to allow kashering between alternate milk and meat uses. Strictly speaking, *libun kal* (a process by which a surface is heated to the point that a piece of paper held to the opposite side will become singed) is enough to remove kosher flavor (*beliyas heter*) absorbed in the walls of an oven. In practice, this is accomplished by leaving the oven on its highest heat setting for 1¼ to 1½ hours. It is also possible to kasher with *ha'agalah*, by applying a steady spray of boiling water on all of the oven's surfaces. A continuous pouring of boiling water from the vessel in which it was boiled (*irui keli rishon*) onto a surface for a sufficient amount of time, is equivalent to *ha'agalah*.

It is important to note that these methods can only be used where the flavor absorbed into the walls of the oven was imparted by a

18. או"ח סי' תק"ט ס"ק י"א

19. עי' במ"ב או"ח סי' תק"ט ס"ק כ"ה מה שהביא בשם הפמ"ג

permissible substance (*beliyas heter*). *Ha'agalah* and *libun kal* would be insufficient to remove a forbidden substance or flavor (*beliyas issur*) that has become absorbed into the walls of an oven.

Separate ovens: Reb Moshe Feinstein, *zt"l*, advised that one should live completely in accordance with the accepted custom of the Magen Avraham, and have separate ovens for milk and meat. The *heter* to kasher an oven between milk and meat was only instituted due to the poverty of Jews who could only afford one oven. Where means permit, one should make sure to own two separate conventional ovens. Following this logic, one should also buy a second microwave oven, perhaps a small, cheaper model that can be used exclusively for milk, and keep the main microwave for meat, or vice-versa.

Kashering a microwave oven between milk and meat: Where that may not be possible, and a person only has access to a single microwave, the following procedures should be followed:

It is best that everything placed into the oven, whether milk or meat, should be double wrapped to avoid potential mix-ups. However, it is acceptable to designate the oven as either meat or dairy, and only double-wrap the other type before heating. A single covering is not sufficient, as the steam on the outside of the wrapping can convey flavor from the oven to the container holding the food. With two wraps, the steam only penetrates the first layer of wrap, and the second layer protects the food. This method is also applicable when the only microwave available has been used for non-kosher food.

INSPECTING CABBAGE[20]

When making stuffed cabbage, whole heads of cabbage are frozen and then defrosted. To check them for infestation, the leaves are held up to the light. Often, it is possible to

20. יו"ד סי' פ"ד

discern a number of black dots in the flesh of the vegetable. Is this a cause for concern?

ANSWER

The cabbage should be in the freezer for about two days so that it will have wilted enough for it to be wrapped around the meat and rice. The bugs that infest cabbage, are usually thrips, which attach to the leaf by embedding their feet into its flesh, but when the cabbage is washed, the main parts of the thrips fall off and only the tips of their feet remain. This may account for the tiny black specks that are seen when the leaf is held up to the light. These miniscule remains are not whole insects (*birya*) and are therefore *batul* to the cabbage leaf. It is important to wash both sides of each leaf to insure that any thrips and cabbage-worms are removed.

Very rarely, cabbage can become infested with burrowing insects. The presence of these insects can be identified by the network of tunnels they leave in the leaf. The tunnels become readily apparent when the leaf is held up to the light. It is only necessary to check the first few layers of leaves in this fashion to ascertain that the rest are insect-free.

'BUG FREE' LEAFY VEGETABLES

There are a number of companies who declare their vegetables, especially Romaine lettuce, to be 'bug free', and have kosher supervision to that effect. How far can we rely on their claims to be 'bug free', especially in such cases where the supervision has changed hands a number of times?

ANSWER

Unfortunately, it is frequently the case that leafy vegetables appearing with as many as three kosher symbols attesting to the absence of insects, are nonetheless infested. Many of the companies that package 'checked' vegetables only allow the mashgichim to take samples of vegetables that have already been packed. The actual cleaning process is totally unsupervised and unregulated.

Inspecting lettuce: If one wants to eat locally produced Romaine lettuce, the best thing is to buy a fresh head and check it by holding each leaf between a strong light and the eye of the observer. This can be accomplished by using a 'light box', which is readily available in art-supply stores. Whatever the source of light, it must be strong enough to shine through the translucent leaf, causing the opaque insects to stand out sharply. Additionally, there are specially produced crops grown in greenhouses under the supervision of expert Rabbinical authorities. These leafy vegetables are completely insect-free.

NON-KOSHER HIND QUARTER[21]

If a Rav paskens that one hind quarter out of a large packet of chicken hind quarters is not kosher, what is the status of the remaining pieces in the packet?

ANSWER

The answer hinges on whether or not parts of the same chicken are generally packaged together. If it can be determined that they are packaged together, and the other hind quarter can be assumed to be in the packet, it would not be *batul b'rov*. A hind quarter is considered to be a significant serving of chicken (*ra'ui l'hiskabeid*), and therefore has the status of a *davar chashuv*, something important.[22] Once the presence of a treif hind quarter is known to exist within a group of items, that group is termed a *ta'aroves* of *issur* and *heter* and the *issur* is not *batul* even among a thousand kosher pieces. If the piece identi-

21. יו״ד סי׳ ק״י
22. עי׳ טור יו״ד סי׳ ק״י ד״ה דבר שאינו בטל, שו״ע יו״ד סי׳ ק״א סע׳ ג׳ ברמ״א

fied as treif was the left hindquarter, then all the right hindquarters are forbidden, even if there are a thousand of them.

The confirmed presence of *issur* in a mixture is called *kevius* or *kevua*. This is a term used in a number of different, yet related ways. Sometimes it is used to indicate an assumption of permanence. In our case, it indicates that a particular item is definitely located within a group of similar items. The definite presence of a prohibited item is referred to as its having *kevius*. If this prohibited item cannot be distinguished from other permissible items with which it was mixed, the result is a *ta'aroves*.

Kevius: In the typical case of packed poultry, however, there is sufficient doubt as to whether or not the second hind quarter from the same chicken is also present in the same pack. Every company has different packaging techniques, as do individual employees, so it is impossible to make a blanket statement about all situations. However, it is the general practice that the tops and bottoms are separated into large piles before being packed, and there is only a very slight chance that a pair of hind quarters from the same chicken will be packaged together. The missing non-kosher hindquarter cannot be assumed to be located in the same package with its pair. This means it has no *kevius*. As such, the question of *ta'aroves* does not apply, and the remainder of the package is permissible.

KASHRUS AGENCY STANDARDS

Nowadays, there are dozens of independent kashrus agencies, each presumably with its own standards, adhering to various stringencies and relying on various leniencies when giving certification. Some basic information is available with respect to the standards regarding bishul Yisroel, pas Yisroel, and chalav Yisroel (products cooked and baked by observant Jewish staff, and milk produced under Jewish supervision, respectively), but by and large, the public is

unaware of the standards employed by each kashrus agency. Are there plans to publish these standards?

ANSWER

Setting the highest standards: First of all, it is important to distinguish between two sets of standards. From the outset, every Kashrus organization establishes certain standards that serve as the benchmark of their certification. This is the *lechatchilah* standard, the level of kashrus that should ideally be met in all circumstances.

Setting the highest standard is of paramount importance for a kashrus agency, and leniencies should never become part of the standard policy. Often, there are certain halachic stringencies which seem impossible to enforce, given the nature of food production today. Yet, there still remains a need to base any decision upon a sincere commitment to analyze the problem from every angle in order to find a solution. The reliability of kashrus certification disintegrates if leniencies are seen as an acceptable way of resolving difficulties that arise. With such an attitude, it would not take long before products were being certified kosher on the basis of a whole series of *heterim* that no one would ever rely upon in their own kitchen.

Clear and unambiguous standards: Reliable kashrus agencies have clear and unambiguous guidelines that standardize their approach to kashrus issues. These guidelines are made available to all the mashgichim. Some agencies publicize their standards in official publications and periodicals, but even those that do not, if requested, are more than willing to discuss their standards, and under what circumstances they employ leniencies.

The b'dieved standard: Though every respectable kashrus organization constantly strives to maintain its goal, mistakes will sometimes be made by employees of the production plant requiring the mashgiach to employ leniencies that have a firm basis in halachah. Batches of food that have accidentally become tainted with uncertified ingredients can justifiably be permitted in accordance with the rules of nullification (*bittul*), and other principles of kashrus that are an integral part of our firm Torah principles, especially if the flavoring is undesirable (*nosein ta'am lifgam*). This is *b'dieved*. It is expected that in the overwhelming majority of cases, there is no necessity to resort to b'dieved standards.

Kulos and chumros: There is no place for *chiddushim* in kashrus standards. There is no obligation to adhere to modern halachic stringencies (new *chumros*) that are not recognized concerns discussed by the Poskim. Similarly, creative halachic leniencies have no place in the policy of a responsible kashrus agency. As for established leniencies of the past, these too should only be relied upon if the circumstances that led to them still exist. In many cases, affluence and the availability of ingredients from kosher sources have rendered the old leniencies employed in Europe obsolete.

Avoiding heterim: When the agency starts off with an eye to maintaining the proper standards, even in difficult situations, then heterim will naturally be limited to the few conditions that truly warrant them, and even then only after a thorough discussion with Poskim of stature who can justify the use of a heter in that particular circumstance. This policy also develops an attitude of responsibility and vigilance on the part of the mashgichim regarding the level of kashrus they provide. The mashgichim in a large kashrus organization are constantly discussing problems that arise, such that an individual mashgiach does not feel he is working in a vacuum. He knows that the decisions he makes will be scrutinized, and this motivates all the members of the organization to maintain their standards.

It is important to note that Poskim of one organization should never feel themselves exempt from discussing their decisions with Poskim of other organizations. The only guaranteed way to ensure that no mistake will ever be made in halachah is to maintain a full-scale transparency. That is, to make the reasons and explanations for their halachic decisions available to the Torah community in printed form, and to avoid at all cost conducting their thought and decision-making processes in secret. This is the Torah way. Any deviation from this standard will eventually result in error. Witness the tragic end of Adoniyahu, son of King David, about whom the possuk attests that he was never rebuked, "ולא עצבו אביו מימיו לאמר מדוע ככה עשית – *His father never saddened him all his days saying, 'Why have you done this?'*" (I Melachim 1:6). His unchecked rebellious spirit was his undoing, as it is written, "וישלח המלך שלמה ביד בניהו בן יהוידע ויפגע בו וימת – *King Shlomo sent by way of Binayahu ben Yehoyada; he attacked him and he died.*" (ibid. 2:25).

Lenient certifications: It is unfortunate that there are various kosher certifications that rely on all manner of heterim. One such *machshir*, who certified the manufacture of certain candies, justified the use of heterim by saying, "Only children eat them." Another Rabbi rationalized the leniencies he instituted, saying, "I would never eat the meat I supervise; it is intended only for less religious Jews."

Halachic issues vs. kashrus standards: It is also important to distinguish between the standards of the kashrus agency, and kashrus issues that are dependent on variant rulings of past *Gedolei HaPoskim*.

Chalav stam: One particular agency, for instance, supervises the production of dairy products that use *chalav stam* – milk and milk derivatives produced by large, government-regulated dairy manufacturers. This does not mean that this agency is 'lenient' in its kashrus standards, nor does it mean that the agency is issuing a *psak* that chalav stam is permissible. The kashrus supervision on these products is as stringent as it is on any of their other products, and is intended to provide quality kashrus for those who rely on the psak of Reb Moshe Feinstein, *zt"l*, and other Gedolim that one may eat chalav stam. Under no circumstances must one who eats only chalav Yisroel consume such products simply because kashrus supervision is in place.

Pas Yisroel and kitniyos: The same is true of non-pas Yisroel products, and Pesach foods containing legumes (*kitniyos*), for Sefardic Jews. All sectors of the religious Jewish public that abide by legitimate halachic opinions in kashrus, need an agency to provide quality certification of foods that they are permitted to eat. Kashrus agencies must fill this need, and it does not reflect in any way whatsoever on the quality of their supervision.

There are organizations that specialize in identifying the status of products with regard to specific *hiddurim*, such as pas Yisroel, *yashan*, and chalav stam. They do not necessarily supervise the production of food, but rather provide information about various products. They can be contacted for up-to-date lists of the products they certify, and the criteria they use to rate products.

COMMUNICATION BETWEEN KASHRUS AGENCIES

Do the various kashrus organizations communicate with each other openly, or does competitiveness prevent trust and the flow of information?

ANSWER

There generally exists a very open atmosphere of communication between the various legitimate kashrus organizations. Even when there is disagreement on a particular issue, and where it might affect the acceptability of a particular product according to the policy of another agency, the senior Rabbanim are straightforward with each other as to what is being done. No one is trying to fool anyone else, *chas vechalila*.

To demonstrate just how cooperative the relationship is between good agencies, one only has to visit a certain well-known slaughter-house. There, members of three 'rival' agencies work closely together at a personal level to resolve any kashrus issues that arise. In one instance, they even inspected each other's knives and jointly carried out the internal and external inspections of the slaughtered animals. Without a doubt, the warm relationship between the Rabbanim of various agencies is responsible for the unprecedented level of kosher shechitah in the United States today.

As for those agencies that are not forthcoming and do not communicate their policies, there is no basis for cooperation.

AIRLINE KASHRUS

What are the differences between the Kosher and Special Kosher meals offered by various airlines, and are there other kashrus concerns when flying abroad?

ANSWER

By far, the best advice is to order the Special Kosher meals, which have Mehadrin supervision. This is particularly important for food prepared in Eretz Yisroel. Standard Rabbanut certification cannot be relied upon without first knowing a host of details. On the other hand, Rabbanut Mehadrin from Eretz Yisroel, which is used at the airport and is actually termed "*Mehadrin min HaMehadrin*," is as good as any quality supervision one could get in the United States at the present time. The package should read, "Mehadrin min HaMehadrin."

Kashrus on Israeli airliners: Special Kosher meals are particularly beneficial when attempting to avoid the specific concerns regarding Israeli airline companies. When leaving Israel, the galleys are stocked with food prepared under the supervision of the standard Rabbanut, which is then served to the passengers without any seal or other indication of kashrus supervision. Even presuming that the initial provisions supplied by the company-owned commissaries adhere to the standard Rabbanut guidelines, plane crews also accept food supplies abroad from other sources. They might re-stock the jetliner's galley in any of fifty locations worldwide, sometimes even after an unexpected landing in a place that might not supply kosher food at all. Additionally, no Rabbinic supervision exists for the preparation of food on individual planes, and these items are unpacked, heated in the galley, and served to the passengers.

A person can only rely on what is served if he personally visits the galley and notes that the original packaging indeed carried the seal of a reliable kashrus agency, and that entrées are heated only while double-wrapped. Thus, by insisting on the individually wrapped and sealed Special Kosher meals, one avoids the pitfalls of the open galley on any plane.

On flights from those companies that originate in the United States, the gap between Kosher and Special Kosher is much smaller. Both come double-wrapped and are from *hashgachos* with similar standards, and therefore the risk of encountering a serious kashrus problem is minimal.

Halachah remains in force: Parenthetically, an international flight is not a no-man's land where the standard rules of Jewish law are suspended. It seems that some people forget about certain halachos while in the midst of a long plane trip. People can be seen eating before davening, when it is clearly daybreak (*alos hashachar*), or eating without washing *netilas yadayim*, and even without making the proper blessings before and after their meal. The author has personally seen almost an entire planeload of passengers eating their meals in the usual fashion, though it was a fast day. Every last one of them was a committed, Torah observant Jew whom we would normally assume to be careful about such things. A Jew must think ahead and consider the unusual circumstances he might face on an extended transatlantic journey. He must know what the halachah requires of him, and not delude himself into thinking he is on some type of vacation from his Jewish responsibilities.

KASHRUS IN ERETZ YISROEL

How can a person ensure that he does not compromise his kashrus standards when travelling abroad?

ANSWER

Just as a person living in the United States knows which kashrus agencies he can rely upon and which he cannot, the same is true in other locales. The people living in Israel, or any other country, know which *hechsherim* are up to par, and which are not. A person visiting abroad should ask the residents there whom they trust, for reliable kashrus information. Question them regarding particular restaurants or hotels, or if there are specific places they can recommend. As in America, the kashrus standard in various institutions fluctuates, and these questions need to be asked anew with each visit.

KASHRUS HASHGACHAH AT A CAMP OR YESHIVAH

Does a camp or yeshivah kitchen require a mashgiach, given that it is not a 'business'?

ANSWER

Kashrus supervision is just as necessary in a yeshivah or camp kitchen as it is in the outside world. Every institution should arrange for a knowledgeable mashgiach who will be respected by the staff and whose word will be followed. In the best scenario, the cook, management, and assistants are all religious Jews, committed to keeping the halachos of kashrus. But any institutional kitchen is hectic; they prepare food for hundreds of people, and it has to be served on time. In the middle of a busy morning, a supply of ingredients may arrive and the distributor may have mistakenly sent a non-kosher variety of a particular spice or sauce. If there is no one specifically in charge of checking deliveries, the non-kosher items might end up being used before anyone notices. Also, yeshivah and camp kitchens prepare both meat and milk dishes, and there is always the possibility that utensils, ingredients, or unwashed hands will inadvertently cross over from one side to the other. If the kitchen hires non-Jewish help, then the mashgiach needs to watch out for *bishul akum*, too. Often, fresh leafy vegetables are served, and the quality of the *bedikas hatola'im* may be compromised if the pressure is great.

Some people claim that it is an embarrassment for the camp if they have a mashgiach, because people will think they are not so religious and therefore need to be supervised. Experience shows that this reasoning is faulty. No large production kitchen escapes sudden dilemmas, even with the best of intentions on the part of the staff and where there are clearly posted rules. With the right attitude and a healthy dose of friendliness and appreciation, the mashgiach can create an environment in the kitchen where all the members of the staff are willing to accommodate the highest kashrus standards.

CHECKING PRODUCT LABELS

Can a person assume that packaged products usually bearing a kosher symbol, are kosher even without the symbol on the package?

ANSWER

Non-kosher runs: If the package does not have a kosher symbol, it was not made under supervision. The kosher consumer must always beware of changes in supermarket products. Even familiar products known to bear a kosher symbol can sometimes appear in a non-kosher variety, without the tell-tale kosher symbol on the label. While no supervising agency should allow a company to market a non-kosher batch of a usually kosher product, the consumer must keep in mind that things like this do happen inadvertently from time to time.

Different varieties: A different problem, one that rests squarely upon the shoulders of the consumer, is the appearance of a new version or flavor of a familiar product. While the old versions might have kosher certification, there is no reason to assume that something new is also certified. Therefore, any new product must be scrupulously examined for kashrus before being served. Only after it is clear that the package bears a reliable kosher symbol should the consumer allow himself to partake of the new item.

SUGAR

Is it true that plain sugar needs no kosher supervision? Does this also apply to the small, unlabeled packets of sugar available in hotels and restaurants?

ANSWER

All regular white sugar is produced using processes that are standard throughout the industry, and there are no additives. There is no need for kosher supervision for year-round use. Even small, unlabeled packets are fine.

NUTS AND DRIED FRUIT

Many stores sell nuts and dried fruits from large sacks and bins, or repackage them without supervision. May the consumer assume these items are kosher, or should one insist on buying only sealed containers that carry kosher certification?

ANSWER

Nuts and dried fruit have always been sold from large sacks. To say that one should never buy these items when sold this way would be an unnecessary restriction, and for many of these products there are no issues at all. On the other hand, any processing or cooking raises potential kashrus issues.

Raw nuts: Raw nuts such as pecans, walnuts, and brazil nuts are not processed in any way, and present no problem.

Incidentally, all almonds as well as peanuts in their shells, are dry-roasted in order to make them edible. No oil is used. Therefore, no hashgachah is needed for these items.

Roasted nuts: Certain roasted nuts are labeled "roasted in oil." Whenever oil is used to process food, reliable kashrus supervision is obligatory. Oil can be derived from many non-kosher sources. Additionally, the utensils used to handle these products must be carefully supervised. Consequently, nuts roasted in oil must bear a reliable kosher symbol.

Cashews: Raw cashew nuts may be infested, and should be inspected before being eaten even if they are packaged with a reliable hashgachah. Roasted cashews present no concern of infestation, because any insects they might contain would be burnt to a crisp in the process of roasting. As mentioned above, all nuts roasted in oil need kosher supervision. Cashews are no exception to this rule.

Kashrus supervision on commonly sold cashews begins only after the large sacks of shelled cashews arrive at the individual processing and packing plants. The process by which the tough adherent shells around the natural cashew are removed is a very complicated one, and is currently done without hashgachah. Although this arrangement is acceptable according to strict halachah, it would be an improvement to have it done under proper supervision.

Raisins: Raisins are supplied to many stores in bulk, in 40–50 pound crates, and they remain open for long periods of time. This means the raisins on top run the risk of drying out. To solve that problem, packers spray the raisins with oils or glycerin, which protect the tenderness of the raisins. In the past, when most brown raisins were sun-dried, the ones packed in consumer-size boxes were not sprayed. Today, most raisins are dried in ovens and sprayed before the completion of drying. In the United States, the oil most commonly used is under kosher supervision.

White raisins (sultanas) are always dried in ovens, and are often sprayed with oil, either on the farm or during the drying process.

Currently, a reliable hechsher is necessary for both brown and white raisins.

Apricots, dates, and figs: Dried apricots are sprayed with sulfur dioxide to keep them from drying out and to protect the color. Sulfur dioxide is a synthetically produced chemical, and therefore dried apricots do not require kosher supervision. Figs must be individually inspected to see if the inside looks damaged or shows other signs of infestation. Dates are often sprayed with dextrose, a type of sugar. Dextrose, and the dates upon which it is sprayed, require supervision for Pesach, but not for the rest of the year.

Banana chips: Banana chips are produced by deep frying slices of banana in oil. Often, companies use the same oil for meat and other products. Therefore, a reliable hechsher is always required.

Dried apples: Dried apples are also processed with antioxidants that are sprayed on the slices. Though most antioxidants used for apples are kosher, there are enough non-kosher formulas used in the industry to make it important to look for reliable supervision. Kosher anti-oxidants include: ascorbic acid, citric acid, and sodium sulfate. Non-kosher varieties include: sorbic acid and calcium stearate.

Pineapples and other tropical fruits: Pineapples are dried in a sugar solution and present no problem. Dried mangoes most likely contain added flavorings, because the taste is all in the juice, which is lost in the drying. Other tropical fruits may have similar problems. Use these with hashgachah only.

Produce from Eretz Yisroel: Nuts and fruit are increasingly imported from Eretz Yisroel. All agricultural products from Israel must have proper hashgachah to ensure that the obligatory *terumos* and *ma'asros* are taken, and that concerns of *orlah* and *shevi'is* are not present.

CANNED VEGETABLES

Kashrus organizations have recently notified the public to keep away from canned vegetables without kosher supervision. What was the cause of this change, and does this apply to all canned goods?

ANSWER

Modernization and diversification: Canning companies upgraded their equipment several years ago to increase the quality and efficiency of their production. The basic process involves placing the raw vegetables into the cans and sealing them. Then the cans, hundreds at a time, are steamed in very large pressure chambers. The combination of pressure and steam cooks the vegetables inside the cans.

It used to be that vegetable canneries would only can vegetables, and that the canning was done seasonally. In such a situation, there was little concern that anything serious could be wrong with canned vegetables.

In today's market, however, there have been some significant changes which introduced serious kashrus concerns. Firstly, the high-tech canneries are fully programmable, and can be adjusted to cook the contents of the cans for a precise amount of time. This allows for a high degree of diversification. Thus, the vegetable canning facilities no longer limit themselves to vegetables, but increasingly schedule canning runs for meat products. Many have begun producing canned bacon and pork. Furthermore, the canneries no longer need to wait for the local vegetables to ripen, but instead import every type of produce from around the globe. This has led to a situation where vegetables and meat are processed on the same equipment, one after the other.

Vegetables: Added to this, is the fact that the intense pressure of the cooking system causes some of the cans to burst. The contents of the burst cans mingle with the steam, and come into contact with all the other cans in that run and in following runs. Thus, if the cannery processes non-kosher meat, particles of the meat may come into contact with the cans of vegetables that are processed afterwards. The Shulchan Aruch[23] rules that if a drop of milk falls onto the outside of a pot of cooking meat, the milk flavor penetrates the food. The same applies to the flavor of the non-kosher meat that is mixed with the steam in the retorts. For this reason, all canned vegetables today require kashrus supervision, to ensure that the machinery is kashered before the run is made.

Beans: Canned beans, of course, have always required kosher supervision, because they are cooked before canning and can contain a number of non-kosher ingredients.

Fruit: Fruit canneries, on the other hand, have not yet diversified. They work only with fruit and, at the time of writing, this particular concern does not apply to them. Thus, most canned fruit is kosher even without supervision, though there are certain issues to be aware of.

Canned fruit labeled "unsweetened" does not need kosher supervision. If the label states "in light syrup" or "in heavy syrup," this means that the fruit is packed in syrup made of plain white sugar and water. Light syrup contains less sugar relative to its water content, and heavy syrup contains more. No kosher supervision is presently required.

If the product states that the fruit is "sweetened," then proper supervision is a must. "Sweetened" is usually a code word for white grape juice concentrate – a sweetener which is derived from grapes processed by gentiles – which is forbidden. Also, any canned fruit containing red cherries needs supervision, because the cherries are usually dyed with carmine, a non-kosher red dye. (See also p. 87.)

23. יו"ד סי' צ"ב סע' ו'

DISPOSING OF CHALLAH[24]

Is it permissible to burn the piece of dough taken for hafrashas challah in the oven, or are there other more preferable methods of disposing of the challah?

ANSWER

Burning challah in the oven: It is best not to burn the dough taken for *hafrashas challah* in the oven. As soon as the dough becomes sufficiently heated, the challah will release its forbidden flavor into the place in the oven where it was set.

Even if one was to put the challah on a piece of aluminum foil to separate it from the oven, this does not eliminate all concerns. Burning challah in the oven is a lengthy process. The dough first bakes, then gradually becomes burnt. This increases the chances of a *beliyas issur*, as the exposed challah must sit for at least an hour in the middle of the oven. During this interval, there is a risk that food or utensils inserted or removed from the oven might touch the challah and absorb its flavor. This is akin to having a piece of non-kosher meat sitting in the middle of an oven while it is being used for cooking and baking.

One way around this is to wrap the challah in foil and then place it in the oven to burn. There are no *beliyos* this way, but it is almost certain that the challah will not burn and instead remain raw under the wrapping material. Burning challah in the oven is not an advisable method.

Burning the challah on the stovetop: The ideal method is to burn the challah on the stovetop. The dough can be placed directly on the grate, with the flame on high. Within a few seconds the dough will be black and within a few minutes, it will be thoroughly burnt. It does not have to be burnt through and through since once it is charred it is not considered fit for eating (*eino ra'ui l'achilas adam*). In any case, it is better to leave it for a couple of minutes so that the insides, while

24. יו"ד סי' שכ"ב

not completely burnt, will have become hard and inedible. If it has been left for a reasonable amount of time, it is not necessary to open up the piece and check that it is thoroughly burnt through.

On the stove, there is no real concern for beliyas issur because the grate is perpetually kashered by the fire, and even in the event that the flavor of the challah did penetrate the grate, the flavor will not transfer to the pot that is placed on it. When the Rema writes, "*Chatzuvah tzarich libbun*, a grate needs to be kashered by flame," he is discussing only the extra stringent requirements for Pesach preparations, not year-round use. [25]

Burning challah on erev Pesach: Some people, who do not want to risk the problems of burning challah in the oven, yet worry about the acrid smell of burning dough on the stove top, instead save up all their challah and burn it erev Pesach. There are two problems with this. First, people tend to wrap the challah in aluminum foil, and the challah hardens over time. These two factors make the pieces of challah quite resistant to fire such that they might not actually burn. Secondly, it is never advisable to leave a forbidden thing in one's home for a long period of time. A person should always consider the possibility, even if it is remote, that someone might eat the challah before it is disposed of. Therefore, it is important to destroy it right away.

WHEY AND OTHER MILK DERIVATIVES[26]

Should one who is accustomed to consume only Chalav Yisroel dairy products avoid dairy derivatives such as whey, whey proteins, and milk sugar (lactose)?

ANSWER

Whey is called *nisyuvei dechalba* by *Chazal*. It is the whitish liquid that remains after the process of curdling milk. Curdling occurs when the

25. או"ח סי' תנ"א סע' ד' ומ"ב ס"ק ל"ד
26. יו"ד סי' קט"ו

milk solids coalesce into curds and rise to the top of the liquid whey. The Tur[27] and the Shulchan Aruch[28] both maintain that whey should be treated as full-fledged milk, and cooking it with meat is a Torah prohibition. This means that the Rabbinical restrictions of *chalav akum* also apply to whey. Barring a pressing need, a person who is careful to drink only *chalav Yisroel* should most definitely avoid whey derived from ordinary milk.

Lactose: Lactose would seem to present less of a problem, as it is not considered milk according to the Torah. Lactose is extracted from whey through either filtration or heating, and is called *mei chalav* by Chazal. Poskim refer to it as "*meimei chalav*." Mei chalav is definitely not considered milk *min haTorah*, but Chazal decreed that it should be treated as milk *miderabbanan*, with regard to the prohibition of mixing milk and meat. One could therefore argue that the restriction of chalav akum was not instituted regarding lactose. However, even according to this way of thinking, the process by which lactose is extracted leaves the flavor of both the whey and the milk solids in the lactose, and it thus remains subject to the same restrictions that apply to milk. Since practically all homeopathic pills contain lactose, they too, should be avoided by one scrupulous to consume only chalav Yisroel, unless, of course, there is proper certification.

Medicine containing whey: There are mitigating factors regarding pills and medicines containing milk sugar, or even whey, that would permit them to be used by those normally careful to avoid chalav stam, that is, milk which was produced and processed under governmental supervision, rather than under the watchful eye of Jewish kashrus supervisors (mashgichim). Pills are not considered 'edible' as they are unfit for human consumption (*nifsal me'achilas adam*). In most circumstances, they are even unfit for animal consumption (*nifsal me'achilas kelev*). Moreover, we see that people are not concerned

27. יו"ד סי' פ"ז
28. שם סע' ט'

whether the pill is palatable. Therefore, swallowing such a pill cannot be considered an act of eating (*achshavei*), as swallowing does not confer upon it the status of food. Since the restrictions of chalav akum only apply to actually eating or drinking dairy food products, they do not apply to these medications.

Vitamins containing whey: Reb Moshe Feinstein, *zt"l*, held that vitamins are possibly considered food supplements, since one swallows them in order to make up for the lack of nutrients in the food. Swallowing a vitamin should therefore be considered an act of eating food (*achshavei*), in light of the Gemara[29] which maintains that the act of swallowing is a simple form of eating: "*Bala matzah yatza*, if one swallowed matzah [on Passover night without chewing it first], he has fulfilled his obligation." Thus, swallowing a vitamin containing whey is tantamount to eating chalav akum, and should be avoided by those who refrain from chalav stam.

Caution: Milk and meat!: Generally, it is highly recommended to avoid all uncertified vitamins and other types of pills and supplements which contain milk or its derivatives, for there are cases where the milk ingredients are combined with animal derivatives such as stearates, creating a question of milk and meat (*basar b'chalav*) if they are heated together. Medicine is only considered inedible due to its bitterness (*irev bo devarim marim*), and the Chavas Da'as maintains that bitterness alone is not enough to render food halachically 'inedible' for humans (*nifsal me'achilas adam*). Bitterness only makes the act of eating 'unusual' (*shelo kedarko*). With regard to eating *basar b'chalav*, however, unusual consumption is also forbidden, and swallowing such a pill would be prohibited.

29. פסחים קטו:

COLOSTRUM

What is the halachic status of colostrum which is taken from cows either immediately before the birth of a calf or during the first few days after giving birth, and sold as a supplement for the immune system? Is it considered milk and therefore subject to the restrictions of chalav akum, or is it not milk at all, and prohibited entirely?

ANSWER

The halachic status of distilled milk plasma (*mei chalav*), the clear liquid component of whole milk, is disputed among the Rishonim. Some opinions maintain that this substance is forbidden, as it is no longer 'milk', which must be white, and is consequently considered *eiver min ha-chai*, a limb from a living animal.[30] Other opinions hold that it is permissible, for it was originally a component of milk, which is permitted by the Torah (with a *gezeiras ha-kasuv*, by Scriptural decree), and it does not lose its permissibility simply by being separated.[31] The halachah follows the lenient opinion.[32]

It would seem, therefore, that colostrum is different, and should be *assur* according to all opinions, because this clear liquid is produced before the regular flow of milk begins, and was never a component of regular white milk. This raises the possibility that animal colostrum is actually *eiver min hachai*.

However, Rashi[33] identifies a liquid which Chazal call "milk from an animal that never nursed" as being colostrum, and the Gemara says concerning this liquid, that it can be seen in two different ways. It may either be considered similar to *chalav zachar*, a milk-like liquid that is sometimes produced by a male animal's mammary glands, which

30. יראים השלם סי' ש"ג וסי' שי"ב, רא"ש חולין פ"ח סי' נ"א, שו"ע יו"ד סי' פ"ז סל"ח בשם יש מי שאומר.
31. רא"ש שם בשם רבינו שמחה, וכן סתם המחבר שם
32. רמ"א שם
33. חולין קג: ד"ה שלא הניקה

is permitted without restriction, or it may be considered as ordinary milk. The Gemara leaves the question undecided.

According to either side of the Gemara's unresolved question, colostrum does not have the status of *eiver min hachai*, for the only question is whether this liquid is parve or dairy. If it is parve, the halachah of *chalav stam* certainly would not apply. Since the Gemara did not conclude what colostrum is, it remains a *safek*, and the overriding principle here is "*safek derabbanan lekula*," a doubt regarding a Rabbinical prohibition is treated leniently. Thus, even the restrictions of chalav akum would not apply to colostrum.

POTATOES AND BISHUL AKUM[34]

Do potatoes hold the status of *oleh al shulchan melachim*, an item that is served at formal dinners? If so, how do we account for the kosher certification given to potato chips without requiring *bishul Yisroel*?

ANSWER

Nowadays, potatoes are definitely *oleh al shulchan melachim*.

Up until the late nineteenth century, the 'humble potato' was almost exclusively eaten by the peasantry as part of a meager subsistence diet. No self-respecting gourmand would have had such a vegetable served at his table. On this basis, some Poskim at that time determined that potatoes were not *oleh al shulchan melachim*.[35] Other Poskim even suggested that potatoes were not considered a normal food, and that the brachah should be '*shehakol*.'

Today, potatoes are a very common and almost universally popular part of our diet, and are commonly served at weddings and state dinners. They are unequivocally *oleh al shulchan melachim* and the correct blessing is clearly '*borei p'ri ha'adamah*.' Though there are halachos that

34. יו"ד סי' קי"ג

35. עי' ערוך השולחן יו"ד סי' קי"ג סי"ח

remain unchanged despite changing historical circumstances, and for which we have a mesorah, this is not one of them, since the principle is specifically based on contemporary conditions.

The manner of serving is the determining factor: It is assumed by some, that the status of *oleh al shulchan melachim* should apply to an entire class of food (בתר המין) if one of its variations can be served at a formal affair. In our case, this would mean that all potato dishes, however they may be prepared (boiled, baked, or fried), would be subject to the rules of bishul akum. Even potato dishes that would never be served at a formal affair, such as French fries, would be subject to the restrictions of bishul akum.

The assumption that bishul akum applies to whole classes of foods is based on a reading of the language of the Shach,[36] who quotes the sefer, *Issur V'heter*: "Entrails and gizzards (*kishka* skin and *pipiks*), truffles, and mushrooms, are *oleh al shulchan melachim* as hors d'oeuvres and are thus subject to the rules of bishul akum." These words may be misinterpreted to suggest that *all* mushrooms are *oleh al shulchan melachim*, whether or not they are prepared as hors d'oeuvres.

However, the Shulchan Aruch, in the previous siman on *hilchos pas akum*,[37] states explicitly that bishul akum applies only to those dishes that are actually served at formal affairs. The Shulchan Aruch writes, "Bread made from legumes, rice, or *dochan*, is not included with regular bread that they [the Sages] forbade [due to pas akum]." The Rema, in his glosses, adds the following important halachah: "Neither are they forbidden because of bishul akum, if they are not served at a king's table." Clearly, rice bread may or may not be subject to the laws of bishul akum, depending on whether this particular type is suitable for a formal dinner.

Similarly, we determine the status of all foods based on the way they are prepared, so that some rice dishes and some potato dishes are *oleh al shulchan melachim*, while others are not. You will not find

36. יו"ד סי' קי"ג סק"ב
37. סי' קי"ב סע' א'

a single source amongst the *Acharonim* and Poskim that states otherwise. As for the previously mentioned Shach, one need only look into the sefer *Issur V'heter* to see that the discussion there is whether hors d'oeuvres (*parparos*) are considered *oleh al shulchan melachim*, and has nothing to do with the issue of whether or not an entire category of food is subject to the restrictions of *bishul akum*.

Different potato dishes: The author has consulted with caterers, Jewish and gentile alike, and they all concur that fries and potato chips are never served at banquets and other formal dinners, except perhaps at the children's table. There are occasionally potato dishes which seem as if they might have been fried because of a little oil found in them, but in every case the caterers have revealed that these dishes have been either baked or cooked. The soft, even texture of the dishes would never result from frying. After its preparation, a small amount of oil is applied to the potatoes as an external seasoning.

Additionally, if one carefully examines the opinions of the *Gedolei Yisroel* over the past forty to fifty years, there is no reliable responsum where the question is presented in detail, and a clear psak given indicating that fried potatoes require bishul Yisroel. Consequently, bishul akum does not apply to fried potatoes, including potato chips, French fries, or any variation thereof. One who thinks that it would be a nice idea to be stringent (*machmir*) and start requiring bishul Yisroel on items which really do not require it, should consider the following:

Creating 'bishul Yisroel': Bishul Yisroel has proven to be one of the more difficult halachic requirements to properly apply with the advent of commercial food production. Bishul Yisroel requires a Jew to participate in a significant way in the cooking process. For Ashkenazim, it is sufficient for the Jew to ignite the flame.[38] Sefardim require more extensive involvement, such as stirring the food while it is on the flame.[39] Practically speaking, the normally acceptable

38. רמ"א יו"ד סי' קי"ג סע' ז'

39. מחבר שם

methods of creating bishul Yisroel frequently require the mashgiach to be present much of the day.

To eliminate this difficulty, some kashrus agencies have 'invented' new, low-cost ways of creating bishul Yisroel. Some use glow-bulbs, and others use timers. There is one case where the Jew turns on the electricity to the entire building. Another Rabbi had a Jewish plumber install the gas piping to the cooking equipment. All of these techniques are entirely unacceptable. There are others that are questionable at best. Given the difficulties, it is far preferable to forego the semblance of bishul Yisroel on products that do not require it, than to resort to halachic innovations that might further entrench these questionable practices in kashrus supervision.

SERVING KOSHER WINE[40]

Is there a risk that wine might be rendered forbidden if it is served by non-Jewish waiters?

ANSWER

The presence of gentiles and non-observant Jews around kosher, uncooked wine is a situation that can easily result in the wine becoming prohibited to drink. Nevertheless, the Sages did not forbid the wine in every situation. If a gentile simply touched the bottle, or even moved it, the wine is still permissible. Only if the non-Jew either, a) touches the wine directly, or even indirectly in certain instances (*negi'ah al yedei davar acher*); b) shakes an opened bottle of wine;[41] or c) pours the wine, does the wine become *assur*. Non-frum Jews should never be allowed to pour non-mevushal wine.

Practically speaking, one should never have non-mevushal wine

40. יו״ד סי׳ קכ״ג–קכ״ד

41. עי׳ שו״ע יו״ד סי׳ קכ״ד סע׳ י״ז, ז״ל המחבר שם: יש מי שאומר שאם אחז עובד כוכבים בכלי פתוח של יין ושכשכו אע״פ שלא הגביה ולא נגע ביין נאסר. אולם כתב הרמ״א: ורבים חולקים לומר דאם שכשך בגופו של הכלי בלא הגבהה לא מקרי שכשוך. ומסיים הרמ״א ולכן אין להחמיר במקום פסידא.

where gentiles are present, as it is nearly impossible to supervise the wine vigilantly at all times. Where there is a necessity to serve wine in the presence of non-Jews, only mevushal wine should be used.

COOKED WINE

Are the wines labeled '*mevushal*,' sufficiently cooked to avoid the problem of *yayin nesech*?

ANSWER

The Shulchan Aruch[42] states that wine is considered '*mevushal*,' or cooked, "once it has boiled while on the fire." The Shach[43] clarifies, in the name of the Rashba, "that its volume must be reduced by being boiled." Reb Moshe Feinstein, *zt"l*, and the Tzelemer Rav, *zt"l*, disagreed regarding the point in the cooking process to which the Rashba referred. Reb Moshe understood that the Rashba defined 'boiling,' as the point where the wine begins to diminish and release steam, which is around 170–180 degrees Fahrenheit (77–82 degrees Celsius).[44] The Tzelemer Rav maintained that the wine must be brought to a full boil. The accepted ruling by practically all Rabbanim follows the lenient opinion, and the great majority of mevushal wine is cooked below the boiling point.

Recently, Rabbanim in Eretz Yisroel raised objections to the accepted practice in America to label wine pasteurized at the above temperatures as '*mevushal*.' Pasteurization involves using a heat exchanger, a closed system wherein the wine enters a network of narrow tubes that pass through boiling hot water in order to rapidly heat the wine and kill any bacteria. Immediately thereafter, the wine in the tubes passes through cold water, instantly cooling it. HaRav

42. יו"ד סי' קכ"ג סע' ג'
43. סק"ז
44. אגרות משה, יו"ד, ח"ב סי' נ"ב

Shlomo Zalman Auerbach, *zt"l*,[45] among others, maintained that such a system maintains the integrity of the wine, as nothing is released. Consequently, the wine is still fit for libations on the Altar in the Beis HaMikdash (*ra'ui lenisuch al hamizbe'ach*). Therefore, it cannot be considered mevushal.

The American Rabbanim, however, led by Reb Moshe and the Tzelemer Rav, examined the pasteurization process, and felt that it satisfied the halachic requirements when brought to the proper temperature. Additionally, the assumption that the wine is unaffected by the heating process is not entirely accurate. High quality wines are never heated, even in a closed system, because such treatment is considered to affect the taste and quality of the wine. In the United States, as well as in many other countries, Rabbanim continue to rely on their opinion.

LIQUOR[46]

Which non-supervised liquors can be used without the concern that either non-kosher ingredients were added, or that they were aged in barrels used for non-kosher wines?

ANSWER

One of the most porous areas of Kashrus is in the hard liquor industry. It was assumed many years ago, that straight (that is, un-blended) whiskies were made in a very standard way, and contained nothing but fermented wheat grain or rye, and the other traditional ingredients.

Sherry casks: It has been known for some years now that many high-quality whiskies are aged in oak casks which were previously used for sherry wine. This is said to improve the flavor of the whiskey.

There are various halachic opinions as to whether or not the tell-

45. שו"ת מנחת שלמה ח"א סי' כ"ה
46. יו"ד סי' קל"ד

tale flavor of the sherry picked up from the casks becomes *batul* to the whiskey itself. According to the Taz,[47] wine is batul at a ratio of one in six, allowing for greater leniency. The Shach[48] holds that only wine in water is batul at a 1:6 ratio, but wine in other food or liquids is not. The Rashba holds that any quantity of wine, if added deliberately, can never become batul. Finally, Reb Moshe Feinstein, *zt"l*,[49] maintained that the *minhag* (and most Poskim agree) is to rely on the Taz, and use a 1:6 ratio for wine in all liquids, whether or not it was added intentionally, but that a *ba'al nefesh*, a scrupulous person, should be *machmir* (stringent).

Blenders: The most recent kashrus problem to surface in the liquor industry is the use of 'blenders.' The traditional method of making and imparting flavor to whiskey is a process that sometimes takes years. Companies looking to save time and money have begun developing specially flavored formulas that are blended into the whiskey. This ensures flavor and quality control, and serves other purposes that are important to the producer. These 'blenders' can contain any number of non-kosher ingredients. In most cases, the quantities of the questionable ingredients are batul, but the time has definitely come to subject the liquor industry to the same rigorous supervision that is applied to all other food and beverage industries. At this point, it is certainly recommended that one look for kosher certification on all hard liquor.

PEYOS HA'ROSH[50]

What are the exact locations of the peyos harosh, the areas on the head which a person is forbidden to shave? How short

47. יו"ד סי' קל"ד סק"ז
48. שם ס"ק כ"א
49. אגרות משה, יו"ד, ח"א סי' ס"ב
50. יו"ד סי' קפ"א

may the hair be cut in those places without transgressing the prohibition?

ANSWER

The Shulchan Aruch[51] states: "The area of the *pe'ah* is across from the hair of the forehead, until below the ear, the place where the lower jaw extends and juts out. One should not touch the entire width of that area."

Upper limit: The author heard directly from HaRav Yaakov Kamenetzky, *zt"l*, that the upper limit of the peyos ha'rosh begins at the highest point of the hairline as it arches over the ear, and extends in a slightly curved line, across to where the hairline of the forehead turns sharply downward towards the sideburns. All the hair from the imaginary line that connects these two points and below, comprises the peyos ha'rosh. (See diagram A.)

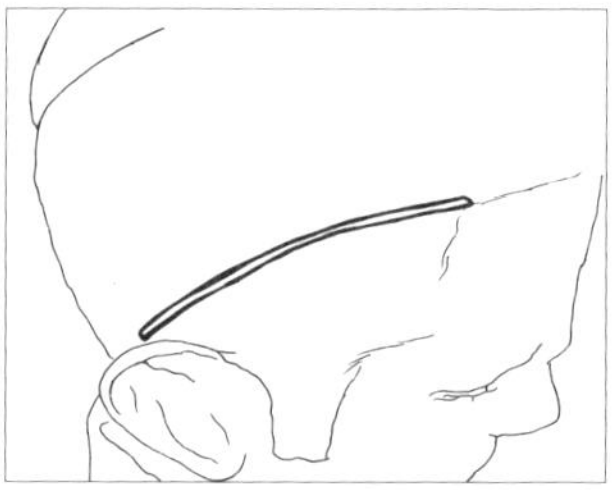

Diagram A

Some Rabbanim have a *mesorah*, a tradition from their Rabbis, that the peyos do not extend above the upper cartilage of the ear (*tenuch ha'ozen*) at all. According to their mesorah, the imaginary line extends horizontally from the point in the hairline above the foremost part of ear, almost until where the downward slope of the frontal hairline angles back towards the ear. (See diagram B.) To compare the two opinions, see diagram C.

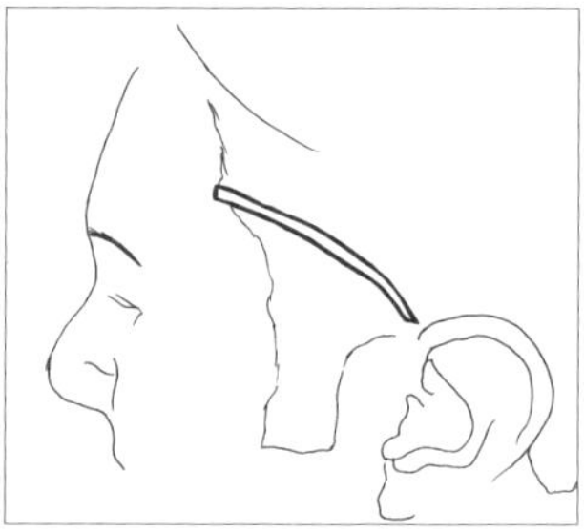

Diagram B

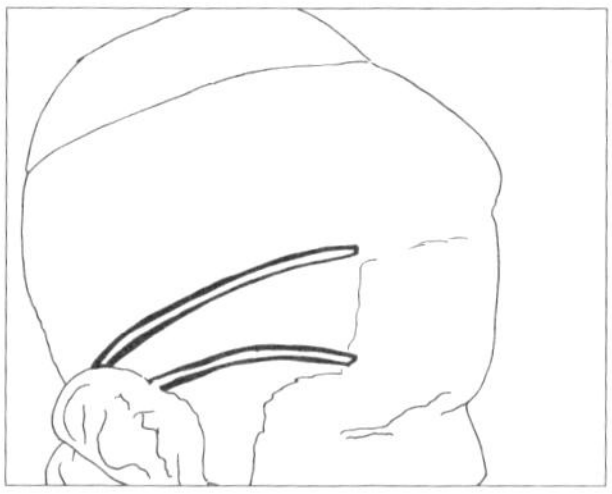

Diagram C

51. יו"ד סי' קפ"א סע' ט'

Lower limit: The bottom end of the peyos is also disputed. The Shulchan Aruch states, "*Lemattah min ha'ozen lo yiga bah* – Until below the ear…one should not touch." Exactly what the Shulchan Aruch means by 'below the ear,' is the subject of much debate.

The hair that grows beside the ear abruptly changes from scalp-type hair to facial-type hair long before it reaches the bottom of the earlobe (*basar ha'ozen*), so it is very likely that the Shulchan Aruch did not literally mean "to the bottom of the lobe of the ear" as we would normally understand it. Furthermore, the Shulchan Aruch identifies the end of the peyos as the "*makom shehalechi hatachton yotzei umispareid* – the point where the lower jawbone extends and juts out." If a person opens his mouth very wide, he will feel the lower jawbone abruptly jut out alongside the ear. This point is higher than the earlobe, opposite the ear canal. It is therefore reasonable to assume that when the Shulchan Aruch states that the peyos should not be touched until below the ear, he means the ear canal. Thus, all the hair down to the bottom of the ear canal, about two-thirds the way down the ear, is to be considered part of the peyos ha'rosh.

Some people's beards are noticeably different in color or texture from their scalp hair (e.g. the hair goes from straight to curly, or from brown to red). In such cases, the point along the sideburn at which the hair changes characteristics is the end of the peyos ha'rosh. Incidentally, this point is almost always opposite the ear canal, which supports the previous opinion.

Those who wish to leave their sideburns until the bottom of the earlobe are not being unnecessarily meticulous, however. The literal understanding of the Shulchan Aruch's words supports this stringency, and this would be considered a *hiddur mitzvah* according to all opinions.

Length of peyos: With regards to the length of the peyos, the *halachah pesukah*[52] is that the hairs must be long enough to take hold of with one's fingers (*kedei achizah*). How long is kedei achizah? Practically

52. עי' נדה נב.

speaking, if a person uses hair clippers with a number two attachment, the hair is probably long enough to grasp. To be on the safe side, it is best to use no less than a number three attachment, which certainly leaves the hair long enough to grasp.

It has been a recognized and widely practiced hiddur throughout the generations to allow the peyos to grow much longer than the minimum requirements discussed above. Yemenite Jews call the peyos, "*simanim*" because they serve as an outward sign that one is a Jew.

Leniencies and hiddurim: There are several leniencies brought in the Rishonim regarding peyos ha'rosh. The Rambam[53] requires that only forty hairs in the entire area be left long enough to grasp; the others can be shaved off. He also maintains that only removing the hairs with a razor (*ta'ar*) is prohibited. It would be allowed to completely remove the peyos with scissors, even if the blade close to the scalp is as sharp as a razor and produces a razor-like shave (*misparayim k'ein ta'ar*).

Klal Yisroel has chosen to fulfill this mitzvah to its fullest extent, and adheres to the more stringent views of the other Rishonim. Thus, the custom today is to leave all the hair in the region of the peyos long enough to grasp, and not to remove them completely, even with scissors. Jews from all backgrounds, communities, and cultures have always shown special devotion to this mitzvah by having longer peyos than that which the halachah strictly requires.

PEYOS HA'ZAKAN

Is there any halachic reason to refrain from shaving the neck or cheeks?

ANSWER

The location of the *peyos ha'zakan*, the corners of the beard, is a matter of dispute. One of these points, the tip of the chin, is easily located.

53. הל' עבודת כוכבים פי"ב ה"ו

Two more, at the tip of the sideburns where they touch the bottom of the peyos ha'rosh (See diagrams on p. 122), are also fairly recognizable. But there are two more, and their location is disputed amongst the Rishonim. Some Rishonim maintain they are below the jawbone, but others hold that they are on the cheeks. Thus, most of the beard is subject to a *safek d'Oraisa*. There are even opinions that hold the peyos to be at the edges of the beard where it reaches down along the neck. But the vast majority of the Rishonim and Poskim hold that the peyos cannot be located further down the neck than the Adam's apple. Therefore it would be considered a very great *chumrah* to forbid using shavers on the area of the neck from the Adam's apple towards the collarbone, unless a shaver is considered to be the exact equivalent of a razor blade. For a discussion of shavers, see the following question.

The greatest concern is where the beard grows on the cheeks. The cheeks protrude slightly in the center, and many Rishonim consider these to be the 'corners' or peyos of the beard. If a person is inclined not to use a shaver out of concern for cutting the peyos too close, in deference to the Poskim that prohibit all shavers, he should be especially careful with regard to the hair on the cheeks.

ELECTRIC SHAVERS

Many observant Jews have ceased shaving their beards with electric shavers, and use trimmers instead. What is the basis for this change? If one plans on using a shaver in any case, which types of electric shaver are permitted?

ANSWER

Two viewpoints: The use of electric shavers has been a subject of much debate amongst the Poskim. There are many Gedolei HaPoskim, past and present, who have declared that shavers are prohibited in the same manner as razors.

The reason for this view is that the Torah does not prohibit a particular shaving device, but rather prohibits the act of shaving and destroying the hair (*gilu'ach* and *hashchasah*). Chazal determined that a razor accomplishes both *gilu'ach* and *hashchasah*, and therefore cannot be used. The shaving machine used nowadays accomplishes both gilu'ach and hashchasah and should be *ossur min haTorah* in the same manner that a razor is ossur.

Secondly, it follows that any device that completely removes the hair and has the exact same effect as a razor, should be considered no different from a razor, regardless of how it functions. Chazal discuss a leniency regarding scissors: *misparayim k'ein ta'ar.* This view maintains that Chazal only permitted the use of scissors that left a visible remainder of hair on the face. Such scissors produced a trim that was *k'ein ta'ar*, similar to, but not exactly the same as that produced by a true razor. Completely removing the hair with any device is never permissible. According to these Poskim, nearly all of today's electric or mechanical shavers are equally forbidden, as they also accomplish *gilu'ach* and *hashchasah.*

The other view amongst the Poskim maintains that only the *gilu'ach* and *hashchasah* of a razor is prohibited by the Torah. They understand that Chazal identified the razor as the only tool to which the prohibition applies. According to this view, there is a fundamental difference between a razor and scissors in the way the hair is cut. A razor cuts the hair directly, due to the sharpness of the blade. Scissors operate in an entirely different manner, squeezing the hair between two opposing blades. The hair is cut by virtue of the pressure applied to it, and not due to the sharpness of the blade.

Consequently, the Poskim who allow the use of shavers maintain that scissors may be used, even if the resulting trim is as exactly the same as that of a razor (*misparayim k'ein ta'ar*). Most mechanical shavers consist of a set of tiny opposing blades or surfaces that cut the hairs in the manner of scissors. According to this second viewpoint, nearly all shavers are permissible under the rule of *misparayim k'ein ta'ar.* Statements can be found in Chazal and Rishonim in support of both views.

In the time of the Chafetz Chaim, mechanical barber clippers were developed. They worked on a scissor principle, yet possessed blades sharp enough to produce a close trim. The Chafetz Chaim agreed with the stringent opinion, and therefore wrote in *Likkutei Halachos*[54] that certain blade numbers should not be used, due to the close shave that they produce. If the device leaves some stubble behind, this indicates that the shave was not 'razor-like', and would be permitted even according to this view. Thus, many b'nei Torah choose instead to use trimmers, which do not cut nearly as close as regular shavers, in order to satisfy the requirements of this halachic viewpoint.

The Shulchan Aruch[55] adheres to the second view, and permits shaving with any scissor-like device, even if it results in a shave which is similar to that of a razor. In the United States, as well as many other places, the view that prevailed was that of Reb Moshe Feinstein, *zt"l*, who also differentiated between the cutting action of scissors and that of a razor, thus permitting the use of most electric shavers.

Recently, a model of a mechanical shaver from the Chofetz Chaim's time was discovered, and it appears that the device in question cut the hair in a manner similar to that of a razor rather than in the manner of scissors. This was attested to by an expert in the field, who examined the machine carefully. It is thus quite likely that the Chofetz Chaim's opinion concurred with that of Reb Moshe and not with the first opinion as was previously assumed.

Very sharp scissors: The Rema[56] quotes the Terumas HaDeshen,[57] who states that it is forbidden to use a pair of scissors if the lower blade (the one close to the skin) is sharp enough to cut the hair by itself were it to be used as a razor.

Thus, if we were to find a shaver where the surface that touches the skin is so sharp that it is capable of cutting the hairs in the manner of a razor, it would be *assur* to use this shaver according to the Terumas HaDeshen. This would be true even if the actual cutting is

54. פ"ג דמכות בעין משפט אות ז'
55. יו"ד סי' קפ"א סע' י'
56. שם
57. סי' רצ"ה

accomplished by the movement of the blades along the inside of that surface in the manner of scissors.

Problematic shavers: There is a design of shaver known as 'microscreen,' which is generally manufactured with one to three thin convex foils, under which is an array of semi-circular blades that slide back and forth against the inside surface of the screen. The hairs enter through the matrix of tiny precision-made holes in the screen, and are then cut with a scissor-like pinch by the blades within. Some wish to suggest that the screen itself is razor-sharp and actually cuts the hairs, with the internal blades merely pressing the hairs against the sharp edges of the screen's perforations. Some companies have actually put this claim into writing and made it available to all inquirers.

If this claim is true, this presents a formidable problem according to the Terumas HaDeshen. Even according to those who argue with this stringency, if the microscreen is sharp enough that hairs would be cut by simply sliding it along the skin, it might be classified as a full-fledged razor.

Upon careful scrutiny, however, it may be observed that the edges of the microscreen perforations are not razor-sharp, leaving the companies' claims unsubstantiated. Nevertheless, one who is reasonably cautious might still want to refrain from using 'microscreen' shavers because of the companies' claims.

The 'lift and cut' shaver presents more of a problem. Based on the company's description, these shavers possess an internal double-blade, the first of which catches the hair and then pulls it beyond the screen and into the shaver. The second blade is then able to cut the hair at a lower point than standard razors, leaving the hair below the surface of the skin once it springs back into place. The manufacturers claim that this results in an exceptionally smooth shave. Accordingly, it might make be forbidden to shave with such devices, even according to the Shulchan Aruch, and certainly according to the Terumas HaDeshen. Removing the hair-catching spring blade would eliminate the concerns of both the Shulchan Aruch and the Terumas HaDeshen.

It must be taken into consideration, however, that the claims of these companies are often exaggerated. They display the unique operation in detail over much of the packaging, in order to bring the potential buyer to anticipate the close shave he will get if he uses this product. The speed at which the blades move would suggest that the sequence of events described above takes place within the tiniest fraction of a second; a possibility that challenges even the most imaginative mind. Nevertheless, it is preferable to remove the spring blade as mentioned above to avoid any doubts.

Most other shavers today satisfy the requirements of the Terumas HaDeshen. Rotary blades and straight vibrating blades do not contain any razor-sharp pieces and operate strictly on a scissor principle.

A razor-like shave: It is important for those who shave to consider that very little is gained by the extra smoothness of the best shavers, which lasts perhaps an hour or two. The hair continues to grow after the shave, and within a short period of time stubble begins to protrude in any case. A person should never risk violating a Torah prohibition, especially when the benefit is so fleeting.

Regarding permission to use shavers, it is worthwhile also to take note of the following: The Gemara (*Yevamos* 5a) seeks a source for the rule that a positive commandment overrides a negative commandment, when the two conflict and one must be observed at the expense of the other (*asseh dachi lo saaseh*). The Gemara proposes that the source could be the commandment of, "וגלח את כל שערו – *He shall shave all his hair*," which requires a *metzorah* whose *tzara'as* has healed, to shave off all the hair on his body, as well as the hair on his head and his beard. The Gemara then says that the extra words, "את ראשו ואת זקנו – *His head and his beard*," come to include the case when the metzorah is also a *nazir*, and is prohibited to shave off the hair on his head; and also the case of a Kohen, who has a special prohibition against shaving off his beard. In each case, we see that the positive commandment of shaving the hair of the metzorah overrides a prohibition: one in the case of a nazir, and the other in the case of a Kohen.

The Gemara concludes that we cannot postulate the rule of *asseh dachi lo saaseh* from either illustration. In the case of a *nazir metzorah*, the prohibition of shaving his hair is *yeshna b'sheilah*. It can be removed by undoing the vow (*hataras nedarim*), and thus eliminating the status of *nazirus*. This shows that the prohibition against the *nazir* cutting his hair is of a more lenient nature (*issur kal*), and the fact that a positive commandment overrides it cannot be used as the source for the rule of *asseh dachi lo saaseh* regarding other Torah proscriptions.

The Gemara also says that the case of a Kohen *metzorah* cannot be the source of the rule regarding any other Torah prohibition. The *issurim* incumbent upon Kohanim are considered to be weaker than other issurim in the Torah, because they apply only to a specific segment of the Jewish nation.

Tosafos poses a serious difficulty with the Gemara's conclusion. As a rule, when two sources are proposed for a certain derivation and each is disqualified on account of a detail that is unique to that case, we can then combine the two and create a new derivation known as a "*tzad hashaveh*," or "common denominator." (The logic of *tzad hashaveh*, is that by combining the cases, the stringencies or leniencies of each case are cancelled out, and the composite case is considered a single one. The composite case thus becomes a legitimate source to extend the shared ruling to other cases in the Torah. It can only be disqualified if an objection common to both is found.)

Tosafos then asks, why should we not be able to combine the two cases (Kohen and *nazir metzorah*), and let them serve together as a *tzad hashaveh*? Together, they would become immune to either of the two disqualifications mentioned above, which are not common to both.

In one answer, Tosafos cites the Gemara in *Maseches Nazir* which contains a reading intimating that the prohibition against shaving with a razor in any case is considered a lenient prohibition (*issur kal*), because it could be avoided by resorting to a scissor shave (*misparayim k'ein ta'ar*), which can produce the exact same result as a razor shave.

It follows then, that since shaving is an *issur kal*, it cannot serve as the source for the rule of *asseh dachi lo saaseh* regarding other mitzvos in the Torah, where the prohibited results cannot be accomplished in a permissible way.

We see clearly from Tosafos, that it is possible to produce a razor-sharp shave without using a razor, but by instead making use of *misparayim k'ein ta'ar*, a scissors shave, without violating the prohibition. Were this not true, and a scissors shave could never produce the exact result accomplished with a true razor shave, the reasoning of Tosafos would be fallacious, for there would be no way of demonstrating the weakness in the prohibition of a razor shave, in order to consider it an *issur kal*.

Although many other answers have been proposed to Tosafos' question, no Rishon, Acharon, nor any other sefer, has ever taken issue with the facts of Tosafos argument. This clearly demonstrates that all major authorities are in consensus, that *misparayim k'ein ta'ar* produces exactly the same result as a razor shave, and that it is not prohibited by the laws that prohibit a razor.

The claim that *misparayim k'ein ta'ar* is only allowed if it produces a different result than that of a razor (that is, some amount of stubble must remain), is thus in error. Since this is the only viable basis for discrediting the use of a shaver, it becomes apparent that there really is no validity to the position of prohibiting shaving machines at all.

Nonetheless, it is preferable for every Jew to wear a beard, just as the Chafetz Chaim proclaimed in his sefer, *Tiferes Adam*.

ALERTING OTHERS REGARDING SHAVERS; SELLING SHAVERS

Should a person go out of his way to warn fellow Jews about the prohibition against using problematic shavers? May a Jewish salesman sell these shavers to other Jews?

ANSWER

While it is certainly no simple matter to use some types of shaver, there are reliable Rabbanim who permit almost every model. There are also Poskim who permit the 'lift and cut' variety mentioned above. This being the case, there is no obligation to attempt to stop Jewish people from buying and using them. The most a person should do is to make sure his own family refrains from using the questionable shavers, and perhaps to inform other receptive individuals about the issues involved.

As for a Jewish store-owner, perhaps those who sell shavers should isolate the halachically problematic models so that they would be accessible to non-Jews only. A vendor who is particularly meticulous in his observance of all mitzvos should avoid carrying these shavers entirely.

COMPLIMENTING & GIFT-GIVING TO GENTILES[58]

Concerning the prohibition of *lo sechaneim*, not to praise or give gifts to non-Jews, are we permitted to praise or give a gift to a gentile employee or service-provider?

ANSWER

In each of the above-mentioned cases, it is perfectly acceptable to give gifts. This applies also to neighbors. Such gifts are given for a specific purpose, namely to promote an atmosphere of goodwill and cooperation or to ensure good service, and there is no prohibition.

It is unusual to find a case where a person gives a gift to people outside his circle of close family and friends with no expectations in return. Thus, this detail of *lo sechaneim* is rarely applicable.

There is another violation of *lo sechaneim* which is far more common in our circles. One is not allowed to admire gentiles or praise them. Admiring and idolizing non-Jewish personalities such as athletes, actors, musicians, and other public figures, is anathema to Yiddishkeit. It is a serious transgression of *lo sechaneim*, when people

58. יו"ד סי' קנ"א

display words or images on their clothing that attest to their great admiration for gentile sports figures, musicians, or other popular heroes. Instead of praising them as individuals, it would be permitted to praise what they do, such as saying, "Her playing is superb; His work is professional, etc."

Baseball cards may also involve the prohibition of *lo sechaneim*. While it may be that some people trade them only for financial gain, the reason for collecting the cards is more likely because of an appreciation and admiration for the personalities depicted on them. This is forbidden.

Of course, as long as some benefit may accrue to Jews individually or collectively, or if praising gentiles personally is necessary as a means of passing on useful information about them, it would be permitted, assuming this could not be accomplished by limiting the praise to their actions and not to them personally, as explained above.

ATTENDING A NON-JEWISH PARTY[59]

May a Jew accept an invitation to attend a non-Jewish party, and may he eat if he is provided kosher food?

ANSWER

The halachah states,[60] "All alcoholic beverages produced by gentiles... are forbidden due to [the possibility of] intermarriage (*meshum chasanus*), but they are only forbidden in the place they are sold...as the decree primarily intended to prevent [the Jew] from joining the gentile in his home (*shema yis'od etzlo*) and becoming high-spirited and overly-friendly with him. [The Sages] only forbade this if he sits down [in a somewhat prolonged and relaxed drinking session] in the presence of the gentile (*k'shekoveah atzmo*)." It should be noted that the leniencies mentioned here hold true for all alcohol, with the

59. יו"ד סי' קי"ד, קמ"ח, קנ"ב
60. יו"ד סי' קי"ד סע' א'

exception of gentile wine, which is categorically forbidden in any place.

Thus, a Jew is not supposed to drink beer, liquor, or any intoxicating drink together with gentiles in their homes, their bars, or any place where they gather to drink alcohol. This is generally the case with 'New Year' parties. An office party may or may not be held for the purpose of drinking; it depends on the character of the party and where it is held. The Rema brings opinions that this entire *issur* only applies to beer made from dates (*shechar*), and on that basis, it became customary to drink alcohol with gentiles despite the fact that most Rishonim forbade every kind of alcohol. As it is, even if there were no halachah to forbid it, it is very sound advice not to let one's guard down in the company of intoxicated gentiles.

A gentile wedding is not a gathering for the purpose of getting drunk, nonetheless it is categorically forbidden for a Jew to attend a gentile wedding.[61]

Suspicion: Another potential pitfall to attending gentile parties, is the possibility of *chashad*, doing something that causes other Jews to suspect that an *aveirah* is being committed. People who see a Jew walk into a non-kosher establishment might suspect him of buying and eating treif food. For this reason, a person should not enter non-kosher restaurants or fast-food establishments. On the other hand, when a person is traveling, he is allowed to stop at the non-kosher store on the highway or at the rest-stop. Here, there is no suspicion that the Jew is about to purchase anything treif, since there is no other place nearby at which he can use the facilities or buy packaged foods with kosher supervision. Thus, if a gentile invites the Jew to a banquet in a treif restaurant, even if the host arranges for a kosher meal it would be forbidden to attend. But if the affair is held in a hall, or any other place that is not designated for non-kosher food, there is no issue of chashad.

61. יו"ד סי' קנ"ב ס"א ובט"ז סק"א

Immodest conduct: It should go without saying that when the behavior at any party or function degenerates and crosses over the boundary of halachic decency, a Jew must leave. If the group begins to sing or dance, then a Jew is obligated to walk out. This applies equally to Jewish and non-Jewish functions.

Holiday parties: There are circumstances under which it is permissible to attend a gentile party, even if it is held in celebration of a religious holiday. The Rema[62] writes: "If we avoid the gentiles on their holidays, there is a concern it might cause enmity, and we live amongst them and need to do business with them the entire year. Therefore, if a person enters the city and finds the gentiles celebrating on the day of their festival, he may celebrate with them, lest they come to hate him, and it is considered only as though he has flattered them. Nevertheless, a sensitive person should refrain from celebrating with them if he can, as long as it will not cause enmity."

If a person cannot avoid going to a party with a religious character, he should go and pay his respects, make sure everyone sees him, and then leave as quickly as possible.

ATTENDING PARTIES ON LEGAL HOLIDAYS[63]

Is it wrong to attend or even make parties on legal holidays such as Thanksgiving and January 1st?

ANSWER

As quoted above, the Shulchan Aruch[64] states that a Jew is allowed to attend such parties *mipnei eivah*, because of the hatred it might engender if he does not participate. Thus, if attending a party is beneficial

62. יו"ד סי' קמ"ח סי"ב
63. יו"ד סי' קמ"ח, קנ"ב
64. יו"ד סי' קמ"ח סי"ב ברמ"א

to one's job or position in the community, or if he might lose his job were he not to show up, he is allowed to make an appearance.

Parties on January 1st are generally quite base. It is inappropriate for a religious Jew to attend these parties.

Regarding a Jew hosting such a party, a little historical perspective is in order. Many years ago, Americans used to be very patriotic, and parades were held regularly commemorating such events as Independence Day, the birthdays of Washington and Lincoln, and other significant national events. Practically everyone displayed a flag in his window. The Jews in America at that time also displayed flags. One who did not would have been suspected of being ungrateful to the United States for its welcoming acceptance of the Jews. The Jewish people have lived in many countries, and America has been by far the kindest, most accepting of them all. This, incidentally, is the proper attitude towards America. The United States should be seen as a benevolent host to the Jewish people in their wanderings.

Nowadays, however, national pride and patriotism are on the wane. The vast majority of Americans do not display flags, even on national holidays. As such, there is no need for a Jew to go out of his way to demonstrate his patriotism. Furthermore, once it is unnecessary, it is also unjustified. The Gemara derives from the possuk, "אל תשמח ישראל אל גיל כעמים – *Rejoice not, O Yisroel, for joy, as the other nations*" (Hoshea 9:1), that a Jew is not to celebrate in the manner of other peoples, and certainly not over the holidays of other nations. Today, it is possible to be grateful, even loyal to the United States, without displaying strong patriotism.

THANKSGIVING

Does this include hosting a private Thanksgiving feast?

ANSWER

Yes. Religious Jews do not generally celebrate Thanksgiving. Those that do are likely continuing the practice of previous times, as we discussed above. The fact that Americans set aside a day to show thanks is quite respectable. Furthermore, Thanksgiving demonstrates religious feeling without any specific sectarian overtones. Nevertheless, even if a Jew should have a reason to make a thanksgiving meal (*seudas hoda'ah*), the *Gedolei Yisroel* frowned upon doing it on the day of Thanksgiving itself. Rather, he should choose a day other than Thanksgiving.

EATING WITH A GENTILE

May a Jew invite a gentile neighbor, business associate, or government official to a *seudas mitzvah* or other simchah, such as a bris or bar-mitzvah?

ANSWER

Many people nowadays are accustomed to inviting gentiles to family celebrations such as bar-mitzvahs and weddings. Technically, it would seem less problematic to invite a gentile than to invite a non-religious Jew. Since an unobservant Jew may be unaware of the obligation to recite blessings on food, or be unwilling to do so, there is an issue of *lifnei iver*, placing a stumbling block before the blind. (See p. 163, for a tactful way to resolve this difficulty.) Such a complication does not exist with gentiles, who are not obligated in these mitzvos.

There is one case where the presence of a gentile creates a potential halachic problem. Chazal[65] explicitly prohibited inviting a gentile to a Yom Tov meal, "*gezeirah shema yarbeh bishvilo* – a decree, lest he add [food to the pot] for the sake of the gentile," and cook food that is not required for Yom Tov. Cooking is permitted on Yom Tov, but only for the physical needs of the Jewish people who observe it. On Shabbos, one is not allowed to cook at all. Therefore, Chazal[66] mention that one is permitted to invite a gentile to a Shabbos meal, for there is no risk

65. ביצה כא:
66. שם.

that one will cook for him. From this statement, it would appear that it is permissible to invite gentiles to any meal, except on Yom Tov.

The Taz[67] is of the opinion that under ordinary circumstances, a Jew should never eat together with a gentile year-round unless there is an urgent need for him to do so. He explains that Chazal never meant to suggest that one may invite gentile guests on Shabbos indiscriminately. The practice is not categorically forbidden as with Yom Tov, but one should avoid extending a Shabbos invitation to a gentile unless the need is pressing.

MAGIC SHOWS[68]

Is it permissible to perform a 'magic' show, if one publicly announces before the show that the effect is simply due to sleight of hand?

ANSWER

One of the prohibitions associated with the occult, is *lo se'oneinu*. There are a number of definitions given by Chazal for this *issur*, and one of them concerns performing magic tricks by sleight of hand (*achizas einayim*, literally "catching the eyes").[69] Many commentaries and Poskim write that this refers to magic tricks that fool people into thinking that something is being done with sorcery, even when no sorcery is being employed.

Chochmas Adam: The Chochmas Adam[70] was critical of *taschen shpiellers* (jesters), who performed sleight of hand at weddings, stating that they were transgressing a Torah prohibition, and that those who engaged them to perform had transgressed the prohibition of

67. או"ח סי' תקי"ב סק"ו
68. יו"ד סי' קע"ט
69. סנהדרין סו:
70. כלל פ"ט הובא בפתחי תשובה יו"ד סי' קע"ט סק"ז

lifnei iver, of 'placing a stumbling block before the blind.' The audience, too, by gathering to watch his show, is encouraging the magician to transgress (*mesaye'a lidei ovrei aveirah*). He does not specifically differentiate between whether or not the audience knows that it is simply an illusion.

If part of the show involves an explanation as to exactly how the trick is performed, then the Chochmas Adam may have agreed that such a performance would be permissible. Knowledge of exactly how the illusion is created might eliminate the element of sleight of hand. However, it is a rare performer who would be willing to reveal the secrets of his trade.

Maharshal: Other early Poskim, such as the Maharshal,[71] differed with the ruling of Chochmas Adam, and maintained that only *achizas einayim* that involves some type of sorcery is prohibited. According to this opinion, sleight of hand alone, which does not employ sorcery, is permissible.

Reb Moshe: Reb Moshe, *zt"l*, took the more lenient attitude in a case where the audience is aware that the performer is using illusion, even where no explanation is given. Nevertheless, he was reluctant to publish his opinion. A number of people close to Reb Moshe understood that this reflected his preference that it is better not to give such performances. Recently, a new collection of Reb Moshe's teshuvos were published,[72] in which Reb Moshe clearly exhibits a strong hesitation to proclaim a heter.

A gentile magician: There is no issur in attending the performance of a gentile magician. Magic and sleight of hand are not prohibited to gentiles, and the audience is thus not encouraging the magician to transgress.

71. הובא בשו"ת רמ"א הנדפס על גליון השו"ע
72. אגרות משה חלק ח' סוף סי' י"ג

Modern-day misconception: An argument that is commonly used to justify the performance of magic shows is that people a hundred years ago were much more prone to believe that sleight of hand was actual sorcery. The assertion is that modern man is more rational and would never consider that a magic show is anything but sleight of hand. This distinction is typical of a common attitude, which seeks to make halachic distinctions between the way things are now and the way they were when the Poskim pronounced their rulings.

In order for such an assessment to have value, as discussed earlier, one must a) be thoroughly knowledgeable of the situation that existed in the times of the earlier Poskim; b) have a full understanding of our current circumstances; and c) be thoroughly knowledgeable in the elements of halachah that would allow distinctions to be made between different cases. Most often, people's opinions are based simply on vague assumptions as to the true nature of changing historical conditions.

One finds that historically, people were not nearly as inclined to attribute mysterious occurrences to supernatural powers two hundred years ago as they are today. In the times of the Chochmas Adam, Europe was undergoing the intellectual revolution known as Rationalism. Many of the great gentile thinkers of that era worked to rid the world's consciousness of all spiritual forces, denying the existence of any mystical or non-rational phenomenon that could not be empirically observed.

In contrast, the past forty years has witnessed an increasing openness to and acceptance of an increasingly bizarre array of mystical and spiritual philosophies. This "New Age" has brought people in our times to embrace all types of mysticism, both that which is rooted in the holy Torah, and, lehavdil, that which is based on other alien and even idolatrous practices. It is reasonable to assume, contrary to what people may wish to believe, that in our current age the average person is quite willing to entertain the possibility that an impressive magic trick is actually accomplished with sorcery or by the harnessing of some sort of supernatural power.

Alternative medicine: A related issue is the expanding market for alternative medicine. The author has encountered and researched several types of alternative medicine. Some may be harmless enough, but a great many of the alternative healing methods available have nothing to do with any form of medicine, and claim to be methods of harnessing and focusing various healing powers that exist in some supposed ethereal realm. Whether or not they actually work, these healing techniques frequently fall into the category of casting spells (*menachesh, kosem kesamim*), or conjuring up spirits (*ov v'yidoni*). Others are actual forms of idolatry (*avodah zarah*). These are methods of healing which purport to channel or focus some type of 'universal energy', and are accomplished by performing some act that placates or persuades that force to work upon the infirm person. In other words, the practitioner is relating to the force as an independent power, and requesting its help. That is avodah zarah.

Sadly, these techniques and the people who practice them have found their way into the observant Jewish community. People in need of a *yeshuah* hear from a friend or a cousin about the miraculous cures a certain person performs, and thousands of otherwise *frum* Jews end up involved with these very questionable healers. Jews must beware of these healing powers; anything that can be categorized as "Eastern" or "Alternative" is suspect. This includes "new age" healing performed by very religious Jews, even those that are supported by well-meaning but ignorant Rabbonim. Keep as far away from these people as possible, "בני אל תלך בדרך אתם, מנע רגלך מנתיבתם – *My son, do not walk on the way with them, keep your feet away from their paths*" (Mishlei 1:15).

LOTTERIES (GORALOS)[73]

Under what circumstances, if any, would a person be permitted to use the *goral haGra*?

ANSWER

The goral haGra is permissible, but it should only be performed when a person is extremely desperate and there seems to be no way out of his dilemma. The great sages of Klal Yisroel who performed a goral HaGra, only did so when it seemed as if the Torah required them to take two separate, contradictory actions.

Seeking to know the future: The Torah writes, "תמים תהיה עם ה' אלוקיך – *You shall faithfully trust Hashem, your God*" (Devarim 18:13). Rashi explains this to mean, "that you should not inquire after the future," even in a permissible manner, even through a legitimate prophet. The Shulchan Aruch[74] writes, "We do not ask astrologers, and do not perform lotteries."

Chazal further tell us that Shaul HaMelech only went to ask Shmuel HaNavi where his flock wandered because he was caught in an insoluble dilemma. The obligation to honor his father simultaneously required him to both continue his search for the missing sheep and to return home, for his father was likely worried about his welfare. In such a situation, a person can avail himself of a permissible channel of higher knowledge.

Under normal circumstances, however, a person must walk with Hashem without worrying about what the future will bring. That is, he should concentrate on fulfilling his obligations to HaKadosh Baruch Hu, himself and his people. There is no need to become overly concerned with what the future has in store as a way of determining what course of action one should presently take. When the future comes,

73. יו"ד סי' קע"ט
74. יו"ד סי' קע"ט ס"א

he will serve HaKadosh Baruch Hu according to the demands of the new circumstances.

Only in certain situations, where there is no clear path to serving HaKadosh Baruch Hu, or it seems that Hashem has confronted him with contradictory paths between which he is unable or unqualified to decide, only then may he avail himself of the navi or the goral.

The importance of bitachon: Most questions of this sort can be avoided by strengthening *bitachon*, one's trust in HaKadosh Baruch Hu. The world is a very uncertain place. We face constant physical and financial threats, ranging from human bombs, to a volatile commodities market. A person can invest all his money and make a fortune, only to see it wiped out in an instant. Nothing in the world seems to have any permanence, and few things seem to follow any discernible pattern. This leads people to become worried and anxious. Instead, a person should fortify his bitachon, and be enjoined to "faithfully trust Hashem, your God." HaKadosh Baruch Hu knows what is good for a person, and He will take care of each and every Jew, providing for his needs in every way.

If a person becomes anxious and begins using mediums in order to know what is in store, then the Ribbono Shel Olam removes His providence, and the soothsayers are in effect, given control of that person's future, a situation described aptly by the possuk, "ואשר יגורתי יבוא לי, לא שלותי ולא שקטתי ולא נחתי ויבוא רוגז – *What I feared will come upon me, I did not rest nor did I remain tranquil, nor was I silent, and the wrath did come.*" (Iyov 3.25–26.)

HaKadosh Baruch Hu constantly protects the Jewish people. He watches after our physical safety and financial security. "הנה לא ינום ולא יישן שומר ישראל – *Behold! He neither slumbers nor sleeps, the Guardian of Israel*" (Tehillim 125:4). Thus, it is very important not to panic from uncertainty, nor to start running to any and every channel of information that might be able to reveal what the future has in store, even if that source is acceptable to the Torah. This is the *middah* of *temimus*, of wholeheartedness. As in every area, a person must seek out advice and stratagems to strengthen his bitachon and his temimus.

Dovid HaMelech writes four possukim[75] that can help strengthen the trust a person has in HaKadosh Baruch Hu:

> זבחו זבחי צדק ובטחו אל ה׳. רבים אומרים מי יראנו טוב נסה עלינו אור פניך ה׳. נתתה שמחה בלבי מעת דגנם ותירושם רבו. בשלום יחדו אשכבה ואישן כי אתה ה׳ לבדד לבטח תושיבני – *Sacrifice offerings of righteousness, and trust in Hashem. Many say, "Who shall show us goodness? Shine upon us the light of Your countenance, Hashem!" You placed gladness in my heart at the very time that their grain and wine abound. In peace, in harmony, I lie down and sleep, for You, Hashem, cause me to dwell solitary and secure.*

Many people get so involved in making their fortunes that they cannot even appreciate their financial success. Even as their 'grain and wine' roll in they still call out, '*Who shall show us goodness*,' asking Hashem for the blessing they dream will someday come. When Dovid HaMelech expressed the 'gladness in his heart,' not everything was going smoothly. He tells us (verse 3), "בני איש עד מה כבודי לכלמה תאהבון ריק תבקשו כזב סלה – *O sons of men, how long will you put my honor to shame, love futility and seek deception*?" Dovid HaMelech's enemies were plotting against him. Yet, "*In peace, in harmony, I lie down and sleep*." Because he trusted in HaKadosh Baruch Hu, Dovid HaMelech could lie down and sleep with his mind at rest, despite the challenges he faced each day. What gave Dovid HaMelech the fortitude to do this? "*For You, Hashem, cause me to dwell solitary and secure*." He lived with the constant awareness that HaKadosh Baruch Hu is the true source of security.

We must first work on eliminating desperation and cease our infatuation with material success, training ourselves to rely on HaKadosh Baruch Hu in all our endeavors. To seek out means of determining the future, even by using the goral haGra, nullifies the positive commandment of *tamim tih'yeh*, to trust faithfully in Hashem. If we want to merit the supreme protection of the Ribbono Shel Olam, then we

75. תהלים ד:ו–ט

must fill ourselves with *simchah* and *menuchas hanefesh*, happiness and tranquility. These, says the Chovos Halevavos,[76] are the foundations of bitachon in Hashem.

DYEING HAIR[77]

Nowadays, some men dye their hair. Does the prohibition of "*lo yilbash gever simlas ishah* – A man shall not don a woman's garment," still prohibit a Jewish man from dyeing his hair?

ANSWER

This question is frequently asked. The Shulchan Aruch[78]states: "It is forbidden [for a man –Rema] to pluck even one white hair from amongst black ones, because of "*A man shall not don* [*a woman's garment*]" (Devarim 22:5). It is similarly forbidden for a man to dye [white hairs to turn them][79] black, even one hair." Consequently, if a man has a few stray black hairs among the white hairs, then he may dye them white, but he must not do it the other way around.

On the other hand, when it comes to the use of mirrors, the Shulchan Aruch[80] distinguishes between locales where the men customarily use mirrors, and places where men do not use mirrors. This is the basis of the heter for men to use mirrors these days, since we live in societies where not only the women, but men too, are accustomed to groom themselves with the aid of a mirror. This would suggest that if the custom has changed, and men dye their hair, that it would be permissible for Jewish men also to dye their hair.

However, the author is unaware of any established custom in the United States for men to dye their hair. If one has heard of a place

76. שער הבטחון
77. יו"ד סי' קפ"ב
78. יו"ד סי' קפ"ב ס"ו
79. הגהת הרמ"א
80. יו"ד סי' קנ"ו ס"ב ברמ"א

where Poskim allow men to dye white or graying hair, it most likely concerns a locale where it was common practice amongst men to dye hair that had grayed prematurely, though the author doubts that such a locality exists.

PULLING OUT HAIR[81]

Nowadays, many men pull out excess hair from their eyebrows. Is it permissible for a Jewish man to do the same, and does it matter if his intention is to beautify himself, or to remove an annoyance?

ANSWER

There have always been men who beautified themselves through depilation, and it is not necessarily true that nowadays the situation differs from former times. Therefore, if the intention is to beautify himself, then a man cannot remove hair, even today. If a hair is causing annoyance or irritation, then he is allowed to remove it.

It would seem that this distinction should also apply to the dyeing of hair. It is not permitted to dye hair from white to black for comfort or beauty, but if a blotch of white hair causes embarrassment and anguish, he should be allowed to dye it. [82]

DYEING HAIR FOR SHIDDUCHIM

If an older man has not yet married, is there a leniency he can rely upon to dye his white hairs a different color?

ANSWER

Whether or not there exists a *heter* to dye white hair for the purposes

81. יו"ד סי' קפ"ב

82. עי' דרכי משה סי' קנ"ו ס"ק א'. ויש להעיר, עי' שו"ת דברי חיים יו"ד ח"ב סי' ס"ב.

of shidduchim is far from clear. If it could be shown that there is indeed a practice amongst men to dye their hair, then this could serve as the basis of such a heter. In circumstances where an individual feels a great need to eliminate gray hair for the purposes of shidduchim, he should decide upon an appropriate course of action by consultation with a qualified Rav.

The 'nowadays is different' fallacy:: As mentioned above regarding magic shows (p. 136), there are those who feel that circumstances today are very different from those of earlier generations, thus necessitating a change in halachic approach. R' Yehudah Al-Charizi, who translated much of the Rambam's commentary on Mishnayos from Arabic to Lashon HaKodesh, mentions in his foreword, that any translator must know three things: he must know the language he is translating from, the language he is translating into, and he has to know the subject matter. Even if he knows both languages, if he does not know the subject, then he might confuse certain ideas.

This concept also applies to determining the halachah based on one's assumptions as to how people conducted themselves in the past, and that certain differences between the former situation and the present one warrant an adaptation of the halachah. To do so, one must have a clear understanding of the context and circumstances pertaining at the time of the psak, and in what way these radical changes in contemporary conditions differ from the former, in addition to possessing a clear grasp of the halachic principles involved. Only then may it be suggested that the halachah should perhaps be applied differently today. The natural assumption of many people that "today is different," is nothing but a gut feeling that things must have been different in earlier times. Without careful investigation on the basis of the three factors mentioned above, no changes may be implemented.

SANCTITY OF TORAH LITERATURE[83]

If printed Torah literature was damaged during shipment, can the distributor file a claim to recover his losses, knowing that the shipping company will keep the sefarim and likely throw them away? Is there a difference between brand new sefarim and sefarim that have been used, and is there a difference between printed material and sheimos, such as *tefillin* and *mezuzos*?

ANSWER

This is a major problem that Judaica distributors face. Shipping companies provide insurance, and if goods are damaged during shipping and the company admits liability, they will reimburse the distributor, and the damaged merchandise is theirs to do with as they please. In most cases, the shipping companies have little use for Jewish sefarim and simply throw them away.

This leaves sefarim distributors in a quandary. If they make a claim to the shipping company, they are indirectly causing the disgraceful treatment of *sifrei kodesh*, sacred books. Not making a claim, however, means that the distributor must absorb the full cost of the damage.

There is, however, a solution to this problem. Most shipping companies operate a policy, whereby, for a fee, they will return the damaged merchandise to the distributor. The agreement is made in advance and the cost is figured into the cost of the shipping. Often, the distributor agrees to pay a certain amount for every piece of damaged merchandise the shipping company returns. Since this is more than the shipping company would receive otherwise, they are generally more than happy to make such an arrangement. Once the damaged sefarim are returned, the distributor can dispose of them properly. Shipping mishaps are not common occurrences, and the total cost of such an arrangement does not usually amount to more than a few hundred dollars a year.

83. יו"ד סי' ר"צ

New and used sefarim: The Gemara[84] discusses the case of a scarf that was designated to be used for wrapping tefillin. "*Azmanei v'lo tzar bei, tzar bei v'lo azmanei, shari l'meitzar bei zuzei* – If he designated it but did not yet wrap his tefillin with it, or if he wrapped his tefillin with it, but did not designate it, one is allowed to wrap up money with it." In other words, if it had not been designated and used for its stated purpose, the scarf does not yet have any *kedushah* and may still be used for mundane purposes. This concept applies to all items that serve objects with inherent holiness (*tashmishei kedushah*). This includes tefillin pouches, mezuzah cases, Torah mantles and crowns, and the velvet bimah covers upon which the open Sefer Torah is placed. Until they have been used for the first time, they possess no holiness.[85]

There are reputable *teshuvos*[86] from many years ago that extend this concept to printed Jewish sefarim. According to this view, new, unused sefarim have no holiness, and do not have to be placed in *genizah*.

Forty or fifty years ago, there was an uproar regarding the practice of using scraps of misprinted Jewish sefarim to reinforce the spines of new sefarim.[87] When a sefer is used often enough, the cover becomes unbound, and at that time, people discovered pieces of Chumashim and Gemaros glued onto the spine of their siddurim and other sefarim. The Rabbanim then moved to forbid the practice. Until that time, the printing houses had been relying on the above *heter*, which was originally given when paper and printing were costly.

It is difficult to justify extending the leniency of *tashmishei kedushah*, which do not possess intrinsic holiness, to sefarim and sheimos that do possess intrinsic kedushah. Intrinsic kedushah is not dependent on whether or not an item has been used. Now that paper is much more affordable, there is really no reason to rely on the old heterim.

All sheimos, including sefarim, have intrinsic kedushah whether

84. ברכות כג:
85. או"ח סי' מ"ב ס"ג ובמ"ב סק"ט
86. עי' אבני נזר יו"ד סי' שע"ו
87. מ"ב סי' קנ"ד ס"ק ל"א

they have been used or not. This means that even new sefarim which become damaged should be placed in genizah. It goes without saying that once sefarim have been used, then even according to the heter, they must be treated as *kisvei kodesh*, sacred writings.

HONORING PARENTS[88]

If a young man wishes to continue his yeshivah studies, but his parents want him to attend college, is he obligated to accede to their wishes?

ANSWER

Since each individual case has its own many and varied aspects, we shall limit the discussion to outlining the major principles involved in making decisions of this nature.

The halachos of *kevod av v'eim*, honoring one's father and mother, are both narrowly delineated, yet broadly applied. The narrow delineation of the obligation is as follows: The Gemara gives several examples of actions that fulfill the requirement of *kevod av*:

> What is considered respect (*morah*), and what is considered honor (*kavod*)? Morah [is given by] not standing in his place, not sitting in his place, not contradicting his statements, and not offering an opinion on his position. Kavod [is given by] serving him food and drink, attending to his clothing and covers, and escorting him in and out.[89]

The Shulchan Aruch[90] adds that all this must be done, "*b'sever panim yafos* – with a pleasant disposition." Many Rishonim understand that the basic obligation of *kevod av* is fulfilled specifically

88. יו"ד סי' ר"מ
89. קידושין לא.
90. יו"ד סי' ר"מ ס"ד

through these actions. Accordingly, a child would not be required to listen to any parental request which does not relate to the above expressions of respect and honor brought by the Gemara. However, these may also be seen as general principles, and it is difficult to strictly define under what particular circumstances a child may be obligated to carry out the wishes of the parent.

For example, there was a case where the father of a yeshivah student felt that the yeshivah he attended was undermining his son's respect for his parents, since he had been instructed to eat a larger measure (*kezayis*) of matzah at the Pesach Seder than was the custom in his family. The father considered that this constituted a type of rebellion against traditional parental authority in the home. Strictly speaking, the son had no obligation to heed the father's request to eat the smaller-sized piece of matzah; it would not have been disrespectful for the son to fulfill mitzvos in the way he felt to be correct, nor would he have honored or served his father in any way by conforming to his father's wishes. He should, however, use tact and show love and respect, and certainly not use offensive language in any case.

As we mentioned, however, though the principles are narrow, their application is broad. Aside from showing the required respect to a parent, one is also obligated not to cause his parents suffering. It requires a degree of common sense, and a healthy dose of courtesy to apply this correctly. In this case, though the son may have been justified in adopting a stricter level of observance than his father, it would have been better for him to have accepted the smaller measure of the middle matzah but to combine with it a piece of the top matzah (the *shleimah*). In this way, the son could have eaten a larger measure of matzah without drawing attention to it and upsetting his father. In each situation, there may be various solutions and compromises that may be employed to ensure that both the sentiments and the honor of all concerned be best preserved. Where possible, common sense, practically applied, may help relieve the stress that sometimes results from acting in accordance with halachah.

Furthermore, parents have an obligation to educate and train their children – including Torah study – and this certainly gives them influence and authority over their children even in areas beyond the obligation of the children to give them honor and respect.

Indeed, the crucial years in a young person's life coincide with the period in which parental rebuke is most effective. The Gemara[91] states that parents can exercise their authority over their children from the age of sixteen or seventeen, until twenty-two or twenty-four. Rashi explains that parents should use these years to rebuke and instruct their children. Children younger than this are not mature enough to fully benefit from all forms of rebuke, while older children might rebel. It stands to reason though, that if the father's instructions run counter to the principles of *chinuch*, then the basis of the father's authority regarding that issue becomes severely diminished.

The Shulchan Aruch[92] nevertheless grants the son the final decision when it comes to his chosen place of study: "A student who wishes to go to another place where he is certain that his Torah studies will be successful with the Rav there, but his father protests because he fears that the gentiles in that city are wont to initiate anti-Semitic actions, [the son] is not required to heed his father in this case." The Rema adds: "Similarly, if the father protests the son's desire to marry a particular woman, he does not have to heed his father." Thus, despite the father's obligation to teach his son Torah and to bring him to the chuppah, the son ultimately makes the decision as to where he shall learn and with whom he shall build a family.

Even when the halachah is clear, a person should never use the halachah as a weapon and justify hurtful actions in the name of the Torah, especially with regard to one's parents. A child must use all the tact, finesse, and gentleness he can muster, even when the halachah does not require him to heed his parent's wishes. In this way, it will be understood that whatever decision the child makes, he is not being disrespectful or rebellious toward his parents. Often, disagreements that arise between parents and children are complicated by other

91. קידושין ל.
92. יו"ד סי' ר"מ סכ"ה

issues, and need to be discussed with great sensitivity and intelligence. The child who avails himself of the sage advice of a talmid chacham will spare himself and his parents much unnecessary emotional pain. An older, more experienced talmid chacham can guide him and help plan his steps and his words with care. By taking this route, the wise son will undoubtedly merit the Ribbono Shel Olam's help and succeed in all he sets out to accomplish.

Regarding the specific question of extended secular studies, many parents feel that without this form of education, their child may be subject to severe hardship, even to the point of actual *pikuach nefesh*, when later on in life he is expected to provide a livelihood for his family. When faced with such a sincere and insistent request from one's parents, it is particularly beneficial to avail oneself of the Torah's wisdom. Both the form and content of a child's response would benefit greatly from the expert guidance that a seasoned talmid chacham can provide. It should be recognized, that leading Torah scholars throughout the ages, began their path in life with a burning desire to devote themselves to Torah, in spite of being faced with many who expressed forceful and sincere opinions in an attempt to dissuade them.

INTERNET

Given the spiritual dangers of the internet, what guidelines may be given to those who require internet access for business purposes?

ANSWER

The internet has already caused terrible problems for young and old alike. The damage is unspeakable. If a person must absolutely have internet access for reasons of parnasah (livelihood), he must take great personal care to access the internet in the safest way possible. This means using any technology available to limit or filter access to any material that could harm a person's *ruchnius*. A combination of a filtered service provider, with surveillance software that can alert designated guardians (*shomrim*) is a good approach. Any protection a person can avail himself of is worth the investment.

No one should think that he is too refined or too righteous to stumble, and should take the necessary steps to ensure that there is no possibility of his being able to access unsuitable material, even if one is sure the temptation will never arise. A few mature and responsible people have been tempted to press a certain combination of keystrokes and view things, create relationships, and do all kinds of transgressions (*aveiros*) that they never before dreamed of doing. Even forums whose stated purpose is to provide an opportunity for discussing questions in learning can foster relationships that can lead to undesirable things.

The above comments are addressed to adults who may be required for reasons of parnasah to use the internet. It goes without saying that the internet should never be made available to children. Sadly, internet-related problems have developed in many homes without the parents having had the slightest clue as to what their children were becoming involved in.

The United States Constitution protects the freedom of all Americans, yet freedom can be abused. There are advocacy groups which defend the right of every American to bear arms. Hundreds of people are shot to death each year, yet these interest groups still work tirelessly to show that this right is protected by the Constitution, and attempt to prove that the guns themselves are not to blame. By and large, in our communities we recognize the danger that guns present to the safety and security of our family and loved ones. Whether or not we have a 'right' to own a gun, it is rare to find such a weapon in an observant Jewish home. We keep far from such dangerous things. The same should be true of the internet. "ואנכי בראתי משחית לחבל – *And I have created a weapon to wreak destruction*" (Yeshaya 54:16), aptly describes the advent of the internet.

SHEITEL CONTROVERSY

The following letter was written by a woman regarding the sheitel (wig) controversy:

"When the sheitel controversy came out this summer (5764), all women were told not to wear their human-hair wigs until the matter was fully investigated and a final determination made. It is now several months later and I have several sheitels put away because I can not determine their origin. I would like to know if a final decision has yet been made. If we are required to burn them, then I would like to know that I can do so, and then buy new sheitels. If I am permitted to wear them, then I would like to know before the upcoming Yamim Tovim. Not knowing what to do is worse than having to burn them, because I can't wear my old sheitels, and due to our financial situation it's difficult to justify buying new sheitels when the necessity of incurring such an expense remains in doubt."

ANSWER

The issue surrounding hair from India is not a new one. Twenty years ago, the question came before the Gedolei Hador, and they looked into the matter and virtually all permitted the use of products that contain Indian hair. The question was reopened recently, although nothing was discovered to indicate that matters were any different from before.

There are two separate and distinct questions regarding the sheitel issue.

Is such hair forbidden?: The first issue has to do with whether or not the hair removed as part of the Indian temple service is in fact an idolatrous offering (*tikroves avodah zarah*). If the hair is considered by the Torah to be an idolatrous offering, it would be forbidden to derive any benefit from it, whether directly or indirectly.

The Gemara (*Avodah Zarah* 51b) discusses various items which become forbidden as *tikroves avodah zarah*. Anything that would normally be brought as a korbon in the Beis HaMikdash, such as meat, wine, and grain, can become forbidden simply by being brought before the idol. Items such as sticks or stones do not automatically become forbidden, even if they are brought as an offering. Some action must be done to them that is in some way similar to the way korbanos were processed in the Beis HaMikdash. A solid object must be broken or smashed, and a liquid offering must be poured or sprinkled in a way that splatters (*zrikah hamishtaberes*). Any other act of worship, even if it is done according to the accepted practice of that particular form of idol worship, does not prohibit the offering from being used by a Jew (though the worshipper has certainly transgressed). This is the view of the Shulchan Aruch,[93] and the halachah follows his opinion.

The author personally consulted with Hindu priests and scholars, including many converts and *ba'alei Teshuvah* (who were once practicing Hindus, and are familiar with this Indian rite), who stated unequivocally that no holiness or sacrificial status is accorded to the hair. On the contrary, hair is a symbol of the ego, is impure, and thus held to be displeasing to their gods. According to these experts, no practicing Hindu with a modicum of knowledge of his religion would ever consider offering his hair as a sacrifice. Cutting off the hair is simply an act of self-degradation, often performed in fulfillment of a vow, whereby the worshipper surrenders his or her beauty and pride in order to purify himself.

At the shrine at Tirupatti, for instance, the worshippers have their hair shaved off in a separate complex by professional barbers hired by the temple. Nothing at all is done to the hair after it is removed from the worshippers' heads. The hair is not even presented to the idol. It is simply collected and placed in a metal bin to be auctioned off later. After bathing, the worshippers make their way to the shrine to pay homage.

Some wish to suggest that the act of shaving off the hair from the head should be seen as a shechitah-like treatment that makes the hair

93. יו"ד קל"ט סע' ג'

forbidden, but this is not the case. The shaving is an act performed upon the worshipper, and not on the hair. This is evident from the above-mentioned Gemara and the writings of the Poskim. Furthermore, only a priest or a worshipper can consecrate an object, turning it into *tikroves avodah zarah*, and in the case of Hindu tonsuring, the act is performed by barbers who are neither the priests nor the worshippers. Thus, the hair shaved off at the Indian shrines never legitimately becomes *tikroves avodah zarah*.

Is Indian temple hair used for Jewish sheitels?: The second issue is whether or not any hair from the Indian temples is actually used in the wig industry, or if the hair we use comes from other sources entirely. Ultimately, this is the more important of the two questions, for if we could determine that none or very little of the temple hair is used for the wigs that Jewish women use, then the halachic status of that hair is no longer relevant.

Brush hair: In the year 5764, extensive research was done to examine the process by which wigs are manufactured, and to determine the source of the hair itself. The report included merchant records, industry reports, in-house publications, and government documents. The fact that India used to be a British colony made the research easier, since many of the documents in the industry were, and continue to be, written in English. These are the findings:

In India, hair is collected in a different manner from most other countries. In Romania, Hungary, Spain and Russia, women interested in selling their hair, grow their hair for up to several years and then cut it all off at one time. The hair must be grown to at least eight inches long in order to be used for a wig. Women in India generally do not cut their hair all at once. Rather, they grow their hair extremely long, not cutting it for years, and whenever they brush their hair they collect the strands that fall out. This is called "brush hair." Every few weeks representatives from hair collection firms visit these women and buy the brush hair in exchange for cash. Indeed, selling brush hair is an important source of income for many poverty-stricken families. It is one of the reasons they do not cut their hair all at once. Were they to do that, the women would only make money once every few years. This way, they can put food on the table each week.

Remy hair: Practically the only time Indian women cut their hair off all at once is in the temples. This hair is called "Indian Remy hair" in the industry. With Remy hair, there is no need for sorting. Before the hair is cut, the hair is gathered together with two ribbons, one at the end near the tip and another close to the scalp. This keeps all the hair strands root to root and tip to tip. Then the hair is cut. Brush hairs are much longer than the Remy hair, yet Remy is by far the better of the two types. There is also European Remy hair, tied and cut in the same way, as mentioned above.

Whether from India or elsewhere, Remy hair is generally used without processing and in its natural color. It is known for its silky texture and natural luster. Almost all Indian Remy hair is solid black and comes naturally in four different shades. Its quality makes it suitable for high-end specialty wigs and for expensive hair extensions used almost exclusively by people with jet-black hair. These products are sold for exorbitant prices; in rare cases, even for as much as five thousand dollars apiece.

Jewish sheitels: Standard wigs in the colors commonly worn by Jewish women, would have to either be made from brush hair, or from European Remy hair but almost certainly not from Indian Remy hair. A 'brush hair' sheitel has an inferior appearance to a Remy hairpiece. This is due to the combing and processing that brush hair undergoes before it can be used, and the fact that not all the strands are aligned root to root. Since practically all Indian hair is black, it must be bleached and then dyed in order to be used for wigs of other colors. This processing removes the outer layers of the hair: the cuticle, and the pigment. Only the bare protein strand of the hair is left intact, without any natural shine or body.

Manufacturers would never subject Remy hair to this process because its quality makes it more valuable in its natural state. For this reason, Indian Remy hair is practically never used in wigs of any color other than black. Standard blonde, brown, dark-brown, and auburn wigs that are made with Indian hair, exclusively contain the lower quality processed and bleached brush hair. Higher quality sheitelach in these colors are made from European Remy hair. Sometimes, a wealthier client will even arrange for a woman with matching hairstyle and color to grow her hair to order.

Sheitel production: There are two very large, multi-million dollar companies that collect the vast majority of the hair in India. They are owned by two relatives, both named Gupta. They purchase brush hair and temple hair. In the year of the sheitel controversy, the amount of hair collected from the temples, including all grades and types, amounted to around three hundred tons. In contrast, the total for brush hair topped four thousand tons, more than thirteen times as much.

The brush hair is processed in 'houses'. These are large facilities where hundreds of peasant women sort the hairs according to quality, shade, and length. This is the only part of the hair processing that is actually done in India. Once the hair is graded and sorted, it is shipped to Romania or Ukraine for bleaching and dyeing. From there the hair makes its way to the wig-weaving factories in China and Korea. Even quality European hair is sent to these countries for weaving.

Doubts still remained after the initial report, and the Guptas asked what they could do to prove that brush hairs are used for standard wigs. The researchers asked to see ten 'houses' where the hair is sorted. The Guptas arranged for them to see eleven such houses. A team of Rabbanim and *askanim* (community leaders) went to India to see first hand the process used to manufacture sheitels from beginning to end. They saw the hair processing factories, talked to the Chinese and Korean merchants, and verified that everything matched the written records and reports that had been procured previously. Brush hair is used for standard wigs, and temple hair is only used for black wigs, specialty wigs and hair extensions.

Some attempts were made to detract from the above findings by claiming that the investigators had actually observed theatrical stagings conducted by the Guptas, who filled the workshops with peasants who acted as if they were doing the work described above. Others said that the work being done in the factories was real, but that it was being done for other purposes. They claimed that the brush hair is used only for floor mats, and that sheitels are made exclusively from the higher quality Remy hair which is purchased from the temples, before being bleached and processed.

The author has seen all the reports, and the first report is far more reasonable, fits the facts, and accounts for all the observations that were made at the factories. Additionally, the need to sort the brush hair into various grades and lengths, which is a complicated and time-consuming process, is entirely unnecessary for the production of floor mats. The assertion that the work observed in the factories was a staged production seems unlikely, although a somewhat reliable investigator echoed that claim.

L-cysteine: As far as other products made from hair, such as L-cysteine, the concern for *issur* is even smaller. Firstly, 10–15% of L-cysteine is extracted from chicken feathers. More importantly, low-grade human hair from which most L-cysteine is manufactured comes from standard sources (barber shops) the world over. This quantity of hair from these places is immensely greater than that which is purchased from the Indian temples. The maximum possible amount of temple hair in any final product is negligible.

A full discussion of the halachic status of Indian temple hair can be found in *Sheilos v'Tshuvos Shulchan HaLevi*. The evidence and arguments presented there support the conclusion that the *Poskei Hador* arrived at twenty years ago, that is, that none of the hair from India carries any shade of issur.

All in all, these conclusions eliminate the worry over temple hair from India, and Jewish women can begin wearing their sheitels once again.

TELEVISION

To what extent is a Jew obliged to convince students, relatives, and neighbors to rid themselves of their television sets?

ANSWER

Rebuke (*tochachah*) is a very difficult thing to deliver properly and effectively.

The Tzelemer Rav, *zt"l*, once gave a fiery *drashah* on Shabbos HaGadol, many years ago, when television was just becoming popular. The Rav said that people were telling him that the television was important for any number of reasons, but he held very strongly that there was no reason important enough to allow that instrument into a Jewish home. He turned to the children and called out, "*Kinderlach*, do you hear me?" A response was heard from the children present. Then the Rav said, "Whoever has a television in his home should see to it that the parents get rid of it. Right after Shabbos, take a stone or a brick or a heavy piece of wood and smash the television. Whoever does this should come to me right away and I'll give him a prize."

Hearing the story now, it may seem extreme, but it was with these methods that they were successful in ridding the entire Williamsburg neighborhood in Brooklyn, New York, of television. The author was in attendance at that drashah.

There is a precedent for using the strong-arm approach in the service of Torah. The most successful generation in terms of *limud HaTorah* that ever existed, was in the time of Chizkiyahu, King of Yehudah. Chazal[94] tell us, "They checked from Dan to Be'er Sheva and did not find even one boy or girl, man or woman who was not completely fluent in the laws of purity and impurity." How did Chizkiyahu accomplish the amazing feat of educating the entire nation in some of the most difficult laws in the Torah? Did Chizkiyahu persuade the people to sit and learn Torah with his beautiful oratory

94. סנהדרין צד:

skill? No. Chazal tell us exactly what he did: "*Na'atz cherev al pesach beis hamidrash v'amar kol mi she'eino osek batorah yidaker bacherev zu* – He stuck a sword above the entrance to the beis midrash and said: Anyone who does not occupy himself with Torah shall be pierced with this sword!" When the people heard Chizkiyahu's simple, yet powerful threat, they ran to the beis midrash for their dear lives, and they became scholars.

Obviously, a person cannot always take this approach. The Tzelemer Rav could do this, but a cheder rebbe cannot do this with his talmidim, lest he slight the child's parents. He must instead use great tact. The rebbe should explain to the child that his parents are the most wonderful people in the world; would it be that every child could have such wonderful parents. But as far as television is concerned, it is like beer. The Rebbe can tell the child to go home and taste a little beer. The child will invariably come back saying that beer tastes awful. The rebbe can then say that the same thing applies to television: for your parents it may be acceptable, but for you it is awful. There are other kinds of tactics that can also be used to keep children away from television without suggesting they rebel against their parents.

The yeshivah once employed a classical first-grade rebbe, Reb Hirsch Vasilsky, *z"l*, who took the responsibility for his students very seriously. One day a huge fellow, who stood a foot taller than the rebbe and was at least one hundred pounds heavier, stormed into the class and said, "Did you tell my child that he's not allowed to have a television?" The rebbe said, "No, I didn't tell your child that." The man flew into a rage, "My child wouldn't lie, and he says that you told him he can't have a television!" Seeing that the man was about to do something dangerous, Rav Vasilsky stood up to his full height and said, "My dear sir, I didn't tell your child that he's not allowed to have a television, I told your child that no Yid is allowed to have a television; him and everybody else included!" The rebbe's unflinching and decisive character had its affect on the man, who walked out without another word. A rebbe must realize that he is responsible for his talmidim.

When it comes to rebuking relatives and neighbors, it depends very much on the situation. The mitzvah of *hoche'ach tochi'ach* – You shall rebuke your fellow, has limitations. Rebuke must be effective. A person cannot just go out in the middle of the street and shout at all the Shabbos desecrators. A rebbe, more than others, has a special obligation to instruct his students in these sensitive areas, but it is rare for *tochachah* to be effective outside of a narrow circle. Some people are endowed with the precious ability to influence and persuade others to do the right thing. They have a great mitzvah to go out and do what they can to right the wrongs of our community. For a more detailed treatment of the *halachos* of tochachah see Shulchan Aruch.[95]

OFFERING FOOD TO A JEW WHO WILL NOT RECITE A BLESSING[96]

May a person invite a non-religious Jew to a meal knowing that he will not recite any blessings?

ANSWER

A person is not allowed to serve food to a Jew who will not recite the proper blessings,[97] or wash before eating bread.[98] However, this does not mean that a person may never invite non-religious Jews to his home, or to a family *simchah*. A person can tactfully ensure that a non-religious guest fulfill his obligation to make blessings. For instance, it is usually enough to simply announce that it is time to wash hands for '*hamotzi*,' and the guest will follow suit. In the case of blessings, a simple instruction that everyone present should answer *Amen* to the blessings that will be recited out loud on behalf of all present, can resolve the issue in a non-confrontational way.

In cases where this approach will not work, it may be permissible

95. או"ח סי' תר"ח ס"ב
96. או"ח סי' קס"ג, קס"ט
97. או"ח סי' קס"ט ס"ב
98. או"ח סי' קס"ג ס"ב ברמ"א, סי' קס"ט ס"א

and advisable to use leniencies for the sake of kiruv. Since this is a very sensitive area, one should consult with a halachic authority before deciding how to proceed.

SELLING TORAH LITERATURE TO GENTILES AND MISSIONARIES

Given that Torah literature and *sefarim* are widely available today, may a Judaica retailer sell these items to non-Jews or missionaries?

ANSWER

Providing a gentile access to Torah: The classic case of *lifnei iver* is discussed by Chazal with regard to presenting a *nazir* with a glass of wine, something that a nazir is forbidden to drink. The Gemara[99] tells us that, one who hands a nazir a glass of wine "from the other side of the river," that is, wine that he could never have obtained without assistance, has caused him to stumble. But if the glass of wine was "on the same side of the river," that is, within the grasp of the nazir in any case, then one has not caused him to stumble simply by handing him the wine, as he would have taken it even without assistance, and thus the *issur* of *lifnei iver* has not been transgressed. The same would apply to handing a limb taken off a living animal to a non-Jew.

Although a gentile should not be learning Torah, just as he is not allowed to eat a limb from a living animal (*eiver min hachai*), Jewish sefarim are accessible to him even without a bookseller's assistance. He simply has to make two trips to a Sefarim store, the first in order to buy a *yarmulke* and the second to walk into another store and buy the sefer. Torah books are therefore considered "on the same side of the river," and it is permissible to sell him sefarim, even if he is not wearing a yarmulke. Today, even the extra effort to buy a yarmulke is

99. ע"ז ו:

unnecessary, because one can buy practically any Jewish sefer using the Internet, without having to enter a sefarim store at all.

Regarding missionaries: Concerning a missionary, however, this *heter* does not apply. By providing him with any material, one is aiding and abetting a transgressor (*mesaye'a lidei ovrei aveirah*) and assisting in his missionary efforts, which are aimed at diverting Jews (*mesis umadiach*) from the Torah, *chas v'shalom*. The prohibition of aiding and abetting a transgressor is not restricted to the limiting parameters of lifnei iver. Heaven forbid that any Jew should have any part in such activities, even if the missionary could purchase his supplies elsewhere. It should not even enter a Jew's mind to do such a thing.

PRINTING INVITATIONS FOR AN EVENT INVOLVING SHABBOS DESECRATION

A Sabbath observant (*shomer Shabbos*) printer once asked the following question: A non-religious Jew ordered invitations for the *bas mitzvah* of his daughter. The *bas mitzvah* was to be held in a hotel on Shabbos Kodesh, virtually guaranteeing that the guests would travel on Shabbos to attend. May the *shomer Shabbos* printer accept the job?

ANSWER

The two separate problems that must be considered were referred to briefly above. One is '*lifnei iver*,' causing another to stumble, and the other is '*mesaye'a lidei ovrei aveirah*,' assisting those who transgress. With regard to placing a stumbling block, since the man could easily find another printer, the *shomer Shabbos* printer is not causing the man to stumble by accepting the job.

With regard to *mesaye'a*, to contribute or assist the transgression is permissible if it is not done at the time of the transgression. By printing the invitations one is not assisting the transgression of Shabbos on Shabbos itself, and indirect assistance is permissible, because of the principle of *darkei shalom*, which enjoins us to ensure that our relationships with all people are as amicable and pleasant as possible.[100]

On the other hand, it is difficult to understand why the *shomer Shabbos* printer would want to take the job, despite it being permissible. If the man is a frequent customer, then refusing him this time might cause him to go elsewhere for his other printing needs. Such a loss might therefore justify the printer's agreeing to print the bas mitzvah invitations. However, if this non-observant Jew is not a regular customer, then the printer's loss will be minimal if declines the job. The printer should weigh this minor financial loss against the great honor he can give to the Shabbos by not printing such invitations.

One may argue that there is possibly a greater loss involved than that of a single customer. High quality work is its own advertisement and may serve to attract other customers. The best answer to this is that the printer should always strive to produce excellent work, and trust that this will itself bring in more business, without having to worry about the loss of a single contract. A Jew must always keep in mind that, "the livelihood of a man is set for him from one Rosh Hashanah to the next."[101] The money he might have earned from a job that is indirectly related to Shabbos desecration would come to him some other way. Only if a person is offered business that he could have and should have taken, but due to laziness or a sense of pride chooses not to accept it, then he will lose out on what was allotted to him, because he intentionally let the money go. A person cannot just go ahead and forfeit an opportunity for livelihood that is entirely permissible, and expect the lost earnings to come to him in another way.

However, if a person gives up the opportunity to print an invitation to a non-kosher simchah, he is not giving up on what the Ribbono Shel Olam has allotted him. It is justifiable to refuse business for the honor of the holy Shabbos. It is certain in cases like this that he will receive his allotted portion. A Jew should accustom himself to think

100. עי' גיטין סא., ע"ז נה:
101. ביצה טז.

this way. Proper bitachon should be a way of life for every single Jew and not just a subject of stories told in tales of tzaddikim.

IMPORTED ISRAELI PRODUCE

What are the main *shmittah* issues that Jews living in the Diaspora have to contend with regarding produce imported from Eretz Yisroel?

ANSWER

There are two levels of concern when it comes to shmittah produce.

Issur sefichim: It is completely forbidden to eat certain shmittah produce, just as it is forbidden to eat non-kosher meat. This prohibition is called *issur sefichim*, and it applies to wheat, lettuce, tomatoes, carrots, beans, and all other herbs and vegetables that grow directly from a seed sown in the ground, either accidentally or intentionally during shmittah, or in some cases from just before shmittah began.

If the seed germinated (*kelitas ha'zera*) after the onset of shmittah, all opinions maintain that its produce is completely forbidden. If the seed germinated before shmittah, but the plant did most of its growth during shmittah, then the permissibility of its produce is subject to a *machlokes Rishonim*, a dispute amongst the early commentators on the Talmud.

Many vegetables from Israeli farms are freshly picked, and shipped via air-freight to international destinations, including the United States. A person should look out for bulletins from Israeli agencies regarding the status of Israeli produce around the time of Chanukah of the shmittah year, and follow that information, adding a few days to the dates listed therein to account for the delay caused by shipping time.

Kedushas shevi'is: Tree-grown produce is not subject to the prohibition of sefichim, and is permitted for consumption. Nevertheless, there are several halachos that govern its handling. Halachically, a tree is defined as any plant whose branches produce fruit from year to year. This category includes grapes, oranges, avocados, nuts, and the like.

Shmittah produce has *kedushas shevi'is*, that is, the produce itself is imbued with the sanctity of the shmittah year. As a consequence, it is subject to four specific restrictions which limit the distribution, sale, and handling of shmittah produce.

Issur sechorah: The first is *issur sechorah*, the prohibition to market shmittah produce. A Jew is not permitted to buy or sell shmittah produce in the usual way. Even when produce is purchased in a permissible way, if someone pays directly for a shmittah item the sanctity of shmittah attaches itself to the money received (*nitfas b'kedushas shevi'is*), and the money becomes subject to all the shmittah restrictions. Therefore, if one must buy a product suspected of being or containing Israeli shmittah produce, one should buy it on credit, and pay the bill the next day so that the money should be considered a debt payment rather than in exchange for shmittah produce. If done this way, the money in question will receive no kedushah.

Issur hefsed: The second is *issur hefsed*, the prohibition to waste or destroy shmittah produce in a direct manner. A person is not allowed to throw into the garbage an edible piece of shmittah fruit or its leftovers for this will quicken its deterioration. People in Eretz Yisroel set aside a special container which they call the *pach shevi'is* into which they place the day's leftovers. They cover this with a piece of paper and put on top of that the next day's leftovers, so that one day's leftovers will not quicken the deterioration of the next day's. Eventually, the lower layers are discarded when they spoil. This is repeated throughout the shmittah season. Outside of Eretz Yisroel this is rarely necessary, as the appearance of Israeli shmittah produce in the market is infrequent.

Bi'ur: The third requirement is to remove all shmittah produce from one's possession once it can no longer be found in the field. This is called *bi'ur*. It is learned from the possuk, "ולבהמתך ולחיה אשר בארצך – *And for your animal, and the wild beast in your land*" (Vayikra 25:7). The Gemara[102] states, "As long as the wild beast eats it from the field, you may feed the animal in your estate. Once it has disappeared, and the wild beast does not have it in the field, you must remove it from the animal in your house." To satisfy this halachah, people consume their shmittah products before the announced date of bi'ur. Whatever remains, they set down outside their property, and announce before three people that the produce is ownerless (*hefker*). Charts are posted announcing when bi'ur is required to be performed for every kind of fruit. Due to the scarcity of shmittah fruit outside of Eretz Yisroel, as it is prohibited to remove shmittah fruit from Eretz Yisroel (see following paragraph), it is unusual for Jews of the Diaspora to be required to perform bi'ur.

Export: Finally, one is not permitted to take shmittah produce out of the borders of Eretz Yisroel. In this sense, there should rightfully be no exports during shmittah at all, with the exception of esrogim, which will be discussed further on. Once produce is brought out of Eretz Yisroel, however, one is allowed to use it. There are exceptional cases whereby shevi'is produce is not limited by the restrictions of bi'ur, and may even be removed from Eretz Yisroel, such as produce falling under the category of *otzar beis din*. A proper treatment of this subject is beyond the scope of this discussion.

Practically speaking, the majority of the issues with tree-grown shmittah produce begin at the end of the shmittah year, when the fruits that budded after Rosh Hashanah ripen and are harvested. All the fruits harvested at the beginning of the shmittah year budded before Rosh Hashanah, and do not have kedushas shevi'is. Canned produce from Israel also arrives in the United States towards the end of the shmittah year. At that time, fruit should not be eaten without proper hashgachah, if there is any suspicion that it might have originated in Eretz Yisroel.

102. פסחים נב:

ARBA MINIM FROM ERETZ YISROEL

What should a person watch out for when buying *arba minim* during *shmittah*?

ANSWER

Lulavim, hadassim, & aravos: There is no shmittah concern with *lulavim*, *hadassim*, and *aravos* (palm, myrtle, and willow fronds), because these plants do not possess any sanctity (*kedushah*).

Chazal[103] discuss the kedushah of a lulav that grew on shmittah, but this does not apply nowadays. In order to have kedushas shevi'is, the use of the produce must resemble the act of eating. Chazal describe eating as *hana'aso u'biuro shoveh*, the pleasure is derived at the moment of its consumption or destruction. This description applied to lulavim in the time of Chazal, since lulavim were used to make brooms. The benefit from the lulav – the swept floor – was derived as the lulav was worn down by the act of sweeping, and it therefore possessed kedushas shevi'is.

Nowadays, we do not use lulavim for brooms, and none of a lulav's other uses are similar to eating. For instance, many people use lulav leaves to make *kaishalach*, the woven hadass and aravah holders, but the benefit from such a holder does not derive from its disintegration. For this reason, all the Poskim rule that lulavim no longer present a shmittah concern. The same is true for hadassim and aravos.

The esrog on the other hand, does have kedushas shevi'is. This means all the limitations of shmittah apply to esrogim. They include the following:

A Jew is not allowed to bring shmittah produce out of the borders of Eretz Yisroel, though for the sake of fulfilling a mitzvah, it is permitted by a number of Poskim.

In addition the esrogim are harvested on behalf of *Beis Din*, and under its supervision. This arrangement releases the produce held under the authority of Beis Din from the requirement of bi'ur according

103. סוכה מ.

to many authorities. Others add that the obligation of bi'ur for esrogim is non-existent, as esrogim remain on the tree from year to year and never truly disappear from the wild. These opinions further maintain that the prohibition to remove shmittah produce from Eretz Yisroel only applies to produce that is subject to the requirements of bi'ur. Thus, esrogim may be removed from Eretz Yisroel.

The great majority of Rabbanim in Klal Yisroel agreed to this unique arrangement. The Rav of Brisk when he lived in Europe, would acquire an esrog from Eretz Yisroel during shmittah. The justification for this leniency applies only to esrogim, and not to any other produce. When purchasing esrogim for Sukkos in the year following shmittah, a person should be especially careful to go to a reliable, God-fearing vendor who will be sure to abide by all the rules of shmittah.

Because it is forbidden to directly cause the destruction of shmittah produce, some people have the practice of sending their esrog back to Eretz Yisroel immediately following Sukkos. This is not because there is a mitzvah to return shmittah produce to the Land of Israel. Rather, the concern is that Jews in the Diaspora are not well-versed in the halachos of handling shmittah produce, and might come to improperly dispose of the esrog, thus showing disdain for the holiness of the fruit. As explained above, in Eretz Yisroel, all Jews have special closed receptacles for disposing of their shmittah leftovers. They are careful to place each day's waste in a different bag, or a different layer, so that yesterday's spoiling fruit will not cause today's fruit to spoil more quickly. A person who wishes to make esrog jam should be sure to learn how to dispose of whatever is removed.

A person should be sure to eat the esrog jam before *Tu b'Shevat*, the fifteenth day of the month of Shevat. A number of Poskim hold that there is a *zeman bi'ur* for esrogim. And it falls out sometime after Tu b'Shevat.

A Jew is not allowed to sell or purchase esrogim in the usual manner. To clarify: There are two ways of selling an item. One is in a business-like way, called *sechorah*. This method of sale is forbidden. The Torah mentions that it is permissible to eat shmittah fruit (*l'achlah*), indicating that some other activity is forbidden. Chazal teach that the reference is to the businesslike handling of shmittah produce (*l'achlah velo l'sechorah*). It is therefore forbidden to sell shmittah fruit to customers, whether from a storefront or a display erected on the street. All other methods of commerce are likewise forbidden under the caveat of *sechorah*.

The alternative, permissible mode of sale, is a private one made between friends or acquaintances, in an informal, unbusiness-like manner. Halachically, this type of sale is called *mechirah*, not *sechorah*. There are cases where it is difficult to determine whether the sale is classified as *mechirah* or as *sechorah*, and a Rabbi should be consulted if questions arise.

As discussed above, if money is paid for the esrog in a direct manner, the money becomes sanctified with kedushas shevi'is. In order to avoid this, reliable merchants will sell the customer a lulav and an esrog together, and stipulate that the payment is for the lulav alone, the esrog being supplied free of charge. Another way is to charge the customer for the esrog box. Some vendors sell all their shmittah esrogim for a set price to cover handling. Each esrog is sealed in a closed box. This method is truly a *hiddur* regarding kedushas shevi'is. Even if a person ends up with an esrog that is less perfect than he had hoped for, the *zehirus*, the special care in upholding the laws of shmittah, gives it an extra level of beauty.

HERBS AND SPICES DURING SHMITTAH

How was it that herbs and spices imported from Eretz Yisroel during the shmittah year of 5761 carried a reliable hechsher?

ANSWER

During the shmittah of 5761, a number of God-fearing Jews in the agricultural community of Eretz Yisroel attempted to produce spices and other goods that would be exempt from the restrictions of shmittah, by selling the fields in a way that would satisfy the objections of the Chazon Ish, *zt"l*, to the *heter mechirah* (the formula for the pre-shmittah sale of Jewish land in Eretz Yisroel employed by the State of Israel). The Chazon Ish did not accept the State's heter mechirah, based on four arguments.

Objections to heter mechirah: Firstly, the Chazon Ish considered the State's general pre-shmittah sale of Jewish land to be invalid, since it is accomplished through a *shali'ach*, an emissary of the parties interested in selling their land. It very much resembles the sale of chametz by the Rav on behalf of his community just prior to Pesach. However, selling Jewish land to a gentile is forbidden by the Torah, and the halachah states, *ein shuli'ach l'dvar aveirah* – one cannot send a representative to perform a transgression. This being the case, the sale is null and void, and the property remains Jewish

Secondly, the Chazon Ish held that any sale that does not follow due process is a mockery, *chuchah utelulah*. Any true real-estate transaction is accompanied by a proper survey of the parcel, a professional evaluation, and a bid. The sale that forms the basis of the heter mechirah does not follow these basic procedures, and thus, it cannot be taken seriously.

Thirdly, the deed and the bill of sale must be legally binding according to the laws that govern such transactions. In Eretz Yisroel, the British set up the Land Authority Registry (*Tabo*), and no sale is valid without first being recorded with the Registry, and this practice was accepted and maintained by the State of Israel. The heter mechirah land sale does not comply with the provisions of the Tabo. The transfer of land to the gentile is not recorded in the Registry, the title is not legally transferred, and the sale is not legitimate, even for religious purposes.

The Chazon Ish's fourth objection concerned the built-in condition that, at the end of the year, the original owners could buy back their land. The Chazon Ish held that a *mechirah l'zman*, a sale of limited duration, is no different than a lease. This condition effectively turns the heter mechirah sale into a one-year rental. Once again, the property remains Jewish.

Mehadrin land sale: The agricultural community in question worked in good faith to make a sale that would satisfy the concerns raised by the Chazon Ish. They made their own private sale of their land, followed due process, registered the sale with the Land Registry, and sold it outright to the gentile with no conditions. To ensure they would get their land back at the end of shmittah, they drew up a separate deed of sale that would go into effect a year later. Once the sale was completed the land was gentile-owned. On the basis of this, the community planted parsley and other spices that were marketed as free of the prohibition of *issur sefichim*, forbidden vegetation.

Eretz Yisroel is always holy: Unfortunately, this *mehadrin mechirah* did not succeed in completely eliminating the problems of shmittah. There are two *minhagim* regarding produce grown on land in Eretz Yisroel owned by a gentile. The *Yerushalmi* minhag is to treat such produce as *chullin*, that is, it possesses no kedushas shevi'is at all. However, the Chazon Ish disagreed. He held that the land of Eretz Yisroel bears kedushas shevi'is even if it is owned by gentiles, and therefore its produce has kedushas shevi'is, which would make it forbidden to destroy, market, and preserve after the time of bi'ur.[104]

(The Chazon Ish also ruled that if the gentile permits the land to be farmed by Jews, then the issur sefichim would also apply. In the above case, however, this was not applicable, as the actual farming was done by gentiles.)

Hence, according to the minhag followed in Bnei Brak, the produce in question possesses kedushas shevi'is and cannot be shipped overseas for ordinary consumption without carrying a warning that it should be treated as kedushas shevi'is.

Many authorities held that the produce should nevertheless be accepted, since the prevailing custom follows that of Yerushalayim. Since the sale of the land was valid according to the Chazon Ish, then its produce was free of kedushas shevi'is.

Eventually it was discovered that the land was owned as a general

104. פ"ד מהל' שמיטה ויובל הלכה כ"ט

partnership by all the members of the community (kibbutz) and that only the officers of the community directly participated in the sale. Despite the fact that the arrangement was one of *shutfus* (partnership), still, one partner acting on behalf of others is considered to be an act of *shlichus*. Thus, the first objection of the Chazon Ish was never really eliminated.

The traditional objection: Other halachic authorities argued that the produce was still unacceptable. The reasons that most of the major Torah communities in the world reject the validity of the sale of land in Eretz Yisroel during shmittah, differed from those given by the Chazon Ish. The most important of these reasons, was that the sale was never intended by the sellers as a real transfer of property, despite all the formal conditions attached to the sale. There is no room to compare the sale of land to the sale of chametz. When chametz is sold, the owner gives up all association with the chametz; he seals it up and has nothing to do with the products until Pesach is over, whereas when land is sold in Eretz Yisroel, the owner continues to control all decisions regarding the land's usage, sells the produce, and keeps the profits earned. Therefore, it would have to be considered a fraudulent transfer, similar to the case described in Shulchan Aruch.[105] This is the traditional and time-honored objection to the sale of the land.

Though their intentions were undoubtedly *l'shem Shamayim*, the procedures followed by those particular agricultural communities could not serve to validate the mechirah. To the author's knowledge, the practice has been discontinued.

105. חו"מ סי' צ"ט סע' ז'

MEZUZOS IN A BUNGALOW COLONY[106]

Should a person recite a blessing when affixing a mezuzah to the door of a rented cottage in a bungalow colony?

ANSWER

Some Poskim claim that according to one opinion cited in the Gemara,[107] if a dwelling is not made to be inhabited in both the winter and the summer, then it is not a considered a "house" (*bayis*) and does not require a mezuzah by Torah law. This would suggest that one should not say a blessing. Other reasons for not reciting a blessing are cited in various sefarim. Despite this opinion, it is decidedly the custom in Klal Yisroel to recite a blessing.

The author once asked a related question to Reb Moshe Feinstein, *zt"l*, when he visited Camp Agudah one summer. There was a question of where to affix the mezuzah to an entrance of a particular building in the camp. The author also asked if a brachah should be made, given that the structure would only be used in the summer. Reb Moshe answered, "Yes, you need to make a brachah." In that situation, the owners of the camp were affixing the mezuzah. It is entirely possible that the halachah would be different regarding a rental where the tenant will not be returning the next year, and the author did not think to ask about this variation. The question of a tenant is not discussed by the Poskim.

Since modern-day bungalow colonies are built to far higher standards than they were years ago, containing the modern conveniences of a standard home, there is more reason to recite a brachah upon affixing a mezuzah, even if the dwellings are not intended for winter residence. Therefore, even if a person is simply renting such a cottage for one summer, he should act in accordance with the prevailing custom, and make a blessing. Regarding a simple bungalow of the old-style, which is not suitable for winter residence, one may affix

106. יו"ד סי' רפ"ו

107. יומא י.

the mezuzah without reciting a brachah, though even in this case, the prevailing custom is to recite the brachah.

MEZUZAH ON RENTED PROPERTY[108]

Must a person wait thirty days before affixing a mezuzah to the doorpost of a bungalow, or can he affix it immediately, knowing he will reside there for at least thirty days? Does this differ from the halachah regarding year-round rentals?

ANSWER

As with any rented property, a person should not affix mezuzos unless he intends to reside there for a minimum of thirty days.[109] Once he knows he will be living there for at least thirty days, exactly when to affix the mezuzah is the subject of a halachic dispute. The Nesivos HaMishpat[110] writes that a person should affix the mezuzah immediately upon taking up residence. Other opinions maintain that he must wait until the thirtieth day.[111]

Rav Yaakov Teitelbaum, *z"l*, used to say in the name of his Rebbi, Rav Meir Arak, that one should only affix the mezuzos to a bungalow on the thirtieth day. The reason he gave was that a summer dwelling should be considered a *diras arai*, a temporary dwelling, until thirty days of actual use. The same idea appears in a teshuvah of the Iggros Moshe.[112] However, it seems that the custom is to follow the procedure used for a permanent dwelling, that is, to affix all the mezuzos except one right away, but without a blessing, and then on the thirtieth day, to affix the last mezuzah with a blessing that includes all the others.

Reb Moshe, *zt"l*, maintained that in the case of ordinary rented

108. יו"ד סי' רפ"ו
109. יו"ד סי' רפ"ו סע' כ"ב
110. מובא בפתחי תשובה סי' רפ"ו ס"ק י"ח
111. עי' פ"ת שם
112. יו"ד ח"א סי' קע"ט

dwellings that are used year-round, all the mezuzos could be affixed right away without a blessing, and that on the thirtieth day the mezuzos should be handled or touched and a blessing recited. Reb Moshe held that *mishmush* (handling), in such a case, necessitates a blessing even if the mezuzah is not removed. This is, in fact, the subject of a great dispute amongst the Rishonim. Reb Moshe therefore recommended that where possible, one mezuzah should be completely removed and reaffixed with a brachah. This halachah pertains to every rented apartment or home, not just rented summer bungalows.

REMOVING MEZUZOS[113]

At which point prior to an intended demolition, is one permitted to remove the *mezuzos* from a house, or should he wait until the last moment, since the removal of *mezuzos* can constitute a sakanah, a danger?

ANSWER

If the house is to be demolished, there is no danger in removing the mezuzos immediately upon moving out. The danger in removing mezuzos only exists if someone else is going to move into the house. Rav Henkin, *zt"l*, used to say that it is even permissible to remove the mezuzos when vacating a home if the new tenant is planning to paint, since in any event the mezuzos will have to be removed before he moves in.

TEACHING CHUMASH[114]

All opinions agree that a father must teach his son *Mikra* (Chumash). Yet, people send their children to yeshivos, and

113. יו"ד סי' רצ"א

114. או"ח סי' רפ"ה, יו"ד סי' רמ"ה

the curriculum (*seder halimud*) does not usually account for finishing Chumash. Parents, too, are willing to hire a tutor to help their children finish Mishnayos before their bar-mitzvah, and perhaps even Shas before their wedding, but the proper study of Chumash is somewhat neglected. Is it enough for a father to rely on the fact that the yeshivah will teach his son the obligation (*chiyuv*) to learn Chumash, and that the son will eventually become accustomed to learning the parshah each week with Rashi?

ANSWER

The study of Chumash is extremely important and requires a special effort. Every Jew should arrange to go over the parshah (*ma'avir sedra*) each week, as stated in the Shulchan Aruch.[115] One should not just mindlessly read each verse twice followed by a reading of the Targum, but should pay attention to every word and its meaning. Additionally, a person should encourage his children and students to learn the parshah with Targum and Rashi, and not simply hope that the child's educational ideology will inspire him to do it sometime in the future.

The author relates an experience from his late 'teens: "On the second day of Shavuos, I was studying *Yatziv Pisgam* (a *piyut* which is recited along with that day's Haftarah from Chavakuk) with my chavrusa. We were having difficulty while examining the meaning of some of the words, when we were approached by a Jew who had come over from Europe after the war. Though he was not a learned man, he had been meticulous in regularly reviewing the Targum, and was sufficiently versed in Aramaic to explain every troublesome word. Even in troubled times, he had set aside time to learn the Targum, something that his parents and rebbis had insisted upon from an early age. From this episode, I clearly saw the great value in emphasizing the importance of learning Chumash with the Targum."

115. או"ח סי' רפ"ה סע' ב'

CHECKING FOR SHAATNEZ[116]

Which types of apparel must be checked for *shaatnez*? When buying clothing from a Jewish store or manufacturer, can it be assumed to be free of *shaatnez*?

ANSWER

Shaatnez issues arise when there is a mixture of linen and wool in any form. The exception to this rule is where either the linen or the wool becomes *batul*, or nullified. Questions of shaatnez occur most commonly when strong linen threads are used to sew buttons onto woolen clothing and upholstery, or to sew seams in places that need strengthening. Especially durable linen material is sometimes used for shoulder pads, collar reinforcements, and other areas in need of support. There are also cases where decorative trimmings often found on women's dresses and other garments, contain various wool and linen components, even if the garment itself is made of synthetic material. Occasionally, the primary fabric of the garment is itself made of a blend of wool and linen. This last concern is almost never present in fabrics produced in the United States. European textile plants, however, weave wool and linen together for reinforcement in a large percentage of their fabrics. The percentage of imported textiles in the U.S. market increases on a yearly basis, and this issue is of growing concern.

As a general rule, any woolen suit regardless of origin, should always be checked by a shaatnez expert to ensure it is free of any concerns. Clothing made of one hundred percent synthetic materials generally does not have to be checked, but to avoid problems, one should keep informed of alerts issued by recognized shaatnez laboratories, such as those in Flatbush, Williamsburg, Lakewood and Monsey, or other reputable shaatnez experts. They are staffed by highly skilled technicians who know the field very well.

With regard to relying on the word of the clothing manufacturers

116. יו"ד סי' רח"צ

and distributors, there are many fine and upstanding religious Jews in the clothes manufacturing business who are very meticulous and careful to avoid any question of shaatnez. Unfortunately, there are others who are not as particular.

The author has personally appeared before a Rabbinical Board to show evidence of *frum*-looking Jews who buy, manufacture, and sell *shaatnez*, whilst reassuring their customers that all their products are totally shaatnez-free. Due to the existence of such disreputable manufacturers and distributers, one must always check with the shaatnez laboratories and ask about a particular garment, or have the garment checked. If a garment is found to contain a mixture of wool and linen, it should be brought to the attention of the Rabbanim who would hopefully raise the proper cry of alarm and protect the public from such deception, as is their sacred duty. The above applies throughout the United States. In other locations one should consult with local Rabbanim who have knowledge of shaatnez issues in their area, and who can advise a person as to how to deal with local circumstances.

RELYING ON SHAATNEZ BATCH-TESTING

If the store says that they had the clothing made especially for them, and they tested several samples from the batch and found them to be free of *shaatnez*, do the garments still need to be checked?

ANSWER

The shaatnez experts say that if a large percentage of a specific company's clothing is found to be consistently free of shaatnez, it is highly unlikely that shaatnez would be found in their other garments. If this is the case, according to the strict letter of the law (*al pi din*), checking every piece of clothing from that company would not be required. To be on the safe side, it is still advisable to have every garment inspected.

CUSHIONS AND PILLOWS

Is one allowed to use pillows and cushions which contain a variety of mixed fibers, given the concern that they might contain *shaatnez*?

ANSWER

There exists a very strong case to permit their use, as will become clear from a brief history of the issue.

The Torah forbids a Jew from wearing a garment made of linen and wool, known as *shaatnez*. According to the Torah, the mixture is only forbidden if the fibers of linen and wool are combed or blended together, spun, and then woven (*shua, tavui, v'noz*) into one piece of fabric.[117] Chazal decreed that even if the fibers are simply spun or pressed together into felt, the substance is forbidden to use. According to the Rambam,[118] felt made from these fibers is *assur min haTorah*.

In olden times, the very greatest *medakdekim b'mitzvos*, those Jews who were exceedingly meticulous in their observance of mitzvos, were careful never to sit on cushions or mattresses made from shredded fibers. It was a very big *chumrah* for two reasons. Firstly, there was only a very slight possibility that these cushions and mattresses were flexible enough to wrap around a person and give him warmth. It is permissible to sit on stiff objects, even if they contain shaatnez.[119] Secondly, such cushions and mattresses only contain linen and wool fibers, not woven shaatnez, and the halachah follows the other Rishonim, that a mixture of linen and wool fibers is only *assur miderabbanan*. Thus, these pious Jews acted in deference to the lone opinion of the Rambam, and were machmir even with stiff cushions and mattresses, that could only vaguely be seen as providing warmth and protection in the manner of a piece of fabric that is worn. For

117. כלאים פ"ט מ"ח
118. הלכות כלאים פ"י ה"ב
119. יומא סט.

these reasons, such cushions were seen by the great majority of Klal Yisroel as entirely permissible, but were avoided by the scrupulous.

The situation with cushion and mattress stuffing today is different than it was many years ago. This is due to the preponderance of cotton and synthetic fibers in the textile industry. By combining the wool and linen with a third substance (*min shlishi*) that is greater in proportion to either the wool or the linen, any shaatnez that might be present is nullified. Once this is done, the fibers can even be spun and woven into a fabric. Halachah permits shaatnez to be nullified even if the wool and linen combination had been created first, before the introduction of the cotton or synthetic fibers.

The fibers used for stuffing cushions are made entirely from offcuts from the garment and upholstery industries. They are sold in bulk to shredding factories, who make the stuffing that is used in anything from baseball gloves to shoulder pads to upholstery. These shredding factories purchase whatever scrap material is available. In today's market, most of the fabrics are synthetic and wool, whilst linen accounts for only a very small percentage of the total. It is always the case that the crushed fiber fillings contain at least enough synthetics to nullify the linen, and often there is enough to nullify even the wool. This means that today, there is no reason at all to be concerned about shaatnez in cushions and mattresses.

Recently, a group of people attempted to restore the concern, claiming that linen threads do not completely unravel in the shredding process and pieces of linen thread an inch or longer could be found in textile stuffing. These threads, they claimed, are considered to be significant (*davar chashuv*), therefore, they can never become nullified, even with the addition of a third type of fiber. Little credence should be given to this claim, however. The reasoning is flawed both with regard to the halachah, and in its portrayal of the reality of the textile industry today. It is of no halachic concern.

REQUIREMENT TO CHECK FOR SHAATNEZ

Is it enough to send a sample of the material in question to a laboratory for inspection, or must a person bring the article of clothing itself to a qualified shaatnez checker?

ANSWER

Everyone should take their clothes to a competent shaatnez laboratory for a thorough checking, and never rely on the perfunctory tests done by drycleaners and manufacturers of the material. More and more often, fabrics and articles of clothing are found to be shaatnez by virtue of some hidden lining, or added trimming or stitching. Qualified shaatnez laboratories are privy to the most recent information, and know where to look for a problem. If a person is unsure which articles of clothing are in need of shaatnez checking, he should call a reliable tester and ask.

SENSITIVE SHIDDUCH INFORMATION

When is the appropriate time to mention important, yet sensitive, personal information that may have a bearing on the outcome of a shidduch?

ANSWER

This is an extremely important question. There is no standard answer, since the circumstances vary from situation to situation. Each case should be discussed individually with a talmid chacham or Rav to ensure that it is handled appropriately, and the details revealed at the proper time and in the most appropriate and sensitive manner. There are two basic guidelines.

There are certain factors which are considered to be major pieces of information. If, for instance, someone was once married and is now divorced, to withhold this information is definitely a deception. A person who discovers basic information like this only after several meetings would be extremely offended. Similarly, a matchmaker (*shadchan*) should never hide such crucial information about the background of the people they wish to introduce. If the man or woman is a convert (*ger tzedek*) this must be made known. A person who becomes engaged only to find out such a fact, can justifiably claim that the shidduch was a mistake, a *mekach ta'us*. Information of this type must be mentioned as a matter of course, even before the couple meets.

There are other pieces of information that are of lesser consequence. An example would be if a person suffers from some minor condition that would not generally interfere with married life. There may be a remote chance that it may have an impact on the couple's lifestyle, but it is a condition that is under control. Things like this must be mentioned before the engagement, but it need only be mentioned when the individuals become more serious about each other, and the possibility of engagement is real.

There are many types of minor personal flaws that people suffer from, and they need not, and indeed should not be mentioned at the very beginning. By mentioning them too early on, the matter can be blown out of proportion and taken as a sign that there is something seriously wrong, and thus ruin a perfectly good shidduch.

Many issues fall somewhere in between these two ends of the spectrum, while other details need not be mentioned at all. Sometimes there is a condition that existed many years ago and has long since been healed. Physical or emotional problems that disappeared fifteen years previously, and are no longer an issue, should generally not be mentioned, and in most cases can be discussed by the couple themselves later in life, once they have married and settled down.

As we mentioned above, these are only general guidelines. Every case needs to be discussed with a mature, responsible, and very wise person steeped in Torah. Such a person will be able to consider all the variables, and can guide the parties involved, based on a clear knowledge of the situation.

In any case, where some piece of information must be revealed to the other party, it should be done with tact and discretion. It should never be presented as if one were disclosing some dark and shadowy secret. This would only alarm the other party unnecessarily, and would be magnified out of proportion to its true significance. For this reason one should always try and mitigate the seriousness of a problem by presenting it matter-of-factly, and as a minor and inconsequential issue. It is almost always the case that the listener will significantly multiply the gravity of any issue. By intentionally downplaying a problem, others will come to judge its true level of importance correctly, without undue exaggeration.

Professional Kashrus Issues

The questions and answers in the following section provide background information for a host of practical kashrus considerations in the kosher meat and poultry industries. Its contents are of particular interest to Jewish professionals and lay-leaders involved in kashrus supervision. The kosher consumer, too, will gain a new appreciation for the multifaceted realm of modern kashrus supervision, and the importance of being aware of current issues as they affect the standards of kashrus in the home.

AVAILABILITY OF GLATT KOSHER RED MEAT

What is the current status of *glatt* meat in the United States? According to one report, there are an insufficient number of truly *glatt* animals, whose lungs have no lesions. Other

information suggests that any meat that is not entirely glatt is immediately sold as treif to the gentiles.

ANSWER

Both pieces of information are correct, and reflect two sides of a growing dilemma in the kosher cattle industry.

Most cattle are not glatt: Each subspecies of steer can be assumed to have a certain percentage of animals that have no lesions (*sirchos*) on their lungs at all, and are popularly referred to as '*glatt Beis Yosef*.' Animals having just a few minor lesions that are easily removed and leave no trace on the lungs, are generally referred to simply as '*glatt*', and are acceptable to those who eat *glatt kosher*. Bulls and older cows, whose tougher, sometimes leaner meat is suitable for salami and frankfurters, have a very low ratio of glatt to non-glatt; only one animal in twenty (5%) may be glatt. Young cows and steers, which are more tender and preferred for fresh cuts of meat, produce more glatt meat, with seven or eight animals out of every twenty (35–40%) being acceptable. Consequently, a high percentage of slaughtered cattle are unsuitable for today's glatt market. Additionally, the custom in the United States is not to process the rear half of the animal by painstakingly removing the forbidden fats (*cheilev*) and the sciatic nerve (*gid ha'nasheh*). Instead the animal is cut in half, and the rear section from the thirteenth rib and back is sold as treif. Ultimately, around eighty-five percent of kosher-slaughtered red meat is labeled treif.

The decline in gentile demand for fresh red meat: This has created a serious financial difficulty. In the early years, when the demand for kosher meat was smaller and the gentile appetite for choice red meat was in its prime, there was no difficulty in selling off the non-glatt animals and rear-sections to gentile slaughterhouses. However, the gentile affinity for quality red meat is waning in response to public awareness of the dangers of high cholesterol posed by a diet rich in red meat. In contrast, the demand for kosher meat is rising along with the numbers and affluence of the observant Jewish community, *kein* *yirbu*, and the desire to celebrate Shabbos and Yom Tov meals with quality red meat. This means that the great surplus of non-glatt kosher meat can no longer be easily sold at its proper value to gentile butchers. Instead, it is sold at a much lower price to processors who grind the meat and supply it to the booming fast-food burger industry.

The loss in revenue is significant enough that kosher slaughterhouses are now spending more money to purchase younger cattle that have a significantly higher proportion of glatt animals in order to cut their losses. For this purpose, kosher slaughterhouses maintain millions of dollars in rollover accounts just to purchase the better cattle, which must be paid for upon delivery, as opposed to older cattle that can be bought on credit. Thus, when all is said and done, there is an adequate supply of high quality glatt-kosher meat in the marketplace. The demand of "תנה לנו בשר ונאכלה – *Give us meat and we will eat it*," can now be satisfied without being met by the hopeless response of, "מאין לי בשר – *From where shall I bring meat...?*" (Bamidbar 11:13).

NIKKUR & MELICHAH[1]

What are the main steps in the process of kashering meat?

ANSWER

Three things must be removed from kosher slaughtered meat before it can be eaten: the sciatic nerve (*gid ha'nasheh*), the forbidden fats (*cheilev*), and the blood (*dam*). In addition, there are other fats and veins that are removed according to Rabbinic law or custom.

Blood: There are two processes that are performed to remove forbidden blood from red meat. The first is the removal of certain blood vessels, and the second is the salting and rinsing of the meat.

The concept of kashering meat through salting is familiar to practically every Jew. Indeed, for generations meat was bought from the

1. יו"ד סי' ס"ד

butcher cut and *menukar* (discussed below), while the salting and rinsing of the meat was done at home. But it is rare these days to find anyone outside the kashrus industry that has ever seen it done. In our generation of mass kosher food production, children grow up never having once witnessed the process.

Kashering involves three basic steps. There is the initial rinsing (*hadachah rishonah*), the salting (*melichah*), and the final rinsing (*hadachah sheniah*). It is a worthwhile endeavor to learn how to kasher meat, and to demonstrate it to one's children so they should know that such a thing exists.

Nikkur: Before kashering red meat, certain blood vessels (*chutei dam*), are removed. There are specific arteries and veins in various cuts of meat that need to be removed. Almost all of them are buried deep inside the flesh. An experienced *menaker* knows just where to cut in order to find them. If an inexperienced person tries to locate these blood vessels, he will likely end up tearing the meat to shreds.

The very tiny blood vessels do not need to be removed; tradition requires only the removal of certain larger vessels. Interestingly, in the United States, we follow the minhag of the Rema and remove several chutei dam that are left by the menakrim in Eretz Yisroel. For instance, we cut into the underside of the tongue and remove four chutei dam, while in Eretz Yisroel the custom is to simply slash through them.

The difference in customs can actually present a problem. In the United States, it is very difficult to find experienced Jewish menakrim. People are not interested in learning the trade. Many young menakrim come to the States from Eretz Yisroel in order to make a living, but they have only been trained in *minhag Eretz Yisroel* which leaves groups of veins and arteries that must be removed according to the practice in the United States, which stems from the custom prevailing in Europe dating back to the Rishonim.[2] This has to be watched, and

2. ראה באגרות רבי חיים עוזר גרודזינסקי זצ"ל (ב"ב תש"ס) אגרת שלט, להגרצ"פ פראנק אב"ד ירושלים: "הנני לשאול את רומעכת"ר ע"ד הניקור מחלק אחוריים...ובכלל הוגד לי כי בעניני החיטוט מקילים ביותר אצלם, והייתי רוצה לדעת בדיוק מה שמקילים. מכבר שמעתי כי אין

the menakrim should be trained to remove all such chutei dam. Anyone who hires a menaker should not simply entrust his new worker with the kashrus of his shop without first ascertaining that he does his job in the proper way.

Cheilev: It is assumed by most people that the fats forbidden by the Torah (*cheilev*) are found in the hindquarters of the animal. In the United States, the hindquarters from the thirteenth rib and back are cut off and processed as non-kosher meat. Thus, a person might be tempted to think that there is little room for concern over *cheilev* in kosher meat, which comes only from the forequarters.

This is not entirely true. Even in the forequarters, there are a few places that contain *cheilev d'Oraisa*, and we use these cuts of meat. There may be a touch of cheilev on the extension of the liver that must be removed (*etzba hakaved*). Also, there is a very expensive cut of meat called the hanging tender. Both of these are connected to the *cheilev ha'kelayos* (kidney fat). According to most opinions, there is also an extension of *cheilev hakesalim* on a cut of meat taken from the abdominal muscle plate by the navel,[3] and if it is not removed, there could easily be a full measure (*kezayis*) of it.

There are also Rabbinically forbidden fats, and other pieces of fat that connect to the cheilev (*yonek min hacheilev*) which are removed according to custom. Though these fats are not nearly as serious as cheilev, they should never intentionally be left.

The author was once asked to inspect a traditionally reliable kosher restaurant, after someone suggested that they were serving cuts of lamb meat with the cheilev still attached. This establishment would buy the freshest meat and perform their own nikkur, and they employed a mashgiach with many years of experience. The owner of the restaurant, the butcher, and the mashgiach each inspected the lambs they showed me, and were at a loss to explain why anyone would suggest there was

מנקרים אצלם חלק הפנים בבית המטבחים וסומכים על חתכי' ומלחי' שפיר דמי, ושאלתי מכבר אצל הגאון קוק זצ"ל והשיב לי כי זהו קלקלה מכבר ואי אפשר לתקן".

3. חולין צג. וברש"י ד"ה שהבשר חופה עליו

any cheilev. Now, all lambs have cheilev attached to the navel, and even though that piece of meat is very tasty, there is no way to clean off the cheilev, and it must simply be cut off and discarded. Unfortunately for this restaurant, they had never identified this piece of cheilev for they mistakenly looked at the meat upside-down, and thought the cheilev was simply a piece of permitted fat. The allegation was indeed true.

GENTILE LABOR IN KOSHER MEAT PROCESSING

Can gentiles be hired to perform *nikkur* and other aspects of kashering meat?

ANSWER

Gentiles can be hired to perform any and every aspect of kashering and processing kosher meat, provided that they are under constant Jewish supervision and that a Jew inspects the meat at the end of the line. Perhaps ninety percent of kashering work is done by gentiles today. It is not as in olden times, when a person could walk into a butcher and see a line of *ehrlicher Yidden* one after the other, working at *nikkur* and *melichah*. There are simply not enough Jews willing to do this kind of work anymore.

Another reason for this is that the bulk of the work is now done at the slaughterhouses, which are located far away from the centers of Jewish population. If the system is to work properly, the mashgiach must see to it that the gentiles are thoroughly trained, and he must constantly test and inspect the standard of their work. Just because a gentile worker did a fantastic job last week does not mean he will do so this week. Even with Jewish workers there should be periodic evaluation, but at least we know that they are aware of the importance of what they are doing and desire to do a consistently good job. A gentile worker has no vested interest in ensuring that he removes every necessary vein or piece of fat. The only motivating factor is that he will be held accountable if even a small piece of these veins and fat are found remaining. In any case, whether the workers are Jewish or gentile, there must always be a mashgiach inspecting each and every cut of meat as it comes off the line.

THE SEVENTY-TWO HOUR RULE (BASAR OVEIR)[4]

At what point does unsalted meat become *treif*? With today's centralized meat processing, have these issues been resolved?

ANSWER

Meat: There is a limit to how much time may elapse between the shechitah and the kashering of the meat. Meat that is not washed and salted within seventy-two hours can only be kashered by roasting (*tzli*).[5] Most people who discover that the meat in their possession had not been salted within seventy-two hours, have no experience in roasting meat for the purposes of kashering. Standard roasting is likely insufficient, for it is not always performed as thoroughly as what Chazal consider true *tzli*. Thus, for all practical purposes, meat that was not kashered within seventy-two hours would not be considered kosher. At the very least, it would be unfit for cooking.

Washing extends the limit: In the days when butchers kashered the meat, it would often be difficult to process the meat within this allotted amount of time. Sometimes, the animals were slaughtered close to Shabbos, with Yom Tov following immediately afterwards. If the butcher waited until after the 'three-day Yom Tov' to kasher the meat, the seventy-two hours would have passed, and the meat would have to be thrown out. To extend the amount of time within which the meat could be kashered, it was washed (*hadachah*), giving the

4. יו"ד סי' ס"ט
5. יו"ד סי' ס"ט סע' י"ב

butcher another seventy-one and a half hours.[6] This washing was one of the processes which required great supervision to ensure it was done properly. Otherwise, the meat could become permanently treif or fit for roasting only.

In former times, when meat was shipped straight after slaughter, it was a common occurrence that the truck would not arrive at the butcher within seventy-two hours. The truck would have to be stopped and the meat taken out and washed. It was not uncommon for the washing to be done entirely improperly. Although currently this happens far less frequently, it is still an issue that arises, especially when freshly slaughtered meat is delivered to butchers in outlying Jewish communities.

Today, kosher meat in the United States does not usually undergo this interim washing; all the processing is done in the packing plants and arrives at the butcher kashered and packaged. It is a great relief to be able to avoid the entire experience of washing the meat en-route, because not everyone considers washed meat to be *mehadrin*, choice kosher meat. Nevertheless, from time to time, it happens that some meat cannot be processed within the requisite seventy-two hours, and the plant will elect to wash the meat so as not to have to sell it to gentiles at a loss. Thus, boxes of washed meat can appear on the market, and they usually end up being sold to smaller Jewish communities under the mistaken assumption that the Jews living there are less concerned about higher kashrus standards than those living in the major Jewish population centers such as New York. An out-of-town Rabbi should keep this consideration in mind, especially if some members of his *kehillah* would never knowingly agree to eat such meat. In the event of washed meat being shipped to the butcher of his community, he will have to decide whether to accept the shipment or not. If he does decide to accept the shipment, the butcher should be instructed to inform his customers that the meat in question is "washed," so as to avoid selling the meat to someone who does not wish to rely on this leniency.

6. יו"ד סי' ס"ט סע' י"ג

Kavush: There is another potential pitfall involving the shipping of meat. Sometimes, meat is delivered in what the industry commonly calls a 'combo.' This is a large container of various cuts of freshly slaughtered meat. If these containers are not drained properly, the meat can end up soaking in a large quantity of blood and other liquids for more than twenty-four hours. In the event that this happens, the meat is considered pickled (*kavush*) in the blood, and is permanently treif. This is a serious concern that presents itself often, even today.

Liver: Livers may be kept for more than seventy two hours, because they will surely be roasted as the halachah requires, but the limit of seventy-two hours still creates a serious and very common concern. While many Poskim, including the Aruch HaShulchan,[7] hold that liver can still be cooked even if it was roasted only after seventy-two hours, many great Poskim disagree, and forbid cooking livers that were roasted after seventy-two hours. This is apparent from the responsa brought by the commentaries on the Shulchan Aruch, and most b'nei Torah follow this standard, as do many others. An indication of the widespread acceptance of this view is its inclusion in the collection of halachos, prepared in Yiddish by HaRav S.Z. Auerbach, *zt"l*, when he was in his early twenties, for one edition of the *Korban Minchah* siddur for women. This suggests that it was common practice in Eretz Yisroel for decades to cook only those livers that had undergone roasting within the seventy-two hour limit.

Butcher stores commonly receive liver that is roasted after three days (seventy-two hours), yet caterers prefer to also cook the roasted liver to give it a smoother texture. As there are many people who are unaware of the higher standard kept by many Jews, caterers and other food establishments might cook liver that was only kashered after the seventy-two hour limit. A Rav needs to be aware of this issue and ensure that any liver delivered to his establishment be certified as roasted within seventy-two hours, if it is to be eventually cooked.

Kavush must also be considered when packaging livers. Many

7. יו"ד סי' ס"ט סע' ע'

processing plants ship chicken livers with the chickens they package by placing them in a small plastic bag to keep the un-kashered livers away from the rest of the chicken. If the juices from the livers are allowed to come in contact with the chicken for an extended period of time, the chicken might be rendered treif. On the other hand, if there is no drainage, the livers themselves can inadvertently soak for more than twenty-four hours in blood. It is therefore important to ensure that livers are packaged properly, with an absorbent pad, or with holes that allow the blood to drain in a way that it does not come in contact with the meat of the chicken.

Last-minute kashering: Wherever there is a time constraint, for instance where the meat arrives at the butcher at the sixty-ninth hour, and the de-veining and nikkur must be done in a rush, a Rav must be present to supervise and assure that the meat will be kashered properly and will not become treif. By making himself available in a crisis, the mashgiach is not only protecting the kosher consumer, but also the investment of the butcher.

It should not be forgotten that nikkur must be performed before the salting. If for whatever reason the salting was done before the forbidden sinews were removed, much of the meat is rendered permanently treif.

FROZEN MEAT AND BASAR OVEIR

If the meat is frozen right after slaughtering, can we then wait more than seventy-two hours?

ANSWER

The Aruch HaShulchan[8] maintains that as long as meat is frozen solid, it is not counted as part of the seventy-two hours. Certainly, a person can always rely upon the word of the Aruch HaShulchan.

8. יו"ד סי' ס"ט סע' ע"ט

On the other hand, meat that was frozen in order to allow for kashering after seventy-two hours is not considered mehadrin by many segments of the Orthodox population these days.

In the United States there is no such thing as official non-mehadrin meat. All meat with reliable kashrus supervision keeps the same standard and only relies upon accepted leniencies in cases of great loss. Thus, kosher meat produced and sold in the United States is not frozen before kashering.

In Eretz Yisroel, however, much of the standard Rabbanut meat is imported frozen, and kashered only after it arrives. All Israeli mehadrin meat is kashered at the place of slaughter and only then is it frozen and shipped.

A particular group once requested that we allow certain products to be marketed in the United States as 'non-mehadrin,' as is the practice in Eretz Yisroel. Our response was that it would create a very complicated situation that would be extremely difficult to supervise and control. Supervising agencies are finding that controlling existing kashrus issues is already a sufficient challenge, without adding the complications involved in having two kashrus standards.

Liver: When it comes to liver, the permission of the Aruch HaShulchan that allows freezing, has a very practical consequence. Generally, one must be sure to roast liver within seventy-two hours. This is to avoid a dispute amongst Poskim about whether liver can be cooked or baked after roasting if the roasting was done after seventy-two hours, as mentioned above. If, however, the liver was frozen, then almost all opinions allow for leniency, and view the liver as still within the seventy-two hours for the purposes of cooking the liver afterwards.

KASHERING LIVER

What must be done to kasher liver?

ANSWER

Livers leave the slaughterhouses unprocessed. It is up to the butchers or their clients to kasher the livers properly. Liver can only be kashered by roasting.

Beef liver: Unlike chicken liver, beef liver has the additional concern of forbidden fats (*cheilev*). The extension of the liver touches the kidney, and the fat surrounding the kidney (*cheilev ha'kelayos*) is forbidden by the Torah, and a person who eats it is liable for *kareis* (a decree of spiritual separation from HaKadosh Baruch Hu, as well as an early death). Some of this fat adheres to the liver, and must be removed. As mentioned above the custom is to also remove the other fats (*yonek min hacheilev*) from the liver. There are also veins that must be removed from a liver. If some of these fats should inadvertently be left in place, even the small piece of actual cheilev, we can rely on the fact that it becomes nullified in the rest of the meat if it is ground up. However, this is never something to rely upon initially, and the fats must always be skillfully and completely removed.

Once, the author visited a particular establishment well-known for its quality beef liver. The owners were God-fearing Jews, and they employed a full-time mashgiach to ensure that the livers were cleaned and roasted according to the strictest standards. There were racks upon racks of liver waiting to be roasted, and each one was perfectly clean of fat, except for a little bit on the extension of the liver (*etzba hakaved*). When asked why they left that small piece of fat when they were so careful to remove everything else, the workers all replied, "Oh, that piece of fat is nothing at all, so we don't remove it." It turned out that the mashgiach had never been informed of the fact that that fat is forbidden, and for years he had trained the workers to leave it. Needless to say, the owners, the mashgiach, and all the employees were aghast at the error and corrected it immediately.

It is noteworthy that no one ran to the streets to make a scandal about this issue. No public furor was raised. This was the wise response, and the problem was corrected without any fanfare. Lamentably, in a similar occurrence of more recent vintage, scandal mongers unnecessarily made a frightening experience out of an honest mistake, causing much worry to great numbers of Klal Yisroel.

Roasting requirements: There are two requirements when it comes to roasting livers. Kosher roasting needs a bright flame, and it has to be hot enough to cause the liver to roast and not just bake. There is a tendency on the part of restaurateurs and caterers to bake liver at a setting of about 180 degrees Fahrenheit for several hours, which leaves the liver soft and smooth. This is unacceptable for kashering, but it was only recently that this practice was abandoned. The author remembers being given a tour of a large liver roasting operation that had certification.

The oven was more of a smoke house; its interior was almost completely dark. Not seeing the heat source immediately, I asked the owner to show me where the broiling fire was located. He told me that, if I close my eyes for a minute or two and get used to the darkness, then by carefully looking in a particular direction, I would be able to discern the faint glow of the heat source. I told him immediately, that this was entirely unacceptable and that certification would have to be withdrawn.

It took much effort by many Rabbanim over a period of several years to implement proper kashering of livers in kosher food establishments across the country.

KOSHER MEAT PROCESSING & HASHGACHAH

Most meat these days comes prepackaged, with kosher certification on the label. Is it still necessary for the mashgiach of a local butcher shop to be trained in the halachos of forbidden fats (*cheilev*) and removal of sinews (*nikkur*)?

ANSWER

The need to know nikkur: Effectiveness and authority are two interrelated reasons why it is important for a Rav or mashgiach involved in kosher meat supervision to know about cheilev and nikkur.

Firstly, practical training in nikkur and cheilev gives the Rav the ability to effectively supervise a butcher's nikkur and verify that he indeed removed the non-kosher sinews. Not long ago, kosher meat was primarily processed by individual butchers. A butcher would purchase a fore-quarter of beef, or a whole cow, and would cut the meat, remove forbidden fats and sinews, and then salt and kasher the meat. The same applied to livers and chickens. This made the supervision of these processes very challenging, for there was no centralized location and little or no control over the hundreds of individual butchers. From time to time there were problems, when a Rav would discover that some delivery of meat was mishandled. Signs would go up throughout the community warning of the *treif* meat. In such circumstances, practical knowledge of nikkur was essential for the Rav.

The move to centralized meat-packing: The situation began to change about thirty years ago, when the kosher meat industry in the United States experienced a very unpleasant incident regarding the quality of nikkur it provided. A certain Jew from Eretz Yisroel, an expert in performing nikkur, inspected several facilities in America and found numerous problems that distressed him. Though many of his complaints were baseless, some were very much on the mark. The American Rabbanim organized a meeting to discuss how to deal with the scandal and respond to the accusations.

Many Rabbanim were reluctant to train themselves in nikkur

because it involved dirty and bloody work. It was argued that even the Rabbanim in Europe did not traditionally receive such training. There was a flaw in this argument. In Europe, the Rabbanim did not need to learn the art of nikkur, because their assistants were butchers who were faithful to the Rav, and these assistants would accompany the Rav on all his inspections and take care of the more disagreeable tasks.

Here in America, the Rabbanim did not have these faithful assistants, and were unable to provide proper supervision. Thus, it was that some of the complaints were justified. Either the Rabbanim had to find assistants, or learn the trade themselves. Seeing that not many others seemed willing, the author worked with butchers and trained himself in all aspects of the meat industry, practicing nikkur in his spare time on treif pieces of meat. Partially as a result of that meeting, the move to centralized kosher meat processing began. In addition, and perhaps more importantly, the slaughterhouses close to New York closed down and the new ones that opened were too far away to permit nikkur at the butchers due to the time gap caused by long distance transportation.

For the above reasons, most kosher meat preparation nowadays takes place in the slaughterhouse. Regular beef cattle are slaughtered in large houses with plenty of Rabbinical supervision and a team of experienced *menakrim*, who remove the forbidden fats and sinews and kasher the meat. Admittedly, this removes much of the need for cheilev and nikkur supervision by the mashgiach of the local kosher meat stores. Nevertheless, there remain many vestiges of the old system.

Veal and specialty meat: Certain types of meat are not processed in the slaughterhouse. A good example of this is veal, tender cuts of meat from young calves. Young calves are only slaughtered in small operations, and they do not have the staff to treat and kasher the meat. It is therefore sent straight to the butchers, and they must perform nikkur and kasher the meat themselves. The Rabbis that supervise these butchers need to be aware of the processes of nikkur and salting in order to properly supervise the kashering of veal.

Additionally, some butchers, restaurants and caterers will only buy whole sides of unprocessed, unkashered beef. They claim that the meat is much fresher and tastier when it is kashered right before cooking. Supervising Rabbis at establishments receiving red meat from these sources have to know the details of nikkur and salting well.

A mashgiach who knows how to perform nikkur also knows what a piece of meat looks like before the sinews have been removed. Thus, he will not simply see a mass of raw cuts of meat, but will immediately recognize the occasional slice of meat that arrived at the butcher unprocessed. Also, butchers sometimes buy kosher meat 'on sale' from suppliers, but the reason for the low price is often due to the fact the meat has not undergone nikkur. Since many butchers today are unfamiliar with nikkur, the mashgiach might be the only one who would notice, but only if he has had the training.

The Rav's authority: The Gemara[9] mentions that Torah sages (*talmidei chachamim*) must learn three things: *k'sav* (the scribal art of *safrus*), *shechitah* (kosher slaughter), and *milah* (ritual circumcision). Though all scholars in Rabbinical positions are challenged from time to time by some aggressive members of their constituencies, none are put to the test more than the young new Rav. The local *klei kadosh*: the professional Jewish scribe, shochet, and mohel, being experienced and knowledgeable in their crafts naturally present the most formidable challenge to the young Rav's authority. It is therefore imperative for a Rav to familiarize himself with these areas of halachah before assuming his position and thereby demonstrate his competency and gain the respect of the community. This also applies to a *Rav Ha'machshir* (certifying Rabbi) or mashgiach when he assumes his position in the food industry.

When it comes to kosher meat, Chazal[10] mention the singular halachah that the shochet "must show his knife to the Rav" every day, before he commences ritual slaughter. This was instituted, the Gemara explains, "Only for the sake of the Rav's honor." The halachah

9. חולין ט.
10. שם י:, יח.

emphasizes that the shochet must accept the will and authority of the Rav.

In the olden days, shechitah simply would not proceed until the Rav had inspected the knife. If there was a bris milah that morning that the Rav had to perform, then the shochet waited. In our times, a shochet receives extensive training before receiving an official letter of certification (*kabbalah*), such that a shochet today is thoroughly versed in all the applicable halachos, including how to sharpen and inspect the slaughtering knife. Today's shochet is therefore considered a "Rav" with regard to shechitah, and can examine his own knife.[11]

A knowledgeable Rav: Yet the esteem in which the Rav is held is no less important today than in days of old, for the value of his hashgachah depends upon it. He must have the authority to inspect the knife and demand its sharpening even today, and his instruction must be seen as authoritative and binding. The staff of a kosher butcher shop or meat plant generally has at least a basic knowledge of what the Torah requires of them. There is a tendency for people, therefore, to justify what they have done in the face of criticism. It is imperative that if the Rav determines a cut of meat or an entire case of goods to be unacceptable, his decision will be accepted and implemented without question. This will only happen if the Rav can demonstrate a working knowledge of the trade, in addition to a mastery of all the pertinent halachos. Conversely, any Rav or mashgiach who is ignorant of the practical side of the industry he supervises can be easily fooled, and this is a serious threat to the effectiveness of his supervision. Thus, small-town Rabbanim must know the meat trade. They are the only ones in a position to test the reliability of the local butcher, and preserve the integrity of the supply of kosher meat to the congregation. This is even true for many Rabbanim in cities with large Jewish populations. At the very least, a modicum of knowledge of the basic issues is essential. In this way, a Rav will be able to spot irregularities, and call in a more knowledgeable Rav for clarification.

11. יו"ד סי' י"ח סי"ז

The author was once asked to inspect a traditionally reliable kosher butcher. The mashgichim knew enough to sense that something had gone awry with the meat, but could not precisely identify the problem. Upon close inspection, it turned out that the meat was not being properly de-veined, despite the fact that this establishment employed their own private menaker, who had been with them for many years. In the early years, the menaker would do the job himself, but as he aged, he began to realize that he was incapable of continuing the work. Nikkur requires strong, steady hands, and his had weakened. Instead, he hired and trained several gentiles to do the work for him, and he supervised. This system worked well for many years, but the menaker continued to age to the point he could not even properly supervise the nikkur. The situation quickly deteriorated, and the nikkur on their meat was consistently neglected.

The importance of a knowledgeable Rav who commands authority cannot be understated. There have been cases whereby restaurant management, despite their desire to maintain a kosher establishment, buckled under the pressure to serve their clients and attempted to use substitute items not certified as kosher, in order to supply unexpected customer demands. The same is true in the meat business, even in a shop where the butcher normally buys only boxed, pre-koshered meat from a reputable kosher slaughterhouse. The Rav must be knowledgeable enough to sink his hand into a barrel of meat cuts, pull out a sample and say, "Excuse me, but this meat was not de-veined the way your usual supplier does it; where did you get this shipment from?" In this way he will act as a deterrent against foul-play on the part of a desperate butcher, eager to service his customers, and afraid to turn away a buyer by saying, "Sorry, I ran out of meat." Only in this way will the butcher understand that the Rav is not to be underestimated.

Ultimately, the source of the Rav's authority rests in his complete knowledge of the halachah and its application in every conceivable situation. If the shochet knows the Rav is competent, then he will respect his authority. On the other hand, if the Rav does not know enough, he hardly deserves the honor which Chazal have decreed should be given to him.

The author would like to share a personal anecdote to demonstrate the difference that practical knowledge makes in kashrus supervision:

> The first time I inspected a particular meat processing plant, I made several important suggestions for improving the quality of the run. Each was greeted with a polite, 'Thank you very much for your suggestion,' and a warm smile. I understood that my words were falling on deaf ears, that my presence was being taken less than seriously, and that nothing would change upon my departure. I continued the inspection of the line and picked up a cut of meat, commenting to all the workers that this piece of meat comes from such-and-such part of the animal, and that a particular sinew was being consistently neglected. One fellow responded calmly, 'Rabbi, that meat doesn't come from that part of the animal, it comes from somewhere else.' At this point, I called for the work to stop, and took all the pieces of meat and set them together in the original form of the animal, proving to all the workers that the cut in question was indeed in need of nikkur. Having made this demonstration, my advice was seen in a much different light.

Experience shows that if the Rav has knowledge, the workers will take note of his words and act accordingly; if he lacks knowledge, they will merely listen politely. Since they are going to ignore his advice in any case, they can afford to be polite.

BUTCHER SHOP MASHGIACH

What knowledge must one acquire in order to supervise a butcher shop?

ANSWER

Proper training takes time. The goal is for the mashgiach to become familiar with the shapes of the various cuts of meat. He should be able to recognize the difference between the chuck and the rib section, and between the inner skirt and the midskirt, for example. He should also be able to spot a cut of meat that has not been sliced correctly in order to remove the sinews, fats, or veins.

To learn the meat industry well, the Rav or mashgiach must "apprentice" himself for a certain amount of time to a butcher and other professionals in the industry. It means putting on a dirty, blood-stained apron, taking a knife in one's hand, standing at the butcher's block and asking how to cut the meat. It means pressing the butcher for details and asking incessant, annoying questions. It requires the patience to endure occasional unkind words far beneath one's dignity, as he slowly learns to master the required skills.

In the end, however, a Rav that is willing to suffer a little for a few weeks will possess the knowledge of meat processing necessary to command endured respect from the personnel, and maintain control over the operation he must supervise. This is indispensable to his effectiveness in assuring the provision of kosher products to the Jewish community. The longer one spends practicing the various skills and reviewing the relevant halachos, becoming familiar with every aspect of the industry, the better and more confident one will be when making decisions.

The badge of experience can be learned from Dovid HaMelech. The Gemara[12] recounts, "Dovid said before HaKadosh Baruch Hu: Ribbono Shel Olam, am I not a pious one, for all the kings of the East and West sit in their courts in their royal garments, but as for me, my hands are filthy with *dam*, *shapir*, *ve'shilyah* in order to permit a woman to her husband." The only way to properly learn the butcher's trade is to don the dirty apron and to be trained by an experienced butcher. This is simply part of the 'sullied hands' approach that one must endure in order to become proficient in mitzvah observance.

12. ברכות ד.

THE LOCAL MEAT STORE: CONTEMPORARY HASHGACHAH REQUIREMENTS

Aside from fresh and frozen meat, butchers also sell many other products. If so, what other issues must be looked after by the attending mashgiach of a butcher shop?

ANSWER

Kashering equipment: Butcher shops do not limit themselves to supplying and cutting up fresh, raw meat. For generations, butcher shops have been roasting meat and supplying ready-to-eat meat products. This means that aside from the standard utensils such as knives, basins, and cutting boards, these shops also use rotisseries, meat slicers, and ovens. Pieces of equipment such as these are often expensive, and butchers seek to purchase used equipment at a discount. A mashgiach of such an operation must therefore see to the kashering of complex equipment.

Indeed, whenever equipment is purchased, the supervising Rav must insist on it being kashered if there is any suspicion that it might have been previously used. Also, if it should ever occur that products of inferior or questionable kashrus are inadvertently cooked or roasted on the establishment's equipment, the affected utensils will need to be kashered once again.

If the need to kasher arises, every effort to use the proper techniques must be made, to ensure that the kashering is effective, and also to avoid damage to the equipment. Thus, a mashgiach in charge of a butcher shop has to be knowledgeable in many areas and not merely know how to identify different types and cuts of meat. He also needs to know how cooking equipment is kashered, when he must insist on applying *libun chamor* (direct heat to the surfaces until they turn red hot or begin to let off sparks), and in which cases it is sufficient to use *libun kal* (applying direct heat until the opposite side of the surface is very hot, or where no direct heat is applied such as an oven wall, when the opposite side gets hot enough for a paper to burn upon contact). It may also be possible to perform *ha'agalah*, and immerse certain items into a cauldron of boiling water.

It should be kept in mind that kashering sometimes does ruin equipment, and this possibility may sometimes bring about a situation where any form of kashering becomes unacceptable. If the mashgiach must be overly cautious so as to avoid damaging the equipment he is kashering, he might fail to perform even a minimally acceptable level of kashering. An example of this would be ordinary ceramic dishes, where the only acceptable way of kashering is to cover them with burning coals, but even this is not allowed in practice. We are afraid that he will be so worried about their shattering (*chas alav dilma pakai*) that he will do an insufficient *libun*. Kashering such items is not allowed, even where the one carrying out the process is confident that he could do it without damaging the item. Halachah forbids it.

Mikvah: Not only do the cooking equipment and utensils need to be kashered, but they must also be immersed in a mikvah before use. The butcher might not be aware of this requirement, or hesitate to immerse equipment that contains electrical components.

Negel vasser: Additionally, any Jewish employees that handle food should be instructed to wash *negel vasser*; otherwise the *tumah* on their hands will contaminate all the food. Though it is true that food touched by someone who did not wash negel vasser is permissible to eat, *b'dieved*,[13] we do not rely on a b'dieved as a first resort (*lechatchilah*).

Respect for kashrus personnel: The Rav Ha'machshir should see to it that his mashgichim are treated with respect. This means he must assure that the mashgiach is not given menial tasks, and that he is paid a proper salary.

Outsourcing: Another concern is a case whereby local food

13. מ"ב סי' ד' ס"ק י"ד וביאור הלכה שם

establishments serve clients from other communities and outlying areas. Caterers especially, may often be hired for a function at a facility far from the company's main quarters. To meet the needs of these clients, the food service company might outsource, hiring other catering firms and renting equipment closer to the event site to cook, reheat, or serve the meals they provide. Depending upon how it is arranged, these situations may present serious kashrus questions. If, for instance, the job is given to a gentile firm, the kosher caterer might unwittingly be providing mehadrin kosher food that will be prepared and cooked by a gentile (*bishul akum*).

New products: People have a tendency to rely upon situations that have remained constant for long periods of time. We call this a *chazakah*, or status-quo. Chazal placed great weight on a reliable chazakah. The Gemara[14] states, "We execute on the basis of a chazakah." When there are conflicting pieces of evidence, Chazal[15] often tell us, "Go with the chazakah."

Anyone familiar with the world of commerce knows there is no status-quo in business. Things are always in flux, always changing. Indeed, a good businessman never stands still; he is constantly considering how he can expand his business and make it more profitable. Salesmen present businesses and stores with samples of new products on a daily basis, suggesting items which the owner may be persuaded to try. Items with a strong marketing potential quickly spread from retailer to retailer. The fiercest competitors share information regarding product availability. Thus, it is not uncommon for a businessman who has been using the same supplier for thirty years to suddenly switch to another brand.

This is just as true for the food industry as it is for any other. This means that the mashgiach or Rav Ha'machshir of a kosher butcher shop has to be on the lookout for new products and new labels, and

14. חולין י:

15. כתובות עה:

be sure that they adhere to the level of kashrus he is providing for the store.

The mashgiach can never rely on last week's inspection. He needs to inspect order forms and deliveries, invoices and inventory. Even if it is once in ten years that a mashgiach catches a mistake and prevents non-kosher meat from accidentally being distributed by a store under his supervision, he has not only done a great service to Klal Yisroel, but he has spared himself the embarrassment of a scandal.

Israeli products: The concern for kashrus extends to Israeli products, too. There are many different kashrus organizations in Eretz Yisroel. Some are reliable and others are not, as in the United States. A careful consumer does his research and determines which agencies he can trust. The presence of Hebrew letters on the package is no assurance that the contents are produced according to the highest standards of kashrus.

Israeli produce: Israel has become a significant exporter of agricultural products. Israeli fruits and vegetables are subject to the laws of terumos and ma'asros, as well as orlah and shevi'is. Unfortunately, it cannot be assumed that these laws are always satisfied prior to export. The mashgiach must therefore verify the source of all produce, and ascertain that these requirements have been fulfilled.

Insects: As we have mentioned, butchers now do a certain amount of food preparation and make ready-to-eat meals. It may be necessary to inspect produce for insects. The mashgiach needs to keep tabs on vegetables and fruits brought into the store, and make sure they are free of worms and insects.

Documentation: Recently, a New Orleans butcher received a shipment of meat from a certain company. Attached was a letter signed by the author attesting to its kashrus:

The butcher called, and asked me to verify the letter. As it turns out, the letter was issued many years ago, and it certified that a particular

Rav Ha'machshir could be trusted. This Rav, however, had left the company long ago. Despite this, the letter was still being used. In such questionable circumstances, the butcher was advised to consider the meat *treif*, and to kasher his equipment.

There is another story which underscores the need to be very careful in reading the documentation and certification of the kashrus of products and even of individuals. A close relative of the author once found a position as shochet of a small town in Kentucky. The job had been left open due to a scandal.

The previous shochet had applied for the position and was told that he would only be hired if the Rav of Cincinnati, Rav Lesser, *zt"l*, would write a letter attesting to his qualifications. (Rabbi Lesser was the Rav of Cincinnati before Rabbi Lazer Silver took the position c.1931.) The would-be shochet traveled to Rav Lesser, who agreed to test him. But after a few questions, it became abundantly clear that the man was not cut out to be a shochet. The Rav said to him, "*Mein kind*, my son, you will never be a shochet." The man asked the Rav, "But what can I do to make a living?" Rabbi Lesser told him he should perhaps apply for the position of shamash and take care of the shul instead. When the man expressed his concern that for this position, too, he would need a letter of certification from the Rav, Rabbi Lesser took out a piece of official stationery and wrote something to the effect of, "Take extreme care and do not let this man become a shochet in your community. However, he is fully qualified to be the shamash of the shul." Rabbi Lesser signed the letter and gave it to the man, who presented it to the leaders of the community. They saw the word shochet, the signature of Rabbi Lesser and his official seal, and installed the man as the town's shochet. A few months later Rabbi Lesser visited the community, only to find that the shamash was the shochet. The matter was immediately corrected, leaving the position of shochet open once again.

Misleading packaging and displays: Another challenge that faces the mashgiach of a butcher shop is the repackaging of meat products. Out-of-town supermarkets that are not owned by observant Jews carry selections of kosher meat products, and may even have a "Kosher

Meat" display, with the OU or other kashrus emblem on a large sign. Beneath the sign are various packages of meat and salami. Sometimes, non-kosher meats are sliced up, packaged, and placed next to the kosher ones, leading to the impression that the OU Kosher sign applies also to these uncertified packages. If the consumer knows to read the package labels, he will quickly realize that the repackaged meat bears no certification and should not be bought. Nevertheless, the out-of-town Rav must beware of this pitfall and see that such deceptions are removed in order to protect less vigilant Jewish consumers.

The problem of repackaging exists also in major Jewish centers. Many of the local *heimishe* markets purchase bulk quantities of meat from extremely reliable sources, open the packages, and then repack the products in smaller containers for their customers. As a service to the customer, they print labels for these containers stating the *hashgachah* that provided the meat. It must be pointed out, however, that no kashrus agency supervises the repackaging of these products, and the customer is relying entirely on the word of the storekeeper that the contents are what he says they are. If a person feels he can trust the proprietor, then well and good. If not, he should only buy products in the original packaging from the supervised company.

A few years ago, a customer bought some kashered, broiled livers from a particular heimishe meat store. The package bore a label that read: "Under the supervision of the Vaad HaRabbanim." He opened the package when he got home and found that they were only broiled on the surface. All the livers were completely raw inside. He returned the livers and the staff were very apologetic. They gave him two fresh packages in exchange. But the customer was surprised to find that the new livers were also completely raw inside.

Knowing a bit about kashering livers, he went into the back of the store and met the owner, and asked him if the Vaad HaRabbanim was really supervising the roasting of the livers. The owner replied that the livers were provided by a slaughterhouse under the supervision of the Vaad HaRabbanim, but that he himself broiled the livers with his own two hands, something he considered far better than the impersonal broiling that is done elsewhere.

The customer asked to see how he broiled the livers. The owner readily explained that he would lay all the livers down and use a propane torch to broil them. When they were brown, he would flip the livers over and torch the other side. The customer now understood why the livers were raw. He told the owner that he had no right to label his livers, "Under the supervision of the Vaad HaRabbanim," and that the Vaad would be shocked to see their name on such a thing. With that, the customer called up the Vaad HaRabbanim, and the situation was dealt with.

Relying on the butcher: In a similar way, the mashgiach should beware of relying on the proprietor's assertion that all his products are above-board and kosher. This is especially true in an out-of-town butcher shop, where the owner might not even be observant, but it also applies to fully observant and otherwise reliable Jewish owners. Chazal[16] say, "A single witness is believed regarding matters of ritual permissibility (*eid echad ne'eman b'issurin*)." However, this does not generally apply to a business where one has a vested financial interest (*noge'ah b'davar*). Generations of Rabbanim have ruled this way, even though it may be permitted by strict halachah.

The mashgiach should get to know the store and the way it runs first hand, so he never will be faced with a situation where he might have to rely solely upon the word of the owner. To this end, arrangements should be made that give the mashgiach sole access to all food inventory. Sometimes, the mashgiach holds the only set of keys to the store; in other establishments, he holds the keys to the storerooms, refrigerators, and freezers. Additionally, the mashgiach should be able to access all the records and accounts at any time. (See above, p. 83.) A mashgiach that is repulsed by the thought of having to put his hand into the garbage heap and retrieve discarded invoices is at a disadvantage. It is through such investigations that a person can discover undisclosed shipments of goods with questionable kashrus.

Sadly, even very observant Jews occasionally fall prey to greed.

16. גיטין ב:

What is more, when they see that others are also willing to rely on leniencies that do not really exist, it only reinforces the impression that such activities are somehow legitimate. This is a problem not only for kashrus personnel, but also for the kosher consumer. There have been incidents in the kosher fish industry for instance, where pre-cut and pre-skinned fish were bought directly from the fishermen without any ability to verify its kashrus, and then marketed as kosher fish in the most heimishe stores. To protect himself from such eventualities, the consumer should only buy fish whose *simanim* (fins and scales) are discernable, and have the fish cleaned in his presence.

It takes little effort to cut up a piece of fish or meat and place them in the display cases with a sign attesting to their kashrus. Thus, even if a person has an intuitive feeling of confidence in the integrity and *Yiras Shamayim* of a store owner, it is always advisable to insist on proper kosher certification.

Non-kosher sister store: A very serious breach in kashrus reliability is encountered when the owner of a kosher butcher shop also owns a non-kosher shop in another community. An entrepreneur is always seeking opportunities to expand his business, and if he can buy out a similar establishment to his in another town, then he can literally double his business. The difficulty here is that deliveries, shipments and service can be provided using the same trucks and equipment that currently service the kosher store, creating a great potential for switched merchandise and contamination of utensils with treif meat. It also raises the possibility that if he should ever experience a shortage at the kosher store, the owner might be tempted to bring over treif supplies as a substitute.

The mashgiach must therefore always be on the lookout for any changes in the tempo of the business he supervises. If it should ever come to light that the owner operates both kosher and non-kosher establishments that provide similar products, then there is no way to properly maintain the hashgachah and the certification must be revoked immediately.

Checking a butcher's sources of meat: Another business gain that needs close watching is the acquisition of large contracts. It is very lucrative for a butcher or caterer to seek to supply institutions such as nursing homes and schools with meals. However, the butcher is then faced with the need for a greater supply of meat and other products. In one case, a kosher meat establishment began to rapidly acquire many high-volume clients. The key to their success was the quality of service they provided, meaning that they were always able to supply any purchaser with whatever he needed without any delay. When the company was investigated, it was found that they would purchase meat from even non-kosher suppliers in order to meet their obligations to their clients. Thus, any time there is an increase in the volume of sales, the mashgiach needs to check the purchase orders and verify that the supplies from kosher, reliable sources are sufficient to cover the new commitments. This is especially true if the company develops a reputation for being able to provide kosher food for any client, even at short notice.

Weights and scales: Another concern that indirectly affects the perceived reliability of a kosher butcher is the accuracy of their scales. Certain unscrupulous merchants rig their scales and short-change their customers. Aside from the horrible desecration of Hashem's holy Name, the scandal that is caused when a kosher butcher like this is caught can ruin the kashrus reputation of the establishment. If the butcher cheats with his scales, how reliable can he be when it comes to the meat? The Rav Ha'machshir should keep this in mind. Finally, let us not forget that it is a Biblical prohibition that the Torah condemns in the strongest terms.

THE KOSHER POULTRY INDUSTRY

What halachic issues present themselves in the commercial kosher slaughtering industry?

ANSWER

Foreword regarding shechitah: In former times, there were no large kosher slaughterhouses in Europe. If a person wanted a chicken he went to the butcher, who would take a live chicken from the coop and hand it to the shochet. After checking his knife, or showing it to the Rav, the shochet would take the bird in his hands and hold it in a special way (called *tefisah*), possibly remove a few feathers from around its throat (*meritas notzos*), and shecht the bird. The customer would cover the blood with some dirt, and the butcher would pluck the chicken.

After that, the chicken would be taken home where it would be kashered. Every single kitchen had what they called a *vekshaffel*, a bucket where they soaked the chicken and did the initial rinsing. Then, the chicken would be carefully cut open, the *vrieden* (veins) would be removed from the neck, and the innards examined. Every housewife knew what to look for: a *buka d'itmah* (a dislocated ball-joint in the thigh), a ruptured *tzomes hagidin* (the junction of vessels and tendons at the narrow end of the drumstick) or punctured or infected intestines (*b'nei me'ayim*), and if there was even the slightest question, she would run to the Rav.

Every Thursday afternoon and Friday morning there would be long lines at the homes of the Rabbanim, and they would inspect one chicken after the other. If there were eggs in the chicken, the children would celebrate. That was a real treat. The eggs had to have their own *melichah* that was performed in a special way. Sometimes they would put the eggs in the cholent.

Description of commercial shechitah: Nowadays, all the work of producing kosher poultry is done in large facilities. Even the smallest slaughterhouse is large by comparison to what was in former times.

Tens of thousands of chickens, all in cages, are taken off the trucks and loaded onto a conveyor belt that enters the slaughterhouse through large open doors. The shochtim stand in a line on either side of the belt. The smaller houses will have three to four shochtim, and the larger ones could have as many as thirty, standing in multiple lines.

Many kosher slaughterhouses employ gentile assistants who pull the live chickens off the conveyor belts and present them to the shochet. They are trained to hold the bird in a particular way that allows the shochet to easily and quickly grasp the chicken's neck with the left hand and draw the knife with the right.

Inspecting the knife: The knives used by today's shochtim are made of highly durable, tempered stainless-steel. They are highly resistant to damage and corrosion. Despite the quality of the knives, this does not obviate the need for routine inspection and sharpening.

According to halachah, any *pegima* (nick) found with a shochet's knife retroactively renders non-kosher all shechitah performed with that knife, up until the last inspection that found the knife flawless.

Thus, when it comes to slaughtering cattle, the shochet's knife is checked after slaughtering each animal. This way, even if a blemish should be found with the knife, the loss is limited to only that one animal.

In poultry slaughterhouses, it would greatly slow down the process of shechting if the shochets' knives were inspected between every bird. Instead, the shochtim inspect their blades approximately every five minutes, and in addition, there are special people hired whose sole job is to circulate amongst the shochtim and check their blades several times during each shift. The efficiency of this system far outweighs the potential loss, even if quite a number of birds might have to be thrown out in the rare event a blemish is discovered.

Bleeding: After slaughtering, each chicken is placed head-first into a funnel-like contraption on another automated conveyor belt, so that the blood will have a chance to drain into the *kisui hadam* trough as the bird is transported to the flicking machines that pluck the feathers.

At the beginning of the day, a thick layer of sawdust is laid down in the trough so there should be dust beneath the blood (*afar lematta*). Throughout the day, the mitzvah of covering the blood (*kisui hadam*) is performed, with huge piles of sawdust to cover the gallons of blood on the floor, or in the trough specially made for the purpose of catching the blood.

Plucking: The flicking machines first remove the large feathers, then gradually remove ever smaller feathers until the chickens are almost completely plucked. This gradual process will have practical consequences, as we shall discuss presently.

Inspecting: Once the chickens have been plucked, the entrances to the chest cavities are cut open and the internal organs pulled outward and displayed, even as the fowl continue on the conveyor hooks. A team of inspectors (*bodkim*) check the birds for any signs of tarfus, and look specifically for common problems. There are three main disqualifications. If the thigh bone is dislocated (*buka d'itmah*), or a rupture is discovered at the junction of tendons at the ankle (*tzomes ha'giddin*), as mentioned above, or if the yolk-sac is ruptured or infected, the bird is treif and removed from the production line. The bodkim keep an eye out for any other abnormalities or fractures that might indicate that a chicken is treif.

Soaking: After the birds have been inspected, the innards are removed and the birds are soaked (*hadachah rishonah*) in large vats of fresh water. They are moved slowly through the water by large vanes. The soaking lasts for a little more than a half hour, after which the birds are automatically removed to drain, until most of the water has dripped off. If the chicken is too wet, the salt will dissolve too quickly and lose the power to draw out the blood. Nor are the chickens left to completely dry, for the salt cannot draw out the blood from the meat without at least a small amount of water.

Salting: The chickens are salted by hand or by machine. Gentile workers may do the salting, while Jewish mashgichim oversee the process. Attention is given to make sure all surfaces of the chicken are completely covered with an adequate layer of salt, both inside and out. They are stacked in large piles on perforated, slanted tables that allow for the unobstructed drainage of the blood, with the open abdominal cavity downwards. They remain covered in salt for a full hour.

Niputz & rinsing: Next, the salt is removed by shaking or spraying it off (*niputz*) with a strong stream of air or water. Once this is done, the chickens are rinsed in a bath three more times (*hadachos sheniyos*). Each rinsing is done in a separate vat with fresh water. By the third time, the water drained from the chickens runs clear, and the chickens are kosher. The chickens are then ready for packaging and flash-freezing.

IMPROPERLY SLAUGHTERED POULTRY

How do slaughterhouses handle improperly shechted poultry?

ANSWER

If a pegima (blemish) is discovered on a shochet's knife, the chickens shechted by that shochet between the previous inspection of his knife and the present one are removed. Thus, if the shochet estimates that he slaughtered no more than thirty chickens since the last time he inspected his knife, then the last thirty birds of his shechitah are removed from his hooks and processed as non-kosher in a separate section of the facility.

It is often the case that two or more shochtim work together, and their slaughtered chickens cannot be distinguished one from the other. It therefore becomes important to address the halachos of *bittul* (nullification). Additionally, a distinction must be made between strict halachic application of *bittul*, and the stringencies and *hiddurim* that are customarily employed by all reliable kosher slaughterhouses in the United States.

Halachic application of bittul: With regard to mixtures of kosher and non-kosher dry items, the Shulchan Aruch[17] rules that in the case of similar items, a minority of non-kosher items is nullified by a majority of kosher ones (*yavesh b'yavesh batul b'rov*). If the mixture is half kosher and half non-kosher, then the entire mixture is non-kosher.

Davar chashuv: Some forbidden items are never subject to bittul. That is, even if only one of these forbidden items (*issur*) were to become mixed with a large amount of similar, yet permitted items (*heter*), the entire mixture would become forbidden (*assur*), because of the one piece of issur which cannot be identified and removed. One example of this is a *chatichah hara'uyah l'hischabed*, an item of value that is appreciated by the one who receives it.

Many authorities[18] maintain that a slaughtered, fully plucked chicken is considered something that would be appreciated, a *chatichah hara'uyah l'hischabed*. If such a non-kosher chicken would become mixed together with other plucked chickens, all of them would be considered non-kosher, for the improperly slaughtered chicken can never become nullified. All opinions agree, however, that a chicken with its feathers, an *oph b'notzasah*, is not an appreciated item and can be nullified.

Minhag Rashi: Whenever *bittul* is applied, it not only spares the kosher items from becoming unusable, but also renders permissible that which was unkosher. Thus, by applying bittul one actually gains the use of previously forbidden items. It is unacceptable according to many opinions to take advantage of bittul in this way. Thus, the Poskim mention the *hiddur* of *minhag Rashi*. Rashi required that a portion of the permitted mixture equal to the amount of forbidden items that were nullified, be removed and destroyed. In this way, one does not derive any financial benefit from the non-kosher items that were rendered permissible through bittul.

17. יו"ד סי' ק"א סע' ג'
18. שו"ע יו"ד סי' ק"א סע' ג'

Applying bittul in a slaughterhouse: Practically speaking, when there are only two shochtim working at the same time, and one finds a nick in his knife, bittul cannot be applied. Each shochet slaughters roughly the same amount of birds each minute, and there is no clear majority of kosher birds. With no way of distinguishing between their slaughtered birds, the entire batch of birds slaughtered by both shochtim since the last inspection of the flawed knife is rendered unfit.

If there are three or more shochtim working at once, all slaughtering at roughly the same pace, there exists a clear majority of kosher to non-kosher birds. According to strict halachah, all the poultry may be permitted by the rule of bittul, as long as they have not yet been plucked.

Typically, it takes about five minutes for the slaughtered chickens to pass through the flicking machines until a sufficient quantity of their feathers are removed to be considered plucked. If the shochtim check their knives at least as often, in the event a blemished knife is discovered, any improperly shechted chickens will still have their feathers, and can be considered *batul*. In the rare case that a *neveilah* inadvertently remained on the line until after that point, it is treated as a *chatichah hara'uyah l'hischabed*. Bittul can no longer be applied, rendering unfit all the chickens with which the unkosher chicken became mixed, from the point that it became a *chatichah hara'uyah l'hischabed* and onward.

Hiddurim in today's kosher slaughterhouse: Nowadays in the United States, every reliable slaughterhouse removes from production any batch of poultry in which even one unkosher bird may possibly have become mixed. This is combined with an additional *hiddur*: Shechitah is carried out in such a way that if a blemished knife is discovered, strict halachah would allow for applying bittul. In particular, shochtim are instructed to inspect their knives frequently enough, so that the chickens they have slaughtered will not have been plucked before verifying that the knife was flawless. This *hiddur* ensures that whenever it is necessary to remove poultry from production, it is not being done to satisfy the strict requirements of halachah, but as a way of going beyond the letter of the law (*lifnim m'shuras hadin*). By following the above procedures, the slaughterhouses go a long way to ensure that not one unkosher bird ever reaches the consumer. The practice of discarding any questionable poultry also satisfies the requirements of *minhag Rashi*, by eliminating entirely the possibility of benefiting from the application of *bittul*. Any questionable poultry is entirely removed from production, and this is many times the amount of any non-kosher poultry that may have been present to begin with.

As mentioned above, poultry removed from the line for any reason is processed in a completely different area of the factory.

Efficiency of processing: Interestingly, the efficiency of the production line can affect the application of bittul. One slaughterhouse developed a system to process the slaughtered chickens more quickly. The streamlining supposedly improved the quality of the meat. However, there was a down side to the improvement. Due to the speed of the new process, the chickens would already have been plucked by the time a blemished knife had been discovered, negating the possibility of applying bittul to the improperly shechted chickens in the batch. This affected the hiddur of the plant, because the mixture of kosher and non-kosher poultry they were faced with was now strictly forbidden by halachah, and great care had to be taken to remove all halachic doubt regarding the presence of the non-kosher chickens.

WORK CONDITIONS AND KASHRUS

What outside factors affect the quality of kosher slaughter? Is the *Rav Ha'machshir* expected to deal with human-relations issues?

ANSWER

Anything that interferes with the physical or emotional comfort of the shochet can potentially have a negative impact on the quality of the shechitah. Once they are identified, it is up to the *Rav Ha'machshir* and the *rosh hashochtim* to work to speedily resolve such issues. Indeed, a good Rav Ha'machshir will pay as much attention to these details as he does to the letter of halachic law. He will imagine what it is like to work in that environment, and try to feel the comfort or discomfort of the employees.

This is true of any facility requiring kashrus supervision, not simply the slaughterhouses. A good mashgiach will spend hours simply observing the facility under his supervision and become thoroughly familiar with the routine of the factory, bakery or restaurant. Having done this, he can begin to analyze the operation and discover where issues exist.

Physical comfort: Once, the author had the opportunity to inspect a very well-run poultry facility:

> There were three *shochtim* positioned next to the conveyor belt that brought the chickens into the plant. The shochtim were doing an exemplary job. They were sincere, God-fearing Jews, something that could be discerned by the quality of their knives and the way they went about their work. The owner of the plant answered in the affirmative when I asked if the shochtim stood in this particular location the year round. I then pointed out to him that in the winter this location presents a problem, because the shochtim are positioned directly across from the entrance and that the cold wind would undoubtedly freeze the shochet's hands, making their work very difficult. The owner was very responsive, and said he would take care of the situation immediately. One of the shochtim came over to me later on and expressed his appreciation for my recommendation. He said that he had been suffering for years from his freezing fingers in the winter months, but the problem had never been addressed.

Similarly, in the heat of the summer, outside temperatures can easily reach 90 degrees Fahrenheit. This means that temperatures inside the slaughterhouse will top 95 degrees. Additionally, the shochet wears a heavy rubber coat and a mask to protect him from the blood and dust flying about, and this means the shochet is working in sweltering conditions of 105 degrees or more. Without proper ventilation, or even air-conditioning, the shochet could very well pass out from heat and exhaustion.

Proper rest: Even the frequency and length of the breaks given to the shochtim should be scrutinized. The rule of thumb is that for every hour of shechitah, the shochet needs one hour of rest. Some plants have their shochtim work for one and a quarter hours, but give them a one and a quarter hour break. However, if the lounge is inconveniently located, the shochet could easily use a third to a half of this time just getting to the lounge and removing his gear. This means that the shochet is getting half the rest he needs, even if he is officially off-duty for an entire hour.

Human relations: The human relations factor is a highly significant one in hashgachah work today. This is especially true of the high-tempo kosher slaughterhouse. The in-house mashgiach should be an esteemed talmid chacham, well-versed in the vocation of shechitah and its halachic requirements. He must carry considerable authority, yet also be sensitive to others. His directives must be definitive and clear, yet he should be capable of dealing with conflict diplomatically. Too strong a confrontation can cause a rift between him and the company, limiting his influence. If his approach is too timid, then his relationship with the shochtim will suffer.

The Rav Ha'machshir and the head of the shechitah operation (*rosh hashochtim*) at the plant must both possess highly developed interpersonal skills. They must be capable of building and maintaining a wide range of relationships with a variety of personalities. It is challenging to find the balance between authority and approachability, and to engage people's cooperation without offending them.

REMOVING FEATHERS

Do the slaughterhouses or the kashrus agencies demand that all shochtim perform *meritas hanotzos*, removing the feathers from the neck of the chicken, before shechitah?

ANSWER

There are two conflicting customs (*minhagim*) amongst shochtim regarding the removal of feathers from the neck of the chicken before slaughtering. One minhag is to remove a few feathers (*meritas hanotzos*), so as to reduce the chances that the stiff spine of the feathers should nick the blade of the knife and make the chicken treif. The other custom, based on the Rema,[19] is to be sure *not* to remove those feathers, for fear that a drop of blood will result, and the esophagus (*veshet*) will be assumed to have been punctured, thus rendering the bird treif. Each shochet is allowed to follow his personal custom in this regard.

Nowadays, neither concern manifests itself practically. It used to be that they would slaughter the old worn out egg-laying hens, whose feathers were very coarse. The chickens today are slaughtered quite young, and the feathers around the neck are silky-soft. They rarely pose a problem to the tempered steel blade of the shochet's knife, which is very strong. Similarly, the feathers are so small that removing them never results in a spot of blood.

Nevertheless, the conflicting minhagim are still cause for concern. In the slaughterhouses employing several shochtim, the one that removes the feathers shechts a few less chickens per hour than the shochet who holds like the Rema, and does not remove the feathers. This can create a sense that one shochet is doing less than another, and may result in competitiveness and bad feelings. If not properly handled, it can even come to the point that the owner of the slaughterhouse might resent the lower productivity of the shochet who

19. יו"ד סי' כ"ג סע' ו'

shechts less in order to keep his minhag. The Rav Ha'machshir has to be sensitive to this situation.

HUMAN RELATIONS

Are there other similar halachic issues that have the potential to turn into a human relations challenge?

ANSWER

There are innumerable opportunities for problems to arise. We shall mention only two additional examples:

Careful knife examination: If a shochet wishes to take an extra moment or two to check his knife before relieving the one who is ending his shift, that may be all well and good. In the meantime, the shochet who is finishing has to continue overtime for those few minutes, and he may resent it. Or, he might just walk off in any case, and the empty space will draw the attention of the other workers, causing embarrassment. The Rav Ha'machshir needs to diplomatically resolve situations such as these without making it seem that he favors one shochet over the other.

Gentile assistants: As we mentioned, the shochtim are able to shecht as fast as they do because of the gentile assistants who present the bird to them for slaughtering. The system works as follows: One worker takes the live bird off the conveyor belt, exposes the neck and presents it to the shochet. As mentioned earlier, the shochet takes hold of the bird with his left hand, while the assistant is also still holding it, and slaughters with his right hand. When the shochet finishes, a process that takes only a second or two, the assistant passes the shechted chicken to a second worker, who puts it in the funnel for *kisui hadam*. Some of the gentile assistants are patient, and they wait for the shochet to release the chicken before passing it on to the other worker. But other assistants are impatient, and tug at the bird even while the shochet is still shechting. If the worker does indeed succeed in pulling the chicken from the shochet in the midst of the shechitah, this can cause the shochet to apply an unacceptable downward pressure on the knife during the act of slaughter. This is called *drasa* (דְּרָסָה) and it invalidates the shechitah, and the bird would not be kosher. Thus, it is extremely important to hire only those gentiles who are cooperative and do not compete with the shochet. Indeed, even the best and most even-tempered assistants have to be well trained by the supervising Rabbanim.

Even with proper training, there are always going to be some assistants who are better than others, and the shochtim know who they are. If they feel that they are always getting the less cooperative assistants, it could easily develop into an aggravated and frustrated situation and thus cause resentment among the shochtim.

MECHANICAL ASSISTANTS

Is there a machine that can be used to present the chickens to the shochtim, by-passing the problems of using assistants?

ANSWER

For years, kosher poultry factories have worked on developing a machine that can do what these assistants do. Until now, none of the prototypes have performed well enough to be implemented. Any such model would have to hold the bird in an immobilized position, as the shochet walks down the line shechting one bird after another. The chickens would then be mechanically removed to the next stages in the process, i.e. bleeding, plucking, etc. However, once the shochet shechts the first chicken, it often begins to forcefully flap its wings, and blood sprays everywhere. Besides, the machines cannot adjust to the spontaneous physical movements of each chicken after slaughter. This makes it very difficult to properly take hold of the second chicken.

The system as it stands today has been modified several times, following the comments and criticism that have been registered over the years. No idea is rejected out of hand. Sometimes, an idea that at first seems implausible can lead to a dramatically positive change in the quality and kashrus of production. Employing shochet's assistants remains, for now, the best procedure.

ACCEPTABLE SPEED OF POULTRY SHECHITAH

What is considered an acceptable rate for chicken shechitah? Are there slaughterhouses that demand greater productivity from their shochtim, and may this affect the quality of the slaughtering? If this is true, why are the kashrus organizations not addressing the issue? Should Rabbis and community leaders attempt to pressure these plants to change by advising the Jewish community not to purchase their products?

ANSWER

Once, a slanderous claim was made against a particular United States slaughterhouse, that it was allegedly overworking its shochtim by requiring them to slaughter at least seven-hundred and fifty chickens per hour. As we shall see, this is a very reasonable quota for a shochet.

The average, experienced shochet working on his own can patiently shecht about fifteen chickens per minute, one chicken every four seconds. Simple math reveals that at this rate, he will slaughter nine-hundred chickens in one hour. There are no slaughterhouses with reliable kashrus certification in the United States that require more than that, and most are satisfied with a rate of around seven-hundred and fifty birds an hour. At this rate, even if the shochet will pause about every five minutes to check his knife, he will still have plenty of time to shecht his quota.

Many slaughterhouses, including the one against which the scandalous claim was made, allow even more time, because the shochet is assisted by a gentile worker who holds the chicken, taking much of the stress off the shochet. The shochet is therefore less apt to tire, and can check his knife every couple of minutes. Additionally, this slaughterhouse actually has a rule that their shochtim are not allowed to shecht more than eight-hundred chickens per hour. As is evident, the claim that shochtim are overworked was found to be patently false, and the kashrus agencies saw no issue that needed addressing.

If the Rabbanim have clear evidence that a particular place is not shechting according to halachah, then they have a solemn obligation to immediately inform the public and save them from transgression. However, there is no obligation to do such a thing in response to second-hand information that has not been verified, and even the more so when the source of the information is itself questionable.

Even HaEzer

DATING AND YICHUD[1]

Are there any precautions that single men and women should take when going out on *shidduchim* in an automobile, or when taking walks in secluded places?

ANSWER

Reb Moshe Feinstein, *zt"l*, always used to say that a person traveling late at night on typically deserted streets and highways with a member of the opposite gender, transgresses the prohibition of *yichud*.[2]

It is forbidden for a man to be alone with one or two women in a secluded area by day, and even with three at night. This is true whether the secluded area is in a house, on a street, in a vehicle, or even while traveling.[3]

A secluded area is a place where no one else is present, and there is no reasonable expectation that another person will enter or pass through that place. In contrast, a room or area that people typically enter is not considered secluded, even if there is no one present at the

1. אבה"ע סי' כ"ב
2. אבה"ע ח"ד סי' ס"ה אות ג'
3. אבה"ע סי' כ"ב סע' ה'

time. Since there is always the chance that someone might appear, the prohibition of *yichud* does not apply.

A particular location may be considered secluded only at certain times. For instance, there are rural and outlying areas in the country, and even areas within cities, that are deserted after a certain hour at night. Though it would be permissible for a man and woman to frequent such an area in the early evening, this is forbidden once it becomes deserted.

YICHUD IN THE OFFICE

Is there an issue of *yichud* for men and women who work together in private offices, or for women who visit the doctor?

ANSWER

Problems of *yichud* do crop up in the workplace and in doctor's offices. A God-fearing doctor who sees patients of the opposite gender will make sure to take precautions against seclusion. For example, a doctor can enlist the presence of his or her spouse, some other acceptable person, or keep the door of the examination room slightly ajar so that someone could enter unannounced.

People who have private offices must also take precautions. A large ground-floor window, unshuttered and looking out onto the street, or a door left ajar to a public thoroughfare, are sufficient in most situations.[4]

Adherence to these standard rules of yichud is all that is needed for two people unfamiliar with each other, even on a *shidduch* date. The boy and girl hardly know each other, so a natural distance exists between them. It is important to remember that there is no justification to ignore the basic requirements of yichud on the basis of this distance alone.

4. אבה"ע סי' כ"ב סע' ט'

There are certain situations which must be treated more cautiously. The environment in many workplaces is casual and the employees may grow to be very familiar with each other, even calling each other by their first names. The Gemara[5] calls this type of situation "*libam gas behaddadei*," that is, they are very comfortable with each other. It is not uncommon that male workers begin to use terms of familiarity and even endearment when addressing certain female co-workers.

Wherever the possibility of such a personal relationship exists, one must tread with extreme caution. The laws of yichud are not a dry and inflexible protocol. Its requirements become more stringent as the distance between the genders disappears and the likelihood of forbidden contact increases. One should never attempt to justify an over-familiar and possibly inappropriate relationship simply because 'the door is open.'

5. קידושין פא.

Choshen Mishpat

PROPER TIME TO WRITE A PROZBUL[1]

When is the correct time to make a *prozbul*, and what happens if one forgets to make one?[2]

ANSWER

The Rambam[3] states, "*Shevi'is* suspends financial obligations only at its conclusion." Thus, the correct time to make a prozbul is at the end of the *shmittah* year, just before Rosh Hashanah.

According to the Torah, shmittah suspends all outstanding debts, and prohibits creditors from requesting payment. In our times, shmittah is only observed *miderabbanan*, by Rabbinic decree, as the conditions for *shmittah d'Oraisa* do not exist.

The prozbul is a legal document by which a creditor effectively transfers all outstanding debts to Beis Din for collection. This instrument bypasses the Rabbinic suspension of debts in the shmittah year, and allows creditors to request payment even after *shmittah*. If

1. שו"ע חו"מ סי' ס"ז סע' י"ח
2. חו"מ סי' ס"ז
3. הלכות שמיטה ויובל פ"ט ה"ד

a person does not write a prozbul for money owed him, he is not allowed to approach the debtor and request payment.

On the other hand, the debtor can approach the creditor and offer to pay. The creditor must then say, "I am prevented from collecting the debt." At that point, the debtor should say, "*Af al pi kein* – nevertheless, I wish to pay it," and the creditor is allowed to accept the payment. If the debtor does not know to say, "*Af al pi kein*," the creditor should prompt him to say it.

The Rosh,[4] however, held that any debt incurred during the shmittah year cannot be collected, unless the creditor makes a declaration ahead of time that all debts over the course of the year should be transferred to Beis Din for collection. The Rosh's opinion is brought by the commentators on the Shulchan Aruch,[5] and a talmid chacham should strive to fulfill this opinion by making the proper declaration before shmittah in the presence of three Jews.

PROZBUL FOR WAGE-EARNING WOMEN

Should a working woman rely on the *prozbul* of her father or husband, or should she make her own?

ANSWER

The head of household: The head of household should always have in mind his family members and others who rely on him for their welfare. When he makes a *prozbul* on erev Rosh Hashanah, he should make sure to word it in the plural and include everyone:

מוסר אני לפניכם פלוני ופלוני ופלוני הדיינים כל חוב שיש לי ולבני ביתי שאגבנו/שנגבנו כל זמן שארצה/שנרצה – I hereby transfer to you before you, *ploni*, *ploni*, and *ploni*, the *Dayanim*, for collection of any debt

4. פ"ד דגיטין
5. סמ"ע חו"מ סי' ס"ז ס"ק נ"ג

owed to me and to the members of my household, that I/we should collect them any time I/we desire [as agents of Beis Din].

This will cover all loans made by family members from their personal money. Money, whose ownership has accrued to the head of the household and was subsequently loaned out, is covered by the prozbul of the head of the household.

Unmarried girl: Often, a father allows his daughter to work for herself and keep her own bank account. This is frequently done with the understanding that the money will help her support her husband in learning once she marries. If she has given a friend a loan from that money, it is no simple thing to rely on her father's prozbul.

Married woman: Similarly, a married woman may also be in a position where she controls a certain amount of assets with the permission of her husband. The basic rule is that all her income (*ma'aseh yade'ah*) belongs to her husband. Investment income (*peiros nichsei melug*) also goes to the husband. But if the husband gives his wife a present, then he has no claim whatsoever to any income derived from it. Here too, if she gives that money as a loan, the husband's prozbul would not prevent shmittah from suspending the loan.

It is not very common for women to lend sizeable sums of money. Yet, as a precaution, the head of household should ask his family members if they have any outstanding loans, and arrange for them to make their own prozbul.

HANDLING OF LOST OBJECTS[6]

What should be done with umbrellas, boots, raincoats, and other items that are left in shuls or at weddings? If someone

6. חו"מ סי' רנ"ט–רס"ב

mistakenly took one of these items instead of his own, is it permissible to use it?

ANSWER

The halachos of *hashavas aveidah* are quite complex. A full treatment of the subject is beyond the scope of this sefer, but a few basic guidelines can be given.

Siman, a proper identifying mark: Lost objects may be divided into two categories: those with an identifying mark, and those without. Any item manufactured in bulk, even if it is less common than other similar products and therefore possesses unique features, (such as a name-brand coat, or a designer purse) is not considered to have a proper identifying mark. This is comparable to a specially shaped loaf of bakery bread (*kikar shel nachtom*). The unique shape itself is not deemed a proper siman by which one can claim ownership of the loaf, because it is shared by many others.[7]

Only marks that would identify the item in question as belonging exclusively to its owner are considered simanim, such as a scratch or other blemish on the product, or a nametag or ribbon tied to it. The location of the object is also a siman, if it was intentionally put there, although later forgotten.

When is an object considered 'lost'?: An object becomes permitted to take when the owner realizes that he has lost it and gives up hope of ever recovering it (*ye'ush*). If there is a siman, we assume that he has not lost hope, unless one definitely knows that this is the case. If there is no siman, then it can be assumed that he has lost hope of ever recovering the item. Strictly speaking, when no proper identifying mark is found, one can claim such an item for oneself right away.

However, it first must be ascertained that the owner of the object was aware that he lost it. Otherwise, the finder would be prohibited from using the item forever, since it came into his hands before the

7. ב"מ כא.

owner actively gave up hope of retrieving it (*ye'ush mida'as*). Such a situation is called *b'issur assa leyadei*, meaning that it came into his hands while it was still the property of the owner and could not possibly be appropriated by the finder. The finder then automatically becomes a guardian (*shomer*) on behalf of the owner with no possibility of ever being relieved of that responsibility. Later, we will discuss certain mitigating factors.

It is generally assumed that when one discovers such an item, with no siman and with no indication that the owner was aware that he lost it, he is not obligated to pick it up, because the Torah clearly connects the mitzvah of picking up a lost object to the obligation (*chiyuv*) of returning it to the rightful owner. Since there will never be a way of returning this unidentifiable object, there is no obligation to take it and guard it in the first place.

There are a number of factors that allow us to assume that the owner already knows of the loss. The first is that if the object is a coin or anything else kept in a wallet or pocket. This follows the rule that *adam asuy lemashmesh b'kiso*, a person frequently touches his pocket or wallet. A second factor is if the item is a heavy one, we assume that he became aware that the item was missing because of the abrupt change in the weight of his load. This follows the rule of *aydi deyakiri meyda yada*, since it is heavy, he must surely know. A third consideration is if the item were precious. Here the rule is *aydi dechashiva meyda yada*, since it is valuable, he must surely know of its loss. Any other solid indication that the owner became aware of the loss of the object and gave up hope, may also justify the assumption that the owner has actively given up hope of retrieving it. In all of these cases, one who finds the object may pick it up and keep it for himself. If, however, the lost object has an identifying mark, one is obligated to pick it up and attempt to return it to the owner.

A lost object in a private domain: The owner of a private domain, such as a house, is never allowed to take an item left on his premises for himself, even if there is no siman, and even if he knows that the owner has lost all hope of recovering it. This is because a private house is a guarded area (*chatzer hamishtameres*). The moment the item becomes classified as an *aveidah,* the homeowner's property automatically gathers the object in, and he becomes responsible for it. This occurs before the owner becomes aware of its disappearance. Thus, the homeowner is considered to have taken hold of the item when it is still forbidden to acquire it (*b'issura assa l'yadei*). Therefore, if the item bears a siman, then the homeowner is obligated in *hashavas aveidah*. If there is no siman, or if the homeowner only discovered the aveidah many weeks later, after the owner of the object surely gave up hope of retrieving it, he does not have to try and return it. Still, neither he nor anyone else is permitted to take it as his own. Some hold that a third party who discovers the item, however, would be allowed to take the object as his own.

A shul or wedding hall is a *chatzer she'einah mishtameres*, an unguarded area. Places such as these are open to the public, and people come and go as they please. Even a private shul is not considered a guarded domain for this reason. Therefore, the owner of the property does not automatically become responsible for items left there.

Since the location of the object can also be considered to be a siman, we can only assume the owner has given up hope of recovering the lost object after a reasonable period of time. If the item was found up to a week after it had been left, it is likely that the owner will consider the possibility of retracing his steps and reclaiming his aveidah. To give the owner the best chance of reclaiming it, the object should be left in the exact place it was found. If it was found after a few weeks have passed, we can assume the owner has already given up hope, and the finder can keep the object.

As we mentioned above, this answer should be understood as a general guideline to a complex and involved subject.

Beyond the letter of the law (lifnim m'shuras ha-din): Even after the owner has lost hope, Chazal emphasize the obligation of a person to act beyond the letter of the law, and return the lost object nonetheless. Wherever possible, one should try to do this.

Switched items: In the event that two similar items are switched, the halachah depends upon where the exchange took place. If the exchange took place in a private home, where someone took the homeowner's hat instead of his own, the homeowner would not be allowed to use the hat left in its place, even if there is no siman, and the hat's owner gave up hope. This is for the same reason that was stated above. The homeowner's *chatzer hamishtameres* gathers the item in and he becomes responsible for it at a time that it was still forbidden to acquire it.

In a case where the hat was switched before Shabbos, it is reasonable to assume that it would be acceptable to the owner that a mitzvah be performed with his property (*nicha lei l'aved mitzvah*), and that he would be happy to know that the finder used his property temporarily in order to avoid embarrassment.

The Gemara (*Bava Basra* 46a) speaks about a switch of merchandise in a craftsman's shop (*ha-machlif keilim b'veis ha'umman*) where it is permissible to make use of the switched item, but the conditions in that case are rarely applicable today.

Reb Moshe Feinstein, *zt"l*, told the author personally,[8] that in a situation where one picked up an item before it was permissible to acquire it, and it is clear that the owner is not going to return to claim it, then after the item has been abandoned for several years, one can have the object evaluated, write down its value, and take it for oneself. If the owner does eventually return, he can be given the cash value of the object in place of the item, in order to fulfill the mitzvah of hashavas aveidah. The possibility of the owner's return is, in any event, highly unlikely.

This is allowed, because the great majority of lost property is inevitably lost permanently or destroyed. This is known as *holech l'ibbud*, literally, on its way to destruction. Considering the vast quantity of lost objects in the world, and the fact that we nevertheless do not see huge storehouses of these aveidos, we can conclude that any lost object that has been abandoned for several years is indeed *holech l'ibbud*. The halachah states that such items can be exchanged for money. In a case

8. ע"ע אג"מ ח"ב סי' מ"ה ענף ד'

where the owner may likely return, one must set the money aside, but in the above case, it is not necessary.

TAKING ITEMS FROM A DEMOLITION SITE

May a person help himself to items of value on the property of a Jewish home which is in the process of being demolished? Should he remove the *mezuzos*?

ANSWER

If it is clear that the owner of the home knows it is being demolished, then it would be classified as an "*ashpah ha'asuyah l'hipanos* – a garbage heap ready for removal."[9] We may assume that he rendered ownerless anything he left behind (*aveidah mida'as*). There is no reason to even attempt to notify the homeowner that one wishes to take possession of such items, except as a gesture of courtesy.

One should not return the mezuzos to the former owner, even as a courtesy, because a person who would demolish a home without first seeing to it that the mezuzos are removed, cannot be trusted to properly care for the mezuzos in any case. One who finds such mezuzos should have them checked, and if kosher, use them in good health.

In the event the owner did not realize his home was slated for demolition, such as where a person left his property for a long time and unbeknown to him the city decided to clear the land, then even if the demolition took place, it is classified as an "*ashpah she'einah asuyah l'hipanos, v'nimlach alav lifnoso* – a garbage heap that was not ready for removal but which they ultimately decided to remove."[10] In this case, the finder is obligated to return whatever objects he removes from the demolition site.

9. שו"ע חו"מ סי' ר"ס סע' י"א. וצ"ע דלא דמי כולי האי, דגבי אשפה לא היה לו להניח שם חפציו מתחילה ולכן הוי אבידה מדעת, אבל הכא שהיה לו רשות ליתנם שם, דילמא שכח ליטלם והוי אבידה שלא מדעת וצ"ע.

10. עי' ב"מ שם

If the finder made an effort to locate the previous owner and did not succeed, it may be justifiable to consider the entire house *zuto shel yam*, i.e. an item found in a tidal basin which is free for anybody to take, or depending on the circumstance a proper *aveidah* which one must protect before reaching the stage of *zuto shel yam*. A sheilah should be asked.

LAW OF THE LAND[11]

The halachah of *dinna d'malchusa dinna* states that we must adhere to the laws of the country in which we reside. When exactly does this halachah apply, particularly with regard to paying taxes, driving and parking laws, recycling rules, and so forth?

ANSWER

The halachos of abiding by the law of the land (*dinna d'malchusa dinna*) are complicated. This is in large part due to the wide range of opinions in the Rishonim, the early commentators on the Talmud.

According to many Rishonim, the obligation to obey the law of the land with regard to taxes, is predicated on the idea that a king, government, or country owns the land and has the power to set the terms and conditions by which an individual may reside there. These conditions consist of abiding by the laws of the land, and paying the appropriate taxes. Thus, one who withholds his taxes is essentially stealing the living space he occupies in that land.[12]

According to this opinion, one may never avoid paying taxes to an official government tax collector. All the *Gedolei Yisroel* with whom the author is familiar, conducted themselves in this fashion, and made sure to pay any and all taxes owed by them

However, some opinions distinguish between an upstanding,

11. חו"מ סי' שס"ט
12. עי' ר"ן נדרים דף כח. בשם תוס' ועוד

trustworthy Jewish tax farmer and any other type of tax collector. These individuals bought the rights to the taxes from the king or other official ruling body. In the case of a Jewish tax farmer, by not paying taxes, one would be causing the Jew a financial loss. Nowadays, this type of arrangement is virtually non-existent. A lenient approach to *dinna d'malchusa* may also be justified, if it can be shown by Torah law, that the governing body does not have a legitimate claim to the land over which it rules.

Despite the above arguments, there is a factor that mitigates against withholding taxes, even if there may be halachic permission to do so (*heter*). It is virtually impossible to avoid taxes without having to lie about one's income, and make a legal declaration that his lie is the truth.

It is written in the Torah explicitly that one should avoid untruths, *mid'var sheker tirchak*. One who is lenient, and permits himself to lie in order to avoid paying taxes, runs the risk of making a way of life out of lies, fulfilling the verse, "*Limdu l'shonam daber sheker* – They taught their tongues to speak falsehood" (Yirmiyahu 9:4). This can easily lead to dishonesty in all financial matters, and a person can begin to make a life of cheating customers and business associates, Jew and gentile alike. Chazal say that where there is a basket-full of sins, *gezel mekatreig b'rosh*, thievery has the greatest power to condemn. If there is a mitzvah that needs strengthening today, it is honesty in monetary affairs.

Most upstanding Jews today only eat glatt kosher meat. The assumption, although not quite accurate, is that the kashrus of glatt kosher meat is self-evident, and no Rav need be consulted (*basar shehorah bo chacham*). We should apply the same standards to our finances, and never accept money from any source that is not obviously free of all suspicion.

One who prides himself on being a sharp and shrewd businessman would be greatly embarrassed if he entered a business deal where he paid an exorbitant price for something of little value. The same applies to someone who sold something of great value in return for a pittance. By gaining a few dollars in a dishonest way, whatever profit a person made is offset by the destruction of his neshamah. The enormity of the loss makes dishonesty the worst 'business deal' of all. Anyone in business should make a point of regularly considering the futility of dishonest practice.

Parking: There are strong grounds to require total compliance to all parking and traffic laws on the basis of the opinion regarding *dinna d'malchusa dinna* that we explained above. In principle, the government only gives permission to use the land, roads, facilities and infrastructure if a person abides by the rules they set down for their use.

Nevertheless, there is a certain amount of flexibility. In some situations it is obvious that deviations from certain minor regulations would cause no harm or inconvenience to anyone. It is customary for law officers to ignore the infraction in these cases. To this extent, such deviations from law would not be halachically considered as disobedience. Major violation of these laws is, of course, forbidden.

Obviously, one should never violate the law in cases where it is meant to guarantee the safety of the inhabitants of the land.

Recycling: The degree to which one must comply with recycling regulations and various types of social legislation, may depend upon the seriousness with which the government takes these laws. According to the Rosh,[13] there may be leniencies that apply if such laws are generally ignored by the authorities and cause undue inconvenience.

The Rashbam[14] maintains that *dinna d'malchusa* is a product of the consensus of the people. The people chose to give the government power to make laws that will benefit the population. Recycling laws are undeniably beneficial, so it does not make sense that someone should desire to ignore *dinna d'malchusa*, and shirk the responsibility to act in a beneficial manner, casting the burden onto others.

Rashi[15] considers *dinna d'malchusa* a fulfillment of the laws of *Bnei*

13. גיטין פ"א

14. ב"ב נד: ד"ה מי אמר

15. גיטין ט:

Noach, one of which is to establish a judicial system. It is arguable that this applies only to monetary matters and the control and punishment of wrongdoers. According to this major opinion, social legislation may not be within the purview of the government. One who is careful about his adherence to halachah should attempt to abide by all of the above opinions.

It should be noted however, that all monetary matters between one Jew and another must only be decided by Torah law, and through the agency of those to whom the halachah grants the right of adjudication. Indeed, any matter involving Jews must always be brought before qualified Rabbanim, who will decide the case and determine how it should be handled.

A full discussion of the parameters of *dinna d'malchusa dinna* is beyond the scope of this work, and each specific case should be presented to a qualified Rav.

TIPS AND WAGES

Is the practice of tipping service providers a halachic requirement?

ANSWER

The Gemara[16] states, "One is not allowed to charge rent for lodgings in Yerushalayim, because Yerushalayim does not belong to its inhabitants.... Therefore, the skins of the offerings may be taken by the proprietors *bizro'a*, by force." This means that the proprietor has a legal claim on the skins and can take his guests to a Jewish court (*Beis Din*) to collect them. Abaye adds, "We learn from this that it is appropriate (*derech eretz*) for a man to leave empty bottles and skins for the proprietor of his lodgings." Even in a case where the proprietor cannot claim them in Beis Din, such as where the proprietor receives rent from the renter, it is still appropriate to leave the skins and bottles.

16. מגילה כו.

The empty bottles and skins are akin to what we nowadays call 'tips'. This Gemara thus teaches us that there are two levels of tipping. Some tips are in place of compensation due for services rendered, as is the case in Yerushalayim where direct rental is forbidden. The obligation to tip in this case is mandatory, and that is why the proprietors can claim the skins in Beis Din.

In Abaye's case, however, the tip is simply a gratuity, given in addition to the rental owed to the proprietor. Even here, one should feel an obligation to show his appreciation and give the customary tip, if he has been a guest, or has received some other service where the custom is to tip the worker.

The difference between these two scenarios is most evident when the service is particularly poor. If the tip is considered part of the wages of the service provider, then there may be an obligation to tip even if the service was inferior; otherwise, he is unfairly withholding his wages. If the tip is simply an addition to a full salary that does not rely on tips to make up the shortfall, as in the case of a taxi driver, or a tip given to a rebbi who makes his salary without the tip being included, then one might justifiably withhold it as a sign of dissatisfaction with the service. The only claim against him might be that he lacks derech eretz, that his withholding of the tip is a violation of *mentshlichkeit*. By saying that it is derech eretz to leave bottles and skins, Chazal are teaching us that giving a tip is proper human behavior, and a person who does not give a customary tip is lacking a certain degree of humanity.

USING EMPLOYER'S PROPERTY FOR PERSONAL USE

To what extent may an employee use his employer's property for personal use? This would include items such as copy and fax machines, telephones, or staying late at work to use the computer.

ANSWER

The prohibition of theft (*gezel*) should not be taken lightly. It is a very serious prohibition. *Chamas*, a form of gezel, was the final sin that brought the flood in the days of Noach.[17] Any time a person avails himself of the property or services of another without consent, he could be transgressing the prohibition of gezel.

Explicit and implicit consent: One might think that asking permission would resolve this issue, but this is not always the case. Some employers do not mind occasional use, but might not want to give official permission to use office supplies out of fear that it will lead to an air of permissiveness. With other employers, the opposite sentiment exists. Asked directly, he might be embarrassed to say no (*meshum kissufa*), though he would rather not allow any personal use at all. The Gemara relates a particular incident that illustrates this point:

> Ameimar, Mar Zutra, and Rav Ashi visited the groves of Mari bar Eisak. His worker brought dates and pomegranates and placed them before the Sages. Ameimar and Rav Ashi partook of the fruits; Mar Zutra did not. In the meantime, Mari bar Eisak returned. He found [the Sages eating his fruits], and said to his worker, "Why did you not bring the Sages from the better ones?" [The implication being that Mari bar Eisak was pleased that the worker had given fruits to the visiting Sages, and that had he personally been there when they arrived, Mari would have presented them with only the very best of

17. סנהדרין קח.

> the crop.] Still Mar Zutra would not partake of the fruits. Ameimar and Rav Ashi asked Mar Zutra, "Now [that it is clear that Mari bar Eisak permits us to eat of his fruits], why is Master not partaking...?" He replied, "...It is only because he is embarrassed [to reveal his reluctance] that he speaks thus."[18]

It is also true that people say things out of anger, or while in a bad mood, which they may later regret. It is therefore unreasonable to rely on what is said in such circumstances in order to judge to what extent company property is permitted for personal use.

The best measure of what is acceptable, is to somehow determine, firstly, which types of office supplies and facilities employees would normally feel comfortable taking or using for their own personal use, and secondly, which supplies or facilities would employers readily allow to be utilized in this way. Anything common to both these principles is most likely permissible.

However, people often imagine that what they want to do is acceptable to all, when this may not be true at all. It requires a great measure of self-honesty to make this assessment accurately. Therefore, unless a person knows beyond the shadow of a doubt that he would never be permissive with other people's property, he should accustom himself to act *lifnim m'shuras hadin*, well within what he might consider to be the accepted boundary, as a safeguard.

Having said that, if the employer specifically forbids a certain thing, especially in a written memorandum, it is prohibited to ignore his orders and rely on what 'everyone does.' Perhaps someone who is close to the boss should go over and tell him that the employees are concerned about gezel, and despite his verbal or written disapproval they think he might not really mind. However, not all employers can be spoken to in such a manner, especially someone who is difficult to communicate with. When in doubt, a person should always refrain from taking or using that which is not his.

18. ב"מ כב.

INHERITANCES[19]

Before his passing, a man expressed the desire to have his estate divided equally among his children, though his eldest son, as the *bechor*, should really receive a double portion. What factors play a role in deciding to what extent the father's wishes should be fulfilled?

ANSWER

There are four issues that must be considered regarding inheritances.

Matnas shchiv m'ra – The gift of a dying man: If the man was sick at the time he made the declaration and he eventually died from that illness, he is considered a *shchiv m'ra*, a dying person. The halachah states, "*Matnas shchiv m'ra k'chesuvim u'chemesurim dami*" – The gift of a dying man is considered as if it had been written in a document, and the document handed to the recipient in a manner which has the power, according to halachah, to transfer ownership of the specified property to him. Whatever he instructed is effective and requires no other act of acquisition (*kinyan*). The actual transfer of title of the property to the beneficiaries that he named will take place upon his death, similar to an ordinary Torah inheritance. The division of the estate must then be done in accordance with the dying man's wishes.

Matnas bari – A healthy man's gift: The proper course of action for a healthy person who knows how he wants to divide his estate, is to write a will while he is of sound mind and body. He should not wait until he is on his deathbed. He should be careful to write the will in accordance with halachah, otherwise it may not be halachically binding. For many generations, the custom (*minhag*) has been to use a special formula for the will, called a *shtar chazi zachar*. HaRav Feivel Cohen, *shilt"a*, printed one recently in booklet form, and it is available in most

19. חו"מ סי' ר"נ

Judaica shops. In case the *shtar chazi zachar* was not drawn up, and only an ordinary will was made, the issue should be brought before qualified Rabbanim, as there are important halachic opinions which consider a standard will to be binding. Nonetheless, the preferred way is to have a *shtar chazi zachar* drawn up by a qualified Rav.

Mitzvah lekayeim divrei hameis: Sometimes, a person will have entrusted a third party with the responsibility of dividing his estate in a certain way, where the control over his estate was transferred to this person during the lifetime of the owner for the specific purpose of carrying out this disbursement. When he dies, there exists an obligation to uphold the wishes of the deceased (*mitzvah lekayeim divrei hameis*), and the man's assets should be distributed according to the instructions given to the third party. The difference between this procedure, and the *matnas shchiv m'ra*, is that in the case of a dying man's gift, his spoken word creates an effective inheritance. Even if someone should attempt to take that which was not intended for him, the Jewish court (*Beis Din*) can take it from him (*motzi'in meyado*). In the case of *mitzvah leykayeim divrei hameis*, the acquisition of the property by the beneficiaries only takes place when they actually receive their allotment. This means that if someone takes hold of some portion of the estate against the wishes of the deceased, that becomes his portion and he cannot be made to return it against his will (*ein motzi'in meyado*). Still, it is proper to try and fulfill the deceased's wishes even though the acquisition only becomes final with receipt of the assets.

As mentioned above, the rule of *mitzvah lekayeim divrei hameis* applies when the third party received prior control of the assets. Notwithstanding the wishes of the deceased, it is recommended to seek everyone's agreement and divide a meaningful amount (perhaps 10%) of the inheritance according to the Torah's instructions. This means giving the firstborn male (*bechor*) a double portion, and dividing the remainder among the other sons. If the inheritance is $200,000, for instance, one might consider taking $10,000 or $20,000 and dividing this portion according to the dictates of the Torah.

Causing pain to a parent: As in all situations, a person must go to great lengths not to upset a parent especially during discussions involving the determination of the future of his or her estate. If the parent's demands are unreasonable, and have no halachic basis, then there is no obligation to comply. Even so, it is important to try and avoid causing a breach. It is of paramount importance to consult with a qualified and experienced Rav, and to calmly and rationally determine the best course of action. Sage advice from an impartial, Torah-based perspective is an essential ingredient in avoiding unnecessary friction.

Throughout their responsa, the Poskim emphasize the pain and enmity that sometimes results from disputes over inheritances. Families have been ruined, and formerly close siblings have severed all ties. It is simply not worth the heartache to do battle with loved ones over an inheritance.

If a person wants to live longer and enjoy his life, he will take the advice of Chazal. The Gemara[20] lists many things that bring longevity. One of the most important is the principle, "I was always yielding with my money." This is not simply a piece of *mussar.* The author saw with his own eyes how his father was forgiving with regard to financial matters. In the end he and his family were privileged to experience health, satisfaction, and happiness within a modest and balanced lifestyle whereas those who retained the bulk of the fortune were for the most part very unhappy people. It is written, "נתתה שמחה בלבי מעת דגנם ותירושם רבו – *You have set joy in my heart, even as their grain and wine increase.*[21] People whose lives revolve almost exclusively around the struggle for money end up with nothing but misery.

One of the greatest qualities a person can nurture is that of *vatranus*, of yielding and flexibility, when it comes to money. People who insist on getting what they feel they deserve might end up a little richer, but will have to live with the burden of knowing that close family members are no longer on speaking terms with them. Perhaps

20. מגילה כח.
21. תהלים ד:ח

even more than seeking sage counsel, vatranus is the key to weathering rough financial storms, and it will bring its bearer long life.

USING THE REGULAR MOHEL

What should be done in a situation when the regular family *mohel* initially says that he will be unavailable, but subsequently says that he can in fact perform the Bris Milah, only after a different *mohel* has been hired? Which *mohel* should be employed?

ANSWER

There are many *teshuvos* written about such situations. The general consensus is that the family mohel takes precedence and should therefore be employed. Nevertheless, the father of the newborn should make an effort to placate the new mohel and compensate him for the loss, by paying him a half or a third of the standard fee.

OPENING AND CLOSING WINDOWS IN SUMMER AND WINTER

What principles govern disputes regarding heating or cooling a communal room or workspace? Should one follow the majority, and in what circumstances must one defer to the preferences of older or more respected individuals?

ANSWER

The classic response to this question is that in the summer, you must listen to the people who want the windows open; and in the winter, you must listen to the people who want the windows closed. This is based on a Mishnah in *Pe'ah*:[22]

22. פ"ד מ"א–ב

> *Pe'ah* [of the field] is left attached to the ground [so that the poor should harvest it themselves]; from a [tree-hanging] vine and from a palm tree, the owner takes [the pe'ah] off and distributes it to the poor.... [Regarding *pe'ah* from the field,] even if ninety-nine [paupers] say it should be distributed, and one says it should be left for collection, we heed this one, for his position is in accordance with the halachah. Regarding a vine or palm tree it is not this way; even if ninety-nine say it should be left for collection, and one says it should be distributed, we listen to this one for his position is in accordance with the halachah.

Pe'ah refers to the 'corners' of a field of agricultural produce. It is a Torah mitzvah to leave the corners for the needy to harvest. Pe'ah is supposed to be left for the poor to collect on their own, as it is written, "לעני ולגר תעזוב אותם – *For the poor man and the sojourner shall you leave them*" (Vayikra 19:10, 23:22). However, collecting the produce from tree-hanging vines and palms is liable to be dangerous for an unskilled picker. In these cases, the owner of the trees must harvest the pe'ah and then distribute it to the poor. Thus, even if all the poor people agree to act otherwise, one dissenting voice is sufficient to oppose them, since he wishes to proceed according to the halachah.

Similarly, when it comes to heating and cooling, the halachah follows the way most people behave in that season. The overwhelming custom is to keep the windows closed in the winter, and leave them open in the summer. Thus, even if the majority of the occupants in a certain space or room agree to act otherwise, one dissenting voice can prevent them from going against the normal practice. This is the opinion of most Poskim, but there are authoritative, dissenting opinions.

Unseasonably hot or cold days: It should be noted that during a particularly hot day in the winter or an exceptionally cold day in the summer, the normal practice in such conditions becomes the measure of action, and not the general practice of the season. The same would be true of a room that is over-heated during winter or over-cooled in the summer.

As in every area of potential confrontation, the rules must be tempered with a healthy dose of common sense. Sometimes, the dissenting voice comes from a person who is exceptionally sensitive to heat or cold. Or, perhaps his seat happens to be right underneath the air-conditioning vent. Often, a chronic debate over heating and cooling a communal room can be permanently resolved by changing the seating arrangement or by adjusting the vanes that direct the blast of air from the vents. If there is a generally cooperative atmosphere, and everyone is willing to compromise a little, a solution agreeable to all can usually be found. If, for some reason, the complainant refuses to cooperate, and the general practice follows his preference, then there is very little recourse. It is not good to maintain a state of confrontation, however. Every effort should be made to persuade him in a pleasant and polite manner. If all else fails, one could always move to another area of the room.

In a classroom, the rebbi or teacher should be considered to be the sole arbiter of such questions.

COPYRIGHTS

Is it halachically forbidden to reproduce copyrighted tapes, books, or discs?

ANSWER

Reb Moshe, *zt"l*, maintained that the practice is forbidden in almost all cases. It is of no relevance whether the copyright is held by a Jew or a gentile. If the copyright is held by a Jew, then there is the additional problem of the fact that a Jew can forbid the use of his property with the force of a *neder*, which includes copying it. A person makes a certain product in order to earn money. He wants people who use it to pay a certain price. By copying it, a person takes away the copyright holder's ability to sell his product.

One leniency is when a person buys a legal copy of the tape or book, and for his personal convenience, makes a duplicate so that he could have one copy at home and another at the office or in the car. A person might also want to make a copy in case the original is lost or damaged. People do not generally buy two copies of a book or tape; if they had to, they would simply make do with one. Thus, making the duplicate for personal convenience does not take away the seller's ability to sell an extra copy. A person must not give out the duplicate to others, however.

There was once a school that needed a particular textbook. To save money, each student contributed a small amount of money to the purchase of one copy of the book, making all the students joint owners (*shutafim*). Then, they made one hundred and fifty copies for the 'convenience' of each of the 'owners'. This was a clever misuse of a good Jewish mind. One should always be vigilant against using cunning loopholes to permit gezel.

Another leniency is when the product is off the market. Here too, making copies does not reduce the copyright holder's ability to sell, since they are not being sold anymore.

Someone once asked: What source is there for granting halachic ownership to a copyright holder, when in fact none of the classical *kinyanim* upon which ownership is generally based have been performed?

The answer to this is simple: A kinyan is necessary only when an object originally existed outside one's ownership; then the item must be transferred into his ownership by means of a kinyan. Something that was created by an individual automatically belongs to him. It was never outside his possession and therefore does not require any of the regular kinyanim.

The Torah itself attests that one's effort confers ownership, as can be seen from the following possuk in Parshas Ki Savo: "כל יגיעך יאכל עם אשר לא ידעת והיית רק עשוק ורצוץ כל הימים – *All your effort shall be consumed by a nation that you have not known and you shall be only plundered and destroyed all the days*" (Devarim 28:33). This person has struggled to create something using his energy, originality and creativity, and he has spent time, money, sweat and toil, to produce something of quality which he hopes will be appealing to the public and can be sold for a profit. Then along comes another, and casually appropriates the fruit of his labors for himself without having invested the least bit of time and money. His act is described in the above Tochachah. The offender is clearly an *oshek* (plunderer) and a *rotzeitz* (destroyer). No other source is needed to prohibit such behavior.

APPROACHING SECULAR COURTS

Are there any circumstances whereby a person can go directly to a secular court without first bringing the complaint to *Beis Din* (Rabbinical Court), for instance, if a person believes that the other party will refuse to abide by the ruling of the *Beis Din*?

ANSWER

No Jewish person should ever go to a secular court without first discussing it with a Rav who is qualified to issue a ruling in such matters. This sefer is not the forum to discuss the details of what makes such a course of action permissible. If one feels that he is in a situation where he may be allowed to go straight to a secular court, he should approach a Rav who knows *Choshen Mishpat* and is qualified to answer questions in *dinei mammonos* (the laws governing monetary loss and transactions), and explain the situation, including why he feels that he should be allowed to bring the case to a secular court.

There are certain circumstances whereby a person may conceivably be permitted to take the law into his own hands (*avid inish dinna l'nafshei*) and do what he must in order to recover what he feels was unjustly taken from him. But let him never decide on his own to go to the secular courts.

Every now and then one encounters a litigant in a secular court who claims that he received permission to take such an action from an important Rabbi, yet refuses to divulge his name. For the most part such "permission" is entirely fictitious. Even if it were indeed true that a qualified Rabbi endowed him with a halachic license to go to civil court, let it be known from this forum that such a *heter* has no halachic validity when given in secrecy. If a Rabbi is unwilling to take responsibility for his halachic pronouncements, then his granting of permission must be considered "שביתין ושביקין, בטלין ומבוטלין לא שרירין ולא קיימין – cancelled and abandoned, null and void, powerless and nonexistent."

Glossary

A

Acharonim – lit. 'latest' or 'more recent ones', refers to Rabbinic scholars who lived around the time of the writing of the *Shulchan Aruch* (16th century CE), and onward

achshavei – lit. 'he considered it significant', a person's consideration of a particular thing can often elevate its halachic status to that of *ikar*, or turn a non-food into a food

amos – cubit (approx. 10.5 in.)

aravos – willow branches, one of the *arba minim*

arba minim – lit. 'the four species', refers to the esrog, lulav, hadassim, and aravos which are waved on the Festival of Sukkos

asher yatzar – blessing recited after using the rest room

Ashkenaz -i, -im, -ic – lit. 'Germanic'; refers to Jews of European origin, their halachic customs, and the formula of their prayers and blessings

assur – halachically forbidden

B

b'dieved – *ex-post-facto*, i.e. if something forbidden was done, it may be acceptable in certain cases

ba'al nefesh – one who is sensitive to his spiritual needs, and a master over his desires, as in the possuk (Bereishis 23:8), "אם יש את

נפשכם – if you desire." (cf. Raavad in his foreword to his sefer, *Ba'alei Nefesh*)

basar b'chalav – a combination of meat and milk

basar oveir – meat that was not salted within seventy-two hours of *shechitah*

basar she'nisalem min ha'ayin – lit. "meat that has disappeared from view," i.e., that is not under constant, close supervision

batim – lit. 'houses', refers to the leather tefillin boxes into which the parchments are inserted

batul – nullified

batul b'rov – nullified by a majority

bedikas tola'im – checking food for insects or worms

Beis Din – court of Torah law, consisting of at least three Rabbis

Beis HaMikdash – the holy Temple in Jerusalem. May refer to either of the historic First and Second Temples, or to the future Third Temple.

beliya – absorption

beliyas heter – absorption of a halachically permitted substance or flavor

beliyas issur – absorption of a halachically forbidden substance or flavor

bentch, bentching – Yiddish, "to recite a blessing". Often used to denote the recital of *Birkas HaMazon*

bi'ur – requirement to remove *shmittah* produce (and *ma'aser*) from one's possession before the required time

Birkas HaMazon – lit. 'Blessing of the food', Grace after meals

birya – a whole fruit or creature

bishul akum – food cooked or prepared by a non-Jew

bishul Yisroel – food cooked or prepared by a Jew

bitachon – trust in Hashem

bittul – nullification

Bnei Noach – lit. 'sons of Noah', gentiles

borei minei mezonos – blessing recited before eating any food made from the five grains (wheat, oats, barley, rye, spelt) that does not have the status of bread, also recited on cooked rice

brachah, brachos – blessing(s); benediction(s) upon performing a mitzvah, to express thanksgiving to Hashem, or before deriving physical pleasure from the world, e.g. eating and drinking

brachah levatalah – a blessing made in vain

bris milah – circumcision performed according to Jewish law

brownstone – A type of semi-attached housing, popular in the northeast United States in the 1920s. As the name indicates, the buildings sport a façade of reddish-brown sandstone bricks

C

Chafetz Chaim – Rabbi Yisroel Meir HaKohen Kagan (d. 1933 CE). Authored the Mishnah Berurah, and the Sefer Chafetz Chaim, a treatise on the laws governing permitted and prohibited speech. His rulings are generally accepted as binding.

chalav akum – milk produced under non-Jewish auspices

chalav stam – milk that is produced under non-Jewish auspices, but is under strict government supervision

chalav Yisroel – milk produced under Jewish supervision

challah – see *hafrashas challah*; commonly used to refer to the braided loaves of bread baked in honor of Shabbos, from which challah is taken

chametz – leavened grain products, unfit for consumption on Pesach

chashad – suspicion

chatzitzah – a foreign substance on the skin that prevents water from making contact

Chazal - an acronym for *Chachameinu zichronam livrachah* – Our Sages of blessed memory. Refers exclusively to the Rabbis of the Mishnah and Talmud, and represents the authoritative opinion of the Talmud

cheilev – forbidden fats

Chizkiyahu (HaMelech) – King Hezekiah of the Davidic dynasty

Chol HaMoed – intermediate days of the Festival

cholent – the traditional Jewish stew-like dish kept hot in a permissible way and served for the second Shabbos meal. Generally consists of any combination of potatoes, meat, beans, and barley.

Chovos Halevavos – lit. 'Duties of the Heart', a book written by Rabbeinu Bachaye ibn Pakudah. Rabbeinu Bachaye lived in Zaragoza, Spain, in the eleventh century. He was a leading Talmud scholar, and an expert in ethics and philosophy. It is common practice to refer to Rabbeinu Bachaye by the name of his book; the Chovos Halevavos.

Chumash – Five Books of Moses, the Torah

chumros – stringencies

chuppah – wedding canopy

D

d'buki be'alma – an ingredient added only to serve as a binder

davar chashuv – an important item

dinei mammonos – laws governing commerce, finance, and transactions

Dovid HaMelech – King David

E

eino ben yomo – lit. 'not within its day', indicates that the absorption of flavor into the walls of a vessel occurred more than twenty-four hours in the past and that certain leniencies may apply

eiver min ha-chai – lit. 'a limb torn from a living animal', refers to the Noahide prohibition of eating meat taken from a living animal and generally applies to Jews as well

Eretz Yisroel – Land of Israel

eruv, eruvin – "*eruv chatzeiros*", lit. 'mixing of courtyards', a halachic process by which communal areas are converted into one large private domain, in order to permit carrying on Shabbos. Often refers to the perimeter wall, fence, or demarcation that surrounds such an area.

ervah – parts of the body that are usually covered by God-fearing Jewish women

esrog – citron, one of the *arba minim*

F

frum – observant

G

Gedolei Hador – Torah leaders of the generation; in some instances, the greatest communal leaders

Gedolei HaPoskim – greatest halachic deciders

Gedolei Yisroel – lit. 'great ones of Israel', refers to the Torah leaders of each generation

Gemara – portion of the Babylonian Talmud redacted by Ravina and Rav Ashi, set as an explanation and expansion on the teachings of the Mishnah

genizah – concealed storage, often in the form of burial

gezeiras ha-kasuv – a Torah decree whose reason is not ascertainable by man, but is derived from the written text of the Torah

gezel – theft

gilu'ach – shaving

goralos – lotteries

H

'*ha'adamah*' – the blessing made on fruit of the earth (vegetables)

ha'agalah – process of kashering vessels through boiling water

hadassim – myrtle branches, one of the *arbah minim*

hafrashas challah – the separation of a portion of every dough as a gift for the Kehunah, as required by the Torah, or Rabbinic decree

halachah, halachos – body of laws regulating every aspect of a Jew's personal and communal life; a specific detail or details of these laws

halachic – of, or having to do with, *halachah*

hamotzi – the blessing recited before eating bread: "*Hamotzi lechem min ha-aretz* – Who has brought forth bread from the earth."

hashavas aveidah – the mitzvah of returning a lost object

hashgachah – formal halachic supervision, particularly concerning foodstuffs *hashgachah temidis* – constant supervision

havdalah – lit. 'distinction', a ceremony marking the conclusion of Shabbos and the onset of the following week

hechsher – certification/authorization of kashrus

hefsek – pause or break

heter, heterim – halachic permissibility, leniencies

heter mechirah – the sale of the Land of Israel by the Chief Rabbinate of Israel before the onset of the Shmittah year, intended to permit continued agricultural pursuits. The sale's validity is contested by virtually every reliable halachic authority.

hiddur, hiddurim – detail(s) that beautify a mitzvah aesthetically and halachically

hotza'as Shabbos – forbidden carrying on Shabbos

I

ikar – the principle element. Often used to refer to the main ingredient in a mixture of foodstuffs.

irev bo devarim marim – bitter things mixed within

irui keli rishon – pouring out the contents of a *keli rishon* onto something

issur d'Oraisa – prohibition stated in the Torah

issur hefsed – prohibition of destroying *shmittah* produce

issur sechorah – prohibition of doing commerce in *shmittah* produce

issur sefichim – prohibition of consuming non-tree *shmittah* produce

K

kasher – to make fit for Jewish consumption

kasher, kashering – to render meat fit for Jewish consumption; expunging non-kosher substances from utensils to be used for preparing kosher food

kashrus – of, or having to do with, the halachic supervision of the food processing industry *katan* – a child or minor, i.e. any Jewish boy under the age of 13, or Jewish girl under the age of 12

keba'alo kach polto – lit. 'as it was absorbed so can it be released', indicates that the process used for kashering must resemble the circumstances in which the vessel became non-kosher. (In some contexts it can mean 'as soon as it is absorbed, it is immediately released.')

kedushas shev'is – sanctity of *shmittah*

keli rishon – lit. 'the first vessel', halachic term denoting a cooking utensil that either is or had been directly on the fire, and its contents

kesidran – in the proper order

kevias seudah – establishing a meal as halachically 'formal' as opposed to being only a snack

kevius – set, permanent

kevod av v'eim – honor due one's father and mother

kezayis – volume equivalent to the size of an olive. The exact measure of the olive is the subject of a long-standing debate amongst *Poskim*.

kiddush – sanctification of Shabbos or festival, generally performed over a cup of wine

kitniyus – legumes

Kohen, Kohanim – Jewish Priest(s)

kosher – fit for Jewish consumption, valid

krias Shema – the Shema prayer, recited twice daily

kugel – Yiddish for casserole

kulah, kulos – leniency, leniencies

L

libbun kal – process of kashering a utensil by lightly scorching its surface. Requires that it reach a temperature whereby a piece of paper held to the opposite surface will become scorched. This method may only be used under certain circumstances.

lifnei iver – lit. 'before the blind [you shall not set a stumbling-block]' (Vayikra 19:14). Prohibition of causing another to transgress *lulav, lulavim* – palm frond(s), one of the *arba minim*

M

ma'asros – tithes; there are three specific tithes mandated by the Torah: *ma'aser rishon* ("first tithe", separated from produce after *terumah*, and given to the Levi of one's choice); *ma'aser sheini*, ("second tithe", separated during the first, second, fourth, and fifth years of the *shemittah* cycle. This tithe must be consumed within the city of Yerushalayim); and *ma'aser oni* ("pauper's tithe", separated during the third and sixth years of the *shemittah* cycle, and distributed to the poor).

machmir – to follow the stricter halachic position in case of doubt or out of piety

mashgiach – one who supervises and verifies adherence to halachic guidelines

matnas bari – healthy man's gift

matnas shchiv m'ra – gift of a dying man

matzah – unleavened bread

me'ikar hadin – lit. 'the fundamental law', i.e. according to the strict definition of the halachah

Megillah, Megillos – lit. 'Scrolls', refers to any of the five Scrolls: Shir HaShirim (Song of Songs), Eichah (Lamentations) , Rus (Ruth), Kohelles (Ecclesiastes), and especially Esther

mehadrin – high standard of kashrus supervision

mei chalav – whey

mekabel tumah – the act or ability to become ritually impure

melachos – creative acts that are forbidden to perform on Shabbos

menaker, menakrim – person trained in removing forbidden fats and sinews

merkachas – compote or blend of foods

metzorah – one afflicted with Biblical *tzara'as*

mevushal – cooked

mezonos – all baked products excluding bread, made from the five grains (wheat, barley, rye, oats, and spelt); Used also as a reference to the blessing made on these foods mezuzah, mezuzos – parchment mandated by the Torah to be affixed to the doorposts of a Jewish residence

miderabbanan – decree or ruling of Chazal, the Sages of the Talmud and Mishnah, or of earlier Sages

mikvah – body or collection of water fit for ritual immersion

minhag, minhagim – custom(s)

Mishnah – body of Oral Torah redacted by Rebbi Yehudah HaNassi at the end of the Second Temple period

Mishnah Berurah – the glosses of Rabbi Yisroel Meir HaKohen Kagan (d. 1933 CE) on the first section of the *Shulchan Aruch, Orach Chaim*. His rulings are generally accepted as binding.

mohel – trained practitioner of *bris milah*

muktzah – item forbidden to handle on Shabbos or Yom Tov

mussar - rebuke, restraint; generally used to refer to the study of character refinement and development of faith and trust in Hashem

N

nazir – nazarite

negel vasser – Yiddish for *netilas yadayim*

netilas yadayim – the ritual washing of the hands in the morning upon awakening, and before breaking bread

nifsal me'achilah – unfit for consumption

nifsal me'achilas adam – unfit for human consumption

nifsal me'achilas kelev – unfit for (even) a dog to eat

nikkur – removing forbidden sinews

niputz – removing salt from meat being kashered

O

orlah – forbidden tree-fruit from the first three years after planting

P

pachos mi'keshiur – less than a specified halachic quantity or measurement

parshiyos – lit. 'passages', refers generally to any designated segment of the Torah; refers specifically to the Torah passages written on parchment and inserted into *tefillin*

parve – food containing neither meat nor milk ingredients

pas akum – bread baked by a non-Jew

pas haba'ah b'kisnin – bread-like mezonos

pas Yisroel – bread baked by Jews

pasken – to pronounce a halachic decision

perek – chapter

Pesach – Festival of Passover

pikuach nefesh – guarding human life

Posek, Poskim – Rabbi, Rabbis qualified to render major halachic decisions

posul – invalid

psak – the binding halachic decision of a qualified Rabbi

R

ra'ui l'achilas adam – fit for human consumption

ra'ui l'hiskabeid – fit to serve to an honored guest

ra'ui lenisuch al ha-mizbe'ach – fitting for the altar libation in the Beis HaMikdash (Temple)

Rabbanim – Rabbis

rakikin dakin meod – very thin crackers

Rambam – Rabbi Moshe ben Maimon, also known as Maimonides. Born 1134, died 1204, the Rambam is one of the most well-known Torah authorities of all time. His most famous work is his *Mishneh Torah* (Review of the Torah) in which he codified the entire body of Jewish law. This was the product of ten years of work and was one of the first systematic codifications of Jewish law. He also wrote *Moreh Nevuchim*.

Ramban – Rabbi Moshe ben Nachman, also known as Nachmanides. He was born in Spain in 1194, and was the foremost halachic authority and kabbalist of his age. He died in 1270 in Eretz Yisroel.

Rashi – Rabbi Shlomo Yitzchaki, born 1040 in France, died 1105. The leading Torah expositor of all time, his greatest contributions to Torah study are his commentaries on the Torah, the Prophets and the Talmud, his authority is one of the most extensive and influential of all commentators

Rav Ha'machshir – certifying Rabbi

Rishonim – lit. 'first ones', refers to the leading Rabbis and *Poskim* who lived approximately from 1000 to 1500 CE, in the era before the writing of the *Shulchan Aruch*.

Rosh Hashanah – Jewish New Year

rov – the majority

ruach ra'ah – impure spirit

S

safek d'Oraisa – a halachic doubt regarding a Torah precept

schach – thatching used for sukkah roof

Sefardi, Sefardim – Jew(s) whose lineage stems from Spain, North Africa, and the East

sefarim – books, usually with Torah content

Sefer Torah – hand written Torah Scroll

sefichim – see *issur sefichim*

seudah – meal

seudas mitzvah – meal in celebration of a mitzvah

shaatnez – mixture of linen and wool forbidden by the Torah to be worn as a garment

Shabbos – the Sabbath, the day of rest

Shabbos HaGadol – Shabbos before Pesach

Shaul HaMelech – King Saul

shechitah – ritual slaughter of animals

'*shehakol*' – "For all came into existence through His word," general blessing recited on any food that does not qualify for a more specific formula

sheilah, sheilos – halachic query, queries

sheitel – Yiddish for wig

shelo kedarko – not according to the regular manner

sheratzim – vermin, specifically the eight species of crawling animals which carry impurity when dead, as detailed in Vayikra 11:29–30

shevi'is – see *shmittah*
shidduch, *shidduchim* – dating according to Orthodox Jewish custom
shifshuf – lit. 'rubbing', requirement to rub hands together after washing for bread
shiur – a prescribed halachic measure or quantity to which certain rules apply
shmittah – Sabbatical year, last year of a seven-year cycle
Shmuel HaNavi – the Prophet Samuel
shnitzel – breaded filets of turkey or chicken breast
shok – upper thigh
Shulchan Aruch – lit. 'The Set Table', written by Rabbi Yosef Karo (d. 1575 CE). It is the authoritative compilation of all halachos governing the life of a Jew in our days.
Simchas Torah – lit. 'The Torah Celebration', Festival after the conclusion of Sukkos
sirtut – scoring applied to parchment before writing a Sefer Torah, tefillin, or mezuzah
sofer – Jewish scribe
stam – acronym for Sifrei Torah, tefillin, mezuzos
sugya, *sugyos* – a topic or topics treated comprehensively by the Talmud
sukkah – temporary hut used for the holiday of Sukkos
Sukkos – Festival of Tabernacles

T

ta'aroves – mixture
tafel – the subsidiary ingredient in a mixture or combination of foodstuffs
tallis, talleisim – four-cornered fringed garment worn by Jewish men
tamei – ritually impure
Tanna – Sage of the Mishnah
tefillin – phylacteries, two leather boxes containing parchment strips inscribed with scriptural quotations that are worn on the

forehead and the left arm by orthodox men during weekday morning worship.

tefiros – stitching

Tehillim – Book of Psalms

terumah – gift to the Kohanim separated out from agricultural products

teshuvah – returning to one's commitment to the precepts of the Torah; a written response to a halachic query

thrips – minute, agile insects commonly found on certain vegetables and fruits, such as lettuce and strawberries.

titura – section of tefillin

Torah – Five Books of Moses; All Torah wisdom, written and oral, transmitted to Moses on Har Sinai

Tosafos - Commentaries which appear on almost every page of the Talmud, which elucidate and clarify every issue discussed there. Together with Rashi, they form the backbone of Torah study. The authors of the Tosafos are known as the Ba'alei Tosafos and include such luminaries as Rabbeinu Tam and the Ri (Rabbeinu Yitzchak), both descendants of Rashi. Forty-four Ba'alei Tosafos are mentioned by name. The rest are anonymous.

treif – lit. 'torn apart', food unfit for consumption by a Jew

Tu b'Shevat – the Fifteenth of the Jewish month of Shevat; the new year for counting the agricultural years of trees

tumah – ritual impurity

tumas meis – ritual impurity conveyed by a corpse

tumas sheretz – ritual impurity conveyed by the corpses of certain small animals

tumas yadayim – ritual impurity conveyed by impurity on the hands

tzitzis – fringes required to be placed on the corners of a four-cornered garment

tzomes ha-gidim – the intersection of tendons found above the ankles of animals and birds

Y

yadayim – hands

yareh shamayim – God-fearing

Yatziv Pisgam – poetic introduction to the Haftarah recited on the second day of the Festival of Shavuos

yavesh – dry

yayin nesech – wine that has been used for idolatrous libations yeshivah, yeshivos – academy, academies for Torah study, the study of Talmud, Rabbinic literature and Responsa; Beis Midrash or Talmudic Academy

yichud – prohibited seclusion of a man and woman in a private area

Z

zeman bi'ur – see *bi'ur*

INDEX

The following index contains the major subject categories included in the questions contained in Shulchan HaLevi, Vol. 1, and can be consulted along with the table of contents to locate specific topics.

About the Machon

Machon Simchas HaTorah is a new and unique publishing house, specializing in high quality Torah publications in both Hebrew and English. Nine years ago, Rabbi Reuven Cohen, founder and executive director of the Machon, began publishing his writings on both Chumash and Gemara, entitled *Livyas Chein* and *Imrei Reuven*, respectively. Since then, he has gradually put together a professional staff of writers, editors, translators and transcribers. The Machon is presently in its fifth year and has earned itself a name as one of the pre-eminent publishing houses in Torah literature.

The Machon's most ambitious project involves the extensive writings and lectures of HaRav HaGaon, Rabbi Yisroel Belsky שליט״א, Rosh Yeshiva of Yeshiva Torah VoDaath. This volume of *Shulchan HaLevi* is the first of a multi-volume series of Rabbi Belksy's halachic responsa in English. This groundbreaking volume includes teshuvos regarding hilchos brachos, Chol HaMoed, tefillin, mezuzah, bishul akum, chukos hagoyim, and more. Also included is a section dedicated to the description of industrial shechitah and related hashgachah issues. Future volumes will address Hilchos niddah and Shabbos, and a host of other contemporary issues.

A Priceless Legacy

The staff of Machon Simchas HaTorah combine literary talent with Torah erudition, and is uniquely suited to working with original Torah material, adapting it for presentation in both Loshon HaKodesh and English. Starting with the basic material, whether it be on tape, hand-written or in computer format, our professional staff will take the project through all the stages of preparation and production, and present you with a finished sefer. We offer comprehensive publication services, including quality printing, jacket design, and worldwide distribution.

Each of us has a favorite Torah shiur; a rabbi or lecturer who inspires us with his breadth of knowledge and his skilled and absorbing delivery. What a privilege it is to be among the fortunate few who benefit from these shiurim, and yet what a shame that the wider community cannot also benefit from these pearls of Torah wisdom. It is to this end that Machon Simchas HaTorah has set itself a primary aim to eternalize the words of our most inspiring Rabbonim and lecturers.

The Machon seeks to uncover the hidden treasures of Torah wisdom that are to be found amongst the manuscripts of talmidei chachamim and the lectures of Rabbonim past and present. Our aim is to set these treasures as sparkling jewels in the ever-expanding crown of Torah, by presenting this wisdom in a polished and attractive format before the Jewish public. What greater gift could there be to an esteemed Rosh Yeshivah, Rav, or teacher, than to have his unique thoughts eternalized in print? Indeed, what greater investment could one make than to transform the words of our most inspiring Rabbis into sefarim that reach out to the hearts and minds of a readership thirsty for Torah wisdom.

Additionally, for the various projects planned by the Machon, we welcome sponsors who wish to share in the great merit of disseminating Torah throughout Klal Yisroel. These projects include:

- Rabbi Belsky on Pirkei Avos
- Rabbi Belsky on Kinnos
- Rabbi Belsky on Eichah
- Scholarly translations of several important Torah works
- Timely publications on a variety of important issues, including Chinuch & Bitachon

Machon Simchas HaTorah invites anyone wishing to discuss the various options that we offer to be in touch with our staff. We look forward to working together with you. Please contact Rabbi Dovid Gelber at:

MACHON SIMCHAS HATORAH

36/1 S'dei Chemed · Kiryat Sefer
Modi'in Illit 71919 · Eretz Yisroel

Tel: 011-972-8-979-8047
Fax: 011-972-8-974-4640
DSL: (718) 337-8490

Simtorah@Neto.bezeqint.net